BACKPACKING OREGON

4TH EDITION

From Coastal Cliffs to Mountain Meadows

BECKY OHLSEN
and
DOUGLAS LORAIN

WILDERNESS PRESS . . . on the trail since 1967

Backpacking Oregon: From Coastal Cliffs to Mountain Meadows

1st Edition 1999
2nd Edition 2007
3rd Edition 2019
4th Edition 2026

Distributed by Publishers Group West
Manufactured in the United States of America

Cover design: Larry B. Van Dyke and Scott McGrew
Book design: Larry B. Van Dyke with updates by Annie Long
Maps by Becky Ohlsen, Douglas Lorain, Steve Jones, and Scott McGrew
Interior photos by Becky Ohlsen except as noted
Color insert photos by Becky Ohlsen
Front cover photos, all photographed by Becky Ohlsen, clockwise from top: Valley near Aneroid Lake in the Wallowas (Trip 21, *page 137*); hiking Little Blitzen Trail in the Steens (Trip 27, *page 177*); Bandon Coast (Trip 2, *page 23*); Twister Falls, Eagle Creek Loop (Trip 5, *page 44*)
Back cover photo: Trail to Eagle Lake in the Wallowas (Trip 22, *page 142;* photographed by Becky Ohlsen)
Title page: View of Drake Peak from the Fremont National Recreation Trail (Trip 29, *page 188;* photographed by Becky Ohlsen)

Cataloging-in-Publication Data is available from the Library of Congress.
ISBN 978-1-64359-104-9 (pbk.); 978-1-64359-105-6 (ebook)

Published by: **WILDERNESS PRESS**
An imprint of AdventureKEEN
2204 First Avenue S., Ste. 102
Birmingham, AL 35233
800-678-7006

Visit wildernesspress.com for a complete listing of our books and for ordering information. Contact us at our website, at facebook.com/wildernesspress1967, or at x.com/wilderness1967 with questions or comments. To find out more about who we are and what we're doing, visit blog.wildernesspress.com.

SAFETY NOTICE: Although Wilderness Press and the authors have made every attempt to ensure that the information in this book is accurate at press time, they are not responsible for any loss, damage, injury, or inconvenience that may occur to anyone while using this book. You are responsible for your own safety and health while in the wilderness. The fact that a trail is described in this book does not mean that it will be safe for you. Be aware that trail conditions can change from day to day. Always check local conditions and know your own limitations.

CONTENTS

Trail Map Legend

Featured route	Alternate trail	Cross-country route
Paved road	Unpaved road	Railroad
River	Creek	State border

40	Interstate		Bridge
9W	US Highway		Dam
28	State Highway	4,050'	Elevation
1234	Forest Service/BLM road		Falls
	Pacific Crest Trail		General point of interest
	Starting point		Gate
	Campground		Lookout tower
	Campsite	4.8	Mileage between points
	Mountain/peak		Overlook
	Pass		Spring
			Tunnel (railroad)

FEATURED TRIPS SUMMARY CHART

	TRIP NUMBER & NAME *(grouped by what is typically the best month)*	PAGE NUMBER
APRIL and MAY		
1	North Coast: Fort Stevens to Nehalem Bay	17
3	Rogue River Trail	31
25	Snake River Trail	162
26	Hells Canyon Bench High Trail	170
30	Honeycombs Loop	193
JUNE		
5	Eagle Creek Loop	44
7	Salmon River Trail	57
24	Hells Canyon Western Rim Summit Trail	154
27	Steens Mountain Gorges Loop	177
28	Desert Trail: Pueblo Mountains Section	183
JULY		
4	Siskiyou–Boundary Trail	37
8	Jefferson Park Trek	63
13	Mount Thielsen Traverse	93
15	Strawberry Mountains Traverse	104
16	Elkhorn Crest Trail	110
18	Minam River Loop	120
19	Bear Creek Loop	126
22	Southern Wallowas Traverse	142
23	East Eagle–Imnaha Loop	149
AUGUST		
6	Timberline Trail Loop	50
9	Mount Jefferson Wilderness Loop	69
10	Three Sisters Loop	74
11	Separation Creek Loop	81
14	Sky Lakes Loop	98
20	Lostine–Minam Loop	132
21	Wallowa River Loop	137
SEPTEMBER and OCTOBER		
2	South Coast: Bandon to Port Orford	23
12	Mink Lake Area	87
17	Wenaha River Traverse	115
29	Freemont National Recreation Trail: Southern Segment	188

RATINGS (1–10)			LENGTH		ELEVATION GAIN	SHUTTLE MILEAGE
SCENERY	SOLITUDE	DIFFICULTY	DAYS	MILES		
8	2	5	5	58	6,240'	42
9	5	4	4–5	40	4,500	49
10	7	8	4–5	41	6,000'	NA
10	8	8	5–8	63	14,900'	46
9	10	8	2–3	17	3,500'	NA
6	4	6	3–4	31	5,100'	NA
6	5	4	2–3	16	4,000'	NA
8	8	5	5–7	53	7,400'	63
10	8	9	2–4	24	4,700'	NA
8	9	7	2–3	22	3,700'	20
8	7	57	4	36	9,100'	25
10	3	6	5–6	36	5,700'	NA
7	6	6	3–4	34	5,500'	25
9	6	7	4	35	7,600'	31
9	6	6	3	27	3,000'	35
7	6	7	3–6	35	5,300'	NA
8	8	8	3–6	39	6,300'	NA
9	6	8	4–5	40	9,400'	42
10	4	6	5–6	39	7,900'	NA
10	2	8	3–5	42	9,600'	NA
9	5	6	3–4	35	6,500'	NA
10	2	6	5–6	55	8,200'	NA
6	7	6	4–6	42	4,700'	NA
7	5	6	5–7	59	6,000'	NA
9	4	6	4–6	43	8,700'	NA
10	2	7	4–5	36	7,100'	NA
8	6	4	3–4	30	600'	27
7	4	3	3	24	1,600'	16
6	7	5	3–4	25	2,100'	21
7	9	5	2	17	3,100'	24

PREFACE

Guidebook authors face a dilemma. Without dedicated supporters, the wilderness wouldn't be protected. The best and most enthusiastic advocates are those who have visited the land, often with the help of a guidebook. On the other hand, too many boots can be destructive. So, as you use this guidebook, remember to tread lightly. It is the responsibility of every visitor to treat the land with respect and to speak out strongly for its preservation.

Even land officially protected as wilderness needs continued attention. If you have the time, seek out a trail maintenance organization in your area and volunteer your time; most such groups offer regular opportunities to pitch in and learn the skills required to keep our beloved trails in shape.

However, in many of Oregon's best-loved wild places, treading lightly isn't enough. The time has come for us to go beyond the well-known Leave No Trace principles. It must be our goal to leave behind a landscape that not only shows no trace of our presence but is also in better shape than before we arrived. Here are some guidelines:

- Leave no litter of your own, and pack out any litter left by others.

- Do some minor trail maintenance as you hike. Kick rocks off the trail and remove limbs and debris. Major trail maintenance problems, such as large blowdowns or washouts, should be reported to trail maintenance groups or land managers, so they can concentrate their limited dollars where they're needed most.

- *Always* camp in sites that are either compacted from years of previous use or can easily accommodate a tent without being damaged (sand, gravel bars, and densely wooded areas are best). Never camp on fragile meadow vegetation or beside lakes or streams. If you see camps being established in inappropriate places, be proactive. Place a few limbs or rocks over the area to discourage further use, scatter horse apples, and remove fire-scarred rocks. Report those who ignore the rules to rangers (or offer to help the offenders move to a better location).

- *Never* feed wildlife, and encourage others to do likewise.

• Do *not* build campfires. This holds doubly true for desert areas, where there is little fuel anyway. You don't need a fire to have a good time, and it is damaging to the land. When you discover a fire ring in an otherwise pristine area, scatter the rocks and cover the fire pit to discourage its use.

• Leave the following at home: soap (even biodegradable soap pollutes); pets (even well-mannered pets are instinctively seen as predators by wildlife); anything loud (bring headphones if you like listening to music or audiobooks in your tent).

• Pack out all waste, including toilet paper. For environmentally conscious backpackers, one good solution to the old dilemma of how to dispose of toilet paper is to find a natural alternative. Two excellent options are the large, soft leaves of thimbleberry at lower elevations and the light-green lichen that hangs from trees at higher elevations. They're not exactly Charmin soft, but they get the job done.

A WORD ABOUT THE FOURTH EDITION

Thanks to the enthusiastic response of hikers in every corner of the state, *Backpacking Oregon* now goes proudly into its fourth edition. Fans of previous editions will recognize the format, but we've made a handful of changes.

As this is a collection of the best and most iconic trails in Oregon, many of the featured trips will be familiar to experienced local backpackers. But we've added several new trips, including a stretch along the evolving and underappreciated Fremont National Recreation Trail, and we've included two coastal adventures that take advantage of continuing improvements to the Oregon Coast Trail. Both the Eagle Creek Trail in the Columbia River Gorge and the Wenaha River Trail in Eastern Oregon are back for this edition, having reopened in the wake of major wildfires; they look a little different now, of course, but these and other areas have a scarred beauty we'll all need to learn to appreciate as huge fires become commonplace across the Northwest. Other trips have been rerouted and redesigned, whether to improve road access or to maximize enjoyment of an area's natural beauty while minimizing time spent on fire-ravaged trails. And speaking of wildfires, we have also included a new section on how to plan around them, where to find out about fire-related closures, and what to do when they interfere with your backpacking plans.

All the trips have been carefully updated to reflect recent changes in trail conditions, access roads, permit details, administrative rules, and the like. We continue to recommend worthwhile side trips and new places to explore on (or off) the trail, and we've added longer or shorter alternatives for several featured trips.

Finally, we hope readers will not feel unduly bound to particular routes as they are outlined in this book. There's more than one way to hike every trail here. Use our recommended itineraries as a springboard, but then get creative: Find a good map, study trail reports, and gradually build the confidence to design your own backpacking adventures according to your ability, schedule, and preferences. Making each trip your own is not only fun but also helps reduce the impact on certain "over-loved" areas.

We hope you enjoy using this guidebook as much as we enjoyed putting it together. Please feel free to contact us, in care of Wilderness Press, at the address listed on the copyright page, with your suggestions and updates, so that this book can continue to be the best and most accurate backpacking guide to the Beaver State.

ACKNOWLEDGMENTS

Douglas Lorain: Years ago, this was my first guidebook (of what would turn out to be many), and more people than it would be possible to list helped turn my stumbling initial efforts into a high-quality book that has stood the test of time. So, a *huge* shout-out is due to all of the hiking partners; conservation-minded people and organizations; dedicated Forest Service, Bureau of Land Management, and Oregon State Parks personnel; fellow hikers met along the way; great editors and other folks at AdventureKEEN/Wilderness Press; and miscellaneous other outstanding people who contributed their time and expertise. I'd also be remiss not to offer my heartfelt appreciation to Becky Ohlsen for taking over this project, adding a huge dollop of her new perspective, wonderful enthusiasm, and endless talents. The book could not be in better hands. Finally, and most of all, much love and appreciation to my wife, Becky Lovejoy, for . . . well . . . everything.

Becky Ohlsen: Thanks to Wilderness Press and to Douglas Lorain for trusting me to update this iconic guidebook once again. Building on Douglas's original work amounted to a masterclass in planning, mapping, adapting, and describing the kind of backcountry adventures that keep readers coming back for more. On that note, thanks to *you,* the person holding this book; we couldn't do this if not for you. For their patience, I also want to thank everyone I've neglected for the past two summers while doing the fieldwork for this guide, and my parents for providing a beautiful place to land when the fieldwork was done and it came time to write. Thanks also to the Sang-Froid Riding Club; Terminal Gravity Brewing in Enterprise, Oregon; Dudley's Bookshop Café in Bend; the Southern Colorado Photography Society; the WatchDuty app; wildland firefighters everywhere; Trailkeepers of Oregon, the Siskiyou Mountain Club, and all the other volunteer organizations dedicated to trail maintenance; and staff in every ranger station and BLM office who put up with my probably baffling questions.

INTRODUCTION

There are many ways to see and appreciate the beauty of Oregon. Many parts of the state can be seen just as easily (sometimes more efficiently) via day hikes, rafting trips, bicycle tours, or even from your car. This book, however, focuses on the best ways for backpackers to see the state. After many years and tens of thousands of trail miles, the authors have listed what they believe to be Oregon's very best backpacking trips. The emphasis is on longer trips—from three days to a week or more. These are beyond a simple weekend outing, but they make terrific vacations and give you enough time to fully appreciate the scenery. Best of all, you'll have the chance to get to know and love the country.

HOW TO USE THIS GUIDE

Each featured trip begins with an information box that provides a quick overview of the hike's vital statistics and important features. This lets you rapidly narrow down your options based on your preferences, your abilities, how many days you have available, and the time of year.

Scenery This is the authors' subjective opinion of the trip's overall scenic quality, on a 1 (an eyesore) to 10 (drop-dead gorgeous) scale. This rating is based on the authors' personal biases in favor of flowers, photogenic views, and clear streams. If your tastes run more toward lush forests or good fishing, then your own rating may be quite different. Also, keep in mind that the rating is a *relative* one. All the featured trips are beautiful, and if they were somehow transplanted to, say, Nebraska, they would justifiably draw crowds of admirers.

Solitude Because solitude is one of the things backpackers are seeking, it helps to know roughly how much company you can expect. This rating is also on a 1 (bring stilts to see over the crowds) to 10 (just you and the juncos) scale. Of course, even on a trip rated as a 9 or 10, there's always an outside chance that you'll end up plagued by a pack of wild Cub Scouts.

Difficulty This is yet another subjective judgment by the authors. The rating is intended to warn you away from the most difficult outings if you're not in shape to try them. The scale is only relative to other backpacking trips. Most Americans would find even the easiest backpacking trip to be a very strenuous undertaking. So, this scale of 1 (barely leave the La-Z-Boy) to 10 (the Ironman Triathlon) is only for people already accustomed to backpacking.

Miles This item lists the total mileage of the recommended trip in its most basic form (with no side trips). For most trips, however, a second mileage number (in parentheses) includes distances for recommended side trips. These side trips are also shown on the maps and included in the "Possible Itinerary" section. (Note: Mileage and elevation gain/loss readings vary from one GPS device to the next, even for two hikers walking the same trail at the same time. The numbers we provide accurately reflect our research, but hikers should always treat these stats as approximate and expect some variability.)

Elevation Gain For many hikers, how far up they go is even more important than the distance. This entry shows the trip's total elevation gain, not the net gain. As with the mileage section, a second number (in parentheses beside the first number) includes the elevation gain in recommended side trips.

Days This is a rough figure for how long it will take the average backpacker to do the trip. It is based on traveling about 10 miles per day. Also considered were the spacing of available campsites and the trip's difficulty. Hard-core hikers may cover as many as 25 miles a day, while others saunter along at 4 or 5 miles per day, a good pace for hikers with children. Most trips can be done in more or fewer days, depending on your preferences and abilities.

Shuttle Mileage This is the shortest one-way driving distance between the beginning and ending trailheads. Be sure to schedule enough time at both ends of your trip to complete the necessary car shuttle.

Maps Every trip includes a sketch map that is as up-to-date and accurate as possible. As every hiker knows, however, you'll also need a good contour map of the area. This line identifies the best available map(s) for the described trip. All references to USGS maps are for the 7.5-minute series.

Usually Open This entry tells you when a trip is usually snow-free enough for hiking (which can vary considerably from year to year).

Best This note lists the particular time(s) of year when the trip is typically at its best (when the flowers peak, the fall colors are at their best, or the mosquitoes have died down, and so on). Unfortunately, the best season may also be the most crowded, so you may prefer to visit when conditions aren't as good, but you'll enjoy more solitude.

Permits Several areas require backpackers to obtain and carry permits, and other areas restrict the number of hikers allowed into traditionally crowded locations. Many of these permits are free, but a few agencies charge for them (and some are technically free but include a processing or reservation fee). Generally, you can reserve these permits online via the recreation.gov website, but if in doubt, call or visit the nearest U.S. Forest Service ranger station. It is always advisable to plan ahead, as permits for some of the most popular hikes are released early in the year and sell out quickly. If you get a coveted permit and then can't use it, be sure to cancel so someone else can take your spot.

Rules This section lists any restrictions on fires, camping, or the number of people in your party, as well as other regulations for the area. Keep in mind that there are often temporary restrictions in place on top of those listed; for example, trail closures or fire bans; follow all posted rules.

Contact This item includes the phone number and website for the local land agency responsible for this area. Be sure to check on road and trail conditions, as well as any new restrictions or permit requirements, before your trip.

Special Attractions This section focuses on attributes of this trip that are rare or outstanding. For example, almost every trip has views, but some have views that are especially noteworthy. The same is true of areas with a good chance of seeing wildlife, with excellent fishing, and so on.

Challenges This is the flip side to the "Special Attractions" section. It lists the trip's special or especially troublesome problems. Expect to see warnings about areas with particularly abundant mosquitoes, poor road access, or limited water.

How to Get There This section includes driving directions to the trailhead(s), as well as GPS coordinates.

Tips, Warnings, and Notes Throughout the text are numerous helpful hints and ideas. These all result from the authors' experiences. We hope these prominently labeled Tips, Warnings, and Notes will make your trips safer and more enjoyable the first time through.

Possible Itinerary This is listed at the end of each trip. To be used as a planning tool, it includes daily mileages and total elevation gains, as well as recommended side trips. Your own itinerary is likely to be different.

WILD AREAS OF OREGON

What follows is a general overview of the principal remaining wild areas in the state of Oregon. All of these have at least one backpacking trip in the featured trips section. Thus, whether you're a desert rat, beachcomber, peak bagger, or canyon lover, there's a choice of outstanding trips for you.

It is appropriate here to say a few words about Crater Lake, probably the best-known scenic attraction in the state. It is also the only major natural wonder for which there is no recommended trip. Construction of the rim road around the lake created one of the most spectacular drives in North America and simultaneously eliminated any chance for developing what would have been one of the most spectacular hikes on the continent. Today the national park features only short (but very scenic) day hikes. The only backpacking is through generally viewless forests, well away from the lake, with little to recommend it other than solitude. The best plan is to visit the park (it really is too good to miss), take a day hike or two, and then head for the longer trails in the nearby Mount Thielsen, Rogue River, or Sky Lakes area.

As you explore these wild places, it's important to keep in mind their long and multilayered history. Backpacking in Oregon means walking through the traditional homelands of Indigenous people, including nine federally recognized tribal groups: the Burns Paiute Tribe, the Confederated Tribes of Coos, the Lower Umpqua and Siuslaw Indians, the Confederated Tribes of Grand Ronde, the Confederated Tribes of Siletz Indians, the Confederated Tribes of the Umatilla Indian Reservation, the Confederated Tribes of Warm Springs, the Cow Creek Band of Umpqua Tribe of Indians, the Coquille Indian Tribe, and the Klamath Tribes.

OREGON COAST

The Oregon coast is world-famous and unmissable. Countless tourists drive up and down this shoreline enjoying some of the continent's best scenery. The coastal highway has also become a popular bicycle tour. Hikers are also drawn to the coast's abundant and diverse wildlife. Long before we *Homo sapiens* built summer homes at the beach, it attracted numerous other species. Keep an eye out for whales, harbor seals, and sea lions. Tidepools teem with life in a dizzying array of forms and colors. The Oregon coast is especially popular with our feathered friends. The cliffs and offshore rocks here support some 1.3 million nesting birds—more than the coasts of California and Washington *combined*, even though the total shoreline mileage of those two states is almost five times longer. Nesting bird numbers peak from about mid-May to the end of June.

NOTE: All offshore rocks are part of a protected wildlife refuge and are strictly off-limits to people. Bring binoculars to get a close-up view.

Visiting midweek will help you avoid crowds, but the best plan is to hike in the off-season. The beach is a great place to visit during a patch of good weather in the winter and is equally scenic in fall (after Labor Day) or spring (before Memorial Day). Whenever you visit, remember to prepare for the notoriously volatile Oregon weather.

KLAMATH AND SISKIYOU MOUNTAINS

Most of southwestern Oregon is a jumbled mass of ancient mountains cut by scenic river canyons. These mountains are much older than the better-known Cascades or Wallowas, and their peculiar geology and botany are a large part of their charm. Unique soils and millions of years of isolation have resulted in Oregon's greatest concentration of rare and unusual plants. This region is truly a botanist's paradise.

The higher Siskiyou Mountains to the east are friendlier terrain for hikers. They feature less-steep trails, small lakes, diverse forests, and cooler summer temperatures. Both ranges provide lots of solitude, wildflowers, and surprisingly abundant wildlife.

COLUMBIA RIVER GORGE

Despite its proximity to a major city and the presence of an interstate freeway, railroads, towns, and dams, much of the Columbia River Gorge remains remarkably wild. Thousands of day hikers hit the trails here every weekend to see the waterfalls, canyons, lush vegetation, clear streams, and views. By hiking a combination of the area's longer trails, backpackers can enjoy these same features, with the added benefit of relative solitude. The Gorge is especially beautiful in late spring, when the wildflowers are blooming and the waterfalls are more impressive, and in late October and very early November, when the dogwoods and maples turn color and people are scarce. Summer, on the other hand, is a poor time for a visit, due to crowds and the often hot and muggy conditions at these lower elevations. The Gorge also has a few hazards. Poison oak is common at elevations below about 1,000 feet. Early-season hikers should expect some trails to be closed due to washouts or landslides. Fires have swept through the area in recent years, destroying some trails and making others less appealing. Darkness comes very quickly in these steep canyons, especially in the fall, so make camp early. Finally, even though elevations are relatively low, hikes here usually require a great deal of climbing, since you start near sea level along the Columbia River. Getting to the tops of those cliffs and ridges requires lots of sweat.

HIGH CASCADES

Many of the trips in this guide are in the High Cascades—centered on well-known volcanic peaks like Mount Hood, Mount Jefferson, and the Three Sisters. These are the signature mountains of the state, and they deserve their popularity. All feature exceptional scenery, wildflower-filled meadows, and miles of trails. Even backpacking snobs who avoid any trail with the slightest whiff of popularity can't resist doing a classic trip like the Timberline Trail at least once in a lifetime. The peaks in the southern part of the range are lower and lack glaciers, but they are also less crowded. Between these peaks, the High Cascades showcase great expanses of forests and numerous lakes. Fortunately, most of the best areas have been set aside as wilderness, so backpackers can enjoy many days of scenic travel without the intrusion of roads, chainsaws, or motorbikes.

The ultimate way to experience these mountains is to hike from one end of the state to the other along the Pacific Crest Trail. A total of about 455 trail miles extend from Fish Lake (east of Medford) to the Columbia River at Cascade Locks. Most people have neither the time nor the energy to tackle this monthlong excursion. A few well-chosen backpacking vacations of 4–10 days, however, can hit all the highlights and provide enough memories to last a lifetime.

Summer in the Oregon Cascades is just about ideal. While you should come prepared for rain, your chances of encountering endless days of wetness are rather small, despite all those stories we tell out-of-staters in an effort to keep them out. You should expect rain perhaps one day in four, and it is even possible to go weeks without any rain. Temperatures are usually in a comfortable range (both day and night) with low humidity. Flowers bloom in profusion, and the quiet hiker has a good chance of seeing wildlife. There are no dangerous animals to worry about because rattlesnakes are found on the east side only at lower elevations, and grizzly bears have been gone for more than a century. Even horse flies and deer flies—so abundant in other parts of North America—are rarely a problem in these mountains. The only issues worth mentioning are mosquitoes (particularly in the lake country) and the need to get permits for some areas, as land managers slowly try to reduce the impact of too many visitors.

BLUE MOUNTAINS

For the most part, northeastern Oregon's Blue Mountains are a gentle region of rolling mountains, open forests, and enticing meadows. In places, however, subranges with snowy crags and sparkling lakes reach dramatically skyward. Elsewhere, rivers have cut impressive canyons into the lava tablelands. At these special places, backpackers can savor not only grand scenery but also lightly traveled trails.

The Wallowas (see the subsection below) are the best-known mountains in this area, but the Strawberry Mountains and the Elkhorn Range have very similar scenery, with only a fraction of the people. Like the Wallowas, these smaller and more compact ranges showcase craggy granite peaks, sparkling lakes, meadows ablaze with wildflowers, and wildlife such as elk, bighorn sheep, and mountain goats. Unlike in the Wallowas, hikers won't have to face trails pounded to dust by heavy horse use or compete with hundreds of other hikers for a campsite.

A big advantage for hikers accustomed to the jungles of the Western Cascades is the open nature of the forests here. The drier climate means less undergrowth, so cross-country travel is much easier. The weather is also generally better, except for afternoon thunderstorms. Mosquitoes present the usual problems near lakes in July, and rattlesnakes are common in the lower canyons.

WALLOWA MOUNTAINS

Though billed as America's Little Switzerland, the Wallowa Mountains of northeastern Oregon are actually more similar to California's Sierra Nevada. (That comparison, however, apparently doesn't carry the same marketing appeal.) The mountains are a stunningly beautiful mix of white granite peaks, shimmering lakes and streams, alpine meadows, and attractive forests, seemingly designed with backpackers in mind. The bulk of the most scenic country is beyond the range of day hikers. For long-distance hikers, however, the Eagle Cap Wilderness is laced with hundreds of miles of interconnecting trails. Because more than 75% of all visits are to the Lakes Basin, Aneroid Lake, and Glacier Lake areas, there are many miles of lonesome trails in other areas to explore.

Relative to the region's attributes, the downsides are so minor that only a true pessimist could dwell on them. Nonetheless, you should be prepared for crowds in a few areas, mosquitoes near the lakes in July, afternoon thunderstorms, and dusty (and aromatic) trails due to fairly heavy horse use.

Most of the range's many highlights are within the areas of the described trips. If, like the authors, you develop a love for this country and want to see more, there are dozens of additional places to explore. Almost any chosen destination will reward you with beautiful scenery and wonderful memories.

HELLS CANYON

The vastness of Hells Canyon is impossible to describe. Neither words nor photographs seem able to capture it adequately. One must personally experience the area to appreciate it properly. Unlike the heavily forested trails familiar to most Oregonians, the mostly treeless routes here present nonstop great views. The gaping chasm, backed by the snowcapped peaks of Idaho's Seven Devils Mountains, presents an incredible expanse of jaw-dropping scenery. The canyon is also one of the best areas for viewing wildlife in the state. Elk, deer, black bears, coyotes, bighorn sheep, mountain goats (on the Idaho side), numerous birds, and various reptiles are all common.

Like the canyon itself, the problems associated with backpacking in Hells Canyon are also on a grand scale. Summer's heat in the shadeless lower canyon is unbearable.

Campsite at Aneroid Lake *(Trip 21, page 137)*

Rattlesnakes, ticks, and black widow spiders are all common, and the canyon supports large populations of black bears and mountain lions. Though no one has been attacked, hikers have reported being stalked by lions. Thickets of poison ivy crowd the lower-elevation trails near water. Even the main trails are often rough, steep, and hard to follow, and lesser-used paths may be nothing more than rumors. Access roads (when they exist at all) are typically long, rough, dirt roads that may be impassable for passenger cars and should generally not be attempted when wet. This is truly the realm of the dedicated adventurer.

Three roughly parallel trails travel the entire north–south length of the canyon. Each is described in the text. Because they are at different elevations, they have different peak seasons. Numerous connecting paths allow for loop trips of almost any length.

SOUTHEASTERN OREGON

Oregon is famous for its dense green forests, rain-soaked valleys, and glacier-clad peaks. Not so well known is that fully one-third of the state is desert. Brown, not green, is the predominant color of southeastern Oregon. Trees are either scarce or nonexistent. Rain falls infrequently, and glaciers are just a distant memory.

Though the landscape differs from western Oregon, it is at least as scenic. The country is especially appealing to those who prefer open views to dense forests, and dry weather to overcast and drizzle. The principal attractions for backpackers are the mountain ranges that rise dramatically from the sagebrush plains. These spectacular mountains have water (due to more precipitation at higher elevations), lots of flowers, and vistas that seem to stretch to eternity. Most of the mountains also have few (if any) people. Wildlife is no more abundant here than elsewhere in Oregon, but the lack of dense vegetation makes it much easier to actually see the animals.

The best-known and most spectacular mountain is Steens Mountain, with its great glacial gorges and towering snowy cliffs. Other nearby ranges like the Pueblo, Hart, and Trout Creek Mountains provide more solitude for those who want to gain a more meaningful distance from the world of crowds and machines. To truly get away from it all, just head off into the seemingly endless sagebrush. A few of the more interesting areas to consider are Beatys Butte, Orejana Canyon, Coyote Lake, Hawk Mountain, Oregon End Table, and Diablo Peak. If you can even find these places on the map, you'll be well on your way to your own desert adventure.

Those unaccustomed to desert travel must beware of some unique hazards. Expect rattlesnakes, ticks (extremely abundant in spring), long distances between water sources, poorly maintained roads, and few established trails.

Hidden in southeastern Oregon near the Idaho border is a land that looks more typical of southern Utah than Oregon. Several spectacularly deep slot canyons and colorful rock formations cut into the sagebrush plains and mountains of the Owyhee River region. The cliffs host bighorn sheep, while pronghorns and wild horses roam the plateaus. It all adds up to a stunningly scenic land, with the added advantage of being a great place to go for solitude. There are *no* crowds here; in fact, you are unlikely to see another human being for weeks of hiking.

The isolation creates unique problems requiring extra precautions. The only trails are those traveled by deer or cattle, so at least one group member must be very good with a map and compass. Many roads here are very poor, especially when wet, and rarely traveled. Carry plenty of emergency gear in your car—extra food, *lots* of extra water, spare parts and tools, and so on. Bring along an especially well-stocked first aid kit (and, of course, you *are* up-to-date on your first aid methods and skills, right?). Except for the bottoms of major river canyons, water is very scarce. In addition, the canyon country throughout southeastern Oregon gets extremely hot during the summer (June–mid-September). Carry *at least* 3 gallons of water in your car, and a gallon per day when hiking. You should always assume water sources are badly polluted by livestock—*double treat* all water. The authors' preference is to first use iodine, wait, and then filter it.

The above precautions aside, this area is well worth the extra effort to explore. Spring (late April–May) is especially nice, with wildflowers, cooler temperatures, and more water. To hike the canyons, however, fall is usually better because water levels are lower and you won't have to do as much wading.

SAFETY

The trips described in this book are long and often difficult, and some go through remote wilderness terrain. In the event of an emergency, supplies and medical facilities may be several days away. Anyone who attempts these hikes must be experienced in wilderness travel, properly equipped, and in good physical condition. While backpacking is not inherently dangerous, the sport *does* involve risk. Because trail conditions, weather, and hikers' abilities all vary considerably, the authors and the publisher cannot assume responsibility for the safety of anyone who takes these hikes. Use plenty of common sense and a realistic appraisal of your abilities so you can enjoy these trips safely.

References to water in the text attest only to its availability, not its purity. All backcountry water should be treated before drinking.

POISONOUS PLANTS

Recognizing poison ivy and oak and avoiding contact with them are the most effective ways to prevent the painful, itchy rashes associated with these plants. Poison ivy ranges from a thick, tree-hugging vine to a shaded ground cover, with three leaflets to a leaf; poison oak occurs as either a vine or shrub, with three leaflets as well. Urushiol, the oil in the sap of these plants, is responsible for the rash. Usually within 12–14 hours of exposure (but sometimes much later), raised lines and/or blisters will appear, accompanied by a terrible itch. Refrain from scratching because bacteria under fingernails can cause infection. Wash and dry the rash thoroughly, applying a calamine lotion or other product to help dry out the rash. If itching or blistering is severe, seek medical attention. Note that oil-contaminated clothes, pets, or hiking gear can easily cause an irritating rash on you or someone else, so wash not only any exposed parts of your body but also clothes, gear, and pets.

MOSQUITOES

Mosquitoes are common in Oregon, especially spring–midsummer. Though it's very rare, individuals can become infected with the West Nile virus by being bitten by an infected mosquito. Culex mosquitoes, the primary varieties that can transmit West Nile virus to humans, thrive in urban rather than natural areas. They lay their eggs in stagnant water and can breed in any standing water that remains for more than five days. Most people infected with West Nile virus have no symptoms of illness, but some may become ill, usually 3–15 days after being bitten.

Anytime you expect mosquitoes to be buzzing around, you may want to wear protective clothing, such as long sleeves, long pants, and socks. Loose-fitting, light-colored clothing is best. Spray clothing with insect repellent. Remember to follow the instructions on the repellent and to take extra care to protect children against these insects.

Mist adds mystery to the coastal forests of Tillamook Head. *(Trip 1, page 17)*

SNAKES

In some of the regions described in this book, you may encounter venomous rattlesnakes. They like to bask in the sun and won't bite unless threatened. Hibernation season is typically October–April. Most of the snakes you will see while hiking, however, will be non-venomous species and subspecies. The best rule is to leave all snakes alone, give them a wide berth as you hike past, and make sure any hiking companions (including dogs) do the same. When hiking, stick to well-used trails, and wear over-the-ankle boots and loose-fitting long pants. Do not step or put your hands beyond your range of detailed visibility, and avoid wandering around in the dark. Step onto logs and rocks, never over them, and be especially careful when climbing rocks. Always avoid walking through dense brush or willow thickets.

TICKS

Ticks are often found on brush and tall grass, where they seem to be waiting to hitch a ride on a warm-blooded passerby. Adult ticks are most active April–May and again October–November. Among the varieties of ticks, the black-legged tick, commonly called the deer tick, is the primary carrier of Lyme disease, but documented cases of Lyme in Oregon are uncommon. Ticks here are more of a nuisance than a serious health risk (though tick bites always carry the risk of infection, so properly disinfecting the area is key). Wear light-colored clothing to make it easier for you to spot ticks before they migrate to your skin.

At the end of the hike, visually check your hair, back of neck, armpits, and socks. During your post-hike shower, take a moment to do a more complete body check. For ticks that are already embedded, removal with tweezers is best. Grasp the tick close to your skin, and remove it by pulling straight out firmly. Do your best to remove the head, but do not twist. Use disinfectant solution on the wound.

BLACK BEARS

Though attacks by black bears are uncommon, the sight or approach of a bear can give anyone a start. If you encounter a bear while hiking, remain calm and avoid running in any direction. Make loud noises to scare off the bear, and back away slowly. In primitive and remote areas, assume bears are present. Most encounters are food related, as bears have an exceptional sense of smell and not particularly discriminating tastes. Hang all food (and anything else with an odor) at night and any time you leave your camp unattended; consider renting a bear canister—it adds weight but also convenience. Several campsites have bear boxes or electric fences; take advantage of these.

WILDFIRES

Unfortunately, wildfires are increasingly becoming a factor in planning any backcountry outing. In recent years, it's been tough to find a region of the state during hiking season that isn't affected by trail closures due to active or recent wildfires, and the places not burning are often plagued by unsightly or even dangerous clouds of wildfire smoke. Unless you have a crystal ball, there's no telling where a fire might roar to life—they can appear overnight and grow unpredictably.

All of this means that you can spend hours or days meticulously planning every detail of an epic backpacking adventure, only to be heartbroken when your chosen trail is suddenly closed. There's no way to completely prevent this, but there are a few precautions you can take.

First, when you plan your hike, choose one or two alternative trips in case your first choice becomes inaccessible. Having a few backup options in mind will allow you to switch gears without being totally disappointed in case your plans have to change. (And if your original plan works out, you'll be ahead of the game on next year's plans!)

Second, use the available technology to keep yourself as up-to-date as possible on fire and weather conditions. Most GPS mapping software includes optional layers that show current and historical wildfire zones. These are useful not only for avoiding smoke and active fires, but also for predicting whether a trail might have a lot of blown-down trees, shadeless areas, or ruined campsites. Studying recent trip reports online can also help with this level of planning.

For up-to-the-minute wildfire information, sign up for text alerts in the region you'll be visiting, as well as statewide emergency alerts at wildfire.oregon.gov. Mobile apps such as WatchDuty and the interactive website InciWeb (inciweb.wildfire.gov) provide constant updates on wildfire activity around the state. Always check in at local ranger stations before you head out on a trip during wildfire season. And this should go without saying, but respect posted closure signs on trails and access roads, for everyone's safety.

GENERAL TIPS ON BACKPACKING IN OREGON

This book is not a how-to guide for backpackers. Anyone contemplating an extended backpacking vacation will (or at least should) already know about equipment, Leave No Trace principles, conditioning, selecting a campsite, first aid, and all the other aspects of this sport. Myriad excellent books cover these subjects. It is appropriate, however, to discuss some tips and ideas that are specific to Oregon and the Pacific Northwest.

1) Most national forests in Oregon require a trailhead parking pass (Northwest Forest Pass). As of 2025, daily permits cost $5, and an annual pass, good in all U.S. Forest Service fee sites in Oregon and Washington, was $30 (actually a pretty good deal). The fees are used for trail maintenance, wilderness rangers' pay, and trailhead improvements. You can order the passes online at discovernw.org or buy them at ranger stations and many outdoors stores.

2) The winter's snowpack has a significant effect not only on when a trail opens but also on peak wildflower times, peak stream flows, and how long seasonal water sources will be available. You can check the snowpack around April 1 and note how it compares to normal. The most accurate information on snowpack is available from the SNOTEL measurements collected in key areas around the state; look up the region you plan to visit on the Natural Resources Conservation Services' handy interactive map (nrcs.usda.gov/oregon/snow-survey). If the snowpack is significantly above or below average, adjust the trip's seasonal recommendations accordingly.

3) When driving on Oregon's forest roads, keep a wary eye out for log trucks. These scary behemoths often barrel along with little regard for those annoying speed bumps known as passenger cars.

4) The Northwest's frequent winter storms create annual problems for trail crews. Early-season hikers should expect to crawl over deadfall and search for routes around landslides and flooded riverside trails. Depending on current funding and the trail's popularity, maintenance may not be completed until several weeks after a trail is snow-free and officially open. Unfortunately, this means that trail maintenance is often done well after the best time to visit. On the positive side, trails are usually less crowded before the maintenance has been completed.

5) Mid-August is usually the best time for swimming in mountain lakes. Water temperatures (while never exactly tropical) are at their warmest, and the bugs have decreased enough to allow you to dry off in relative peace. A swimsuit makes a good addition to your gear for any trip to the mountains at this time of year, or you can go with a birthday suit in less popular areas.

6) General deer-hunting season in Oregon runs from the first weekend of October to the end of the month or early November. Also, for a week in early to mid-September, Oregon holds a High Cascades deer hunt in the wilderness areas of the Cascade Mountains. For safety, anyone planning to travel in the forests during these periods (particularly those doing any cross-country travel) should carry and wear a bright red or orange cap, vest, pack, or other conspicuous article of clothing.

7) Elk-hunting season is in late October or, more often, early November. The exact season varies in different parts of the state, but the same precautions apply: Wear bright red or orange somewhere conspicuous.

8) Mushrooms are an Oregon backcountry delicacy. Though our damp climate makes it possible to find mushrooms in any season, late August–November is usually best. Where and when the mushrooms can be found varies with elevation, precipitation, and other factors.

WARNING: Make absolutely sure that you know your fungi. Several poisonous species exist in our forests, and you do not want to make a mistake.

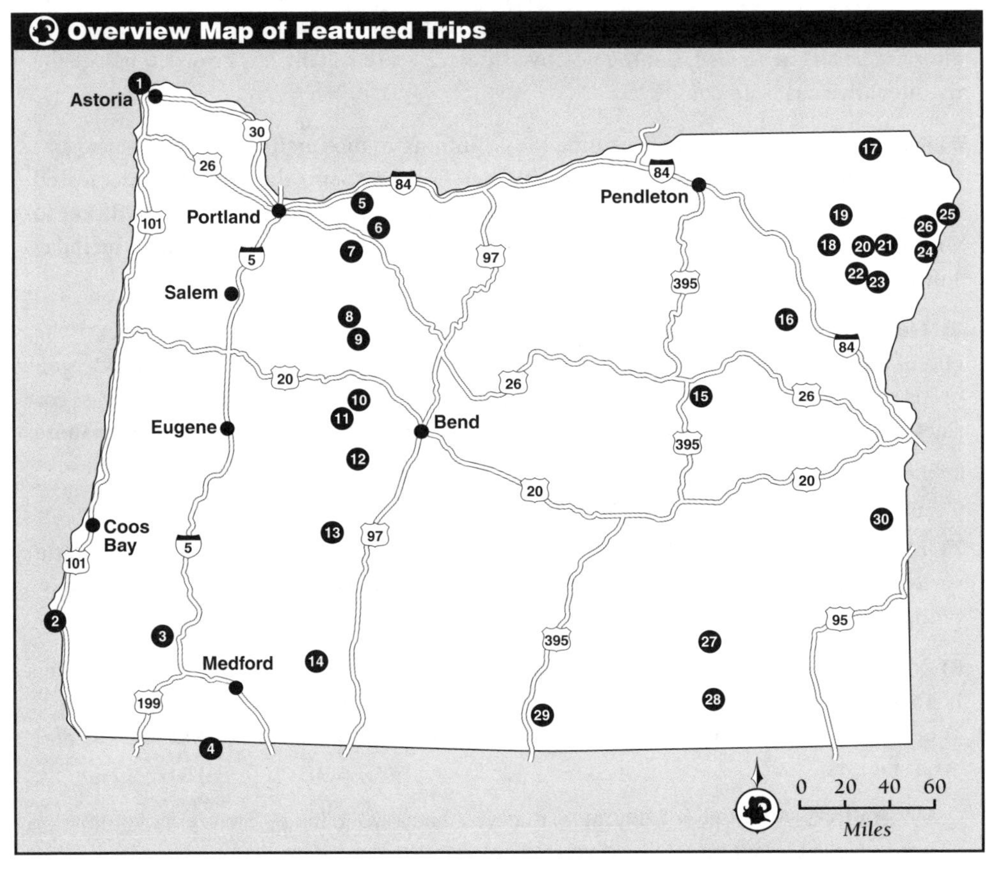

OPPOSITE: A view up the coastline from Neahkahnie Mountain
(Trip 1, page 17)

FEATURED TRIPS

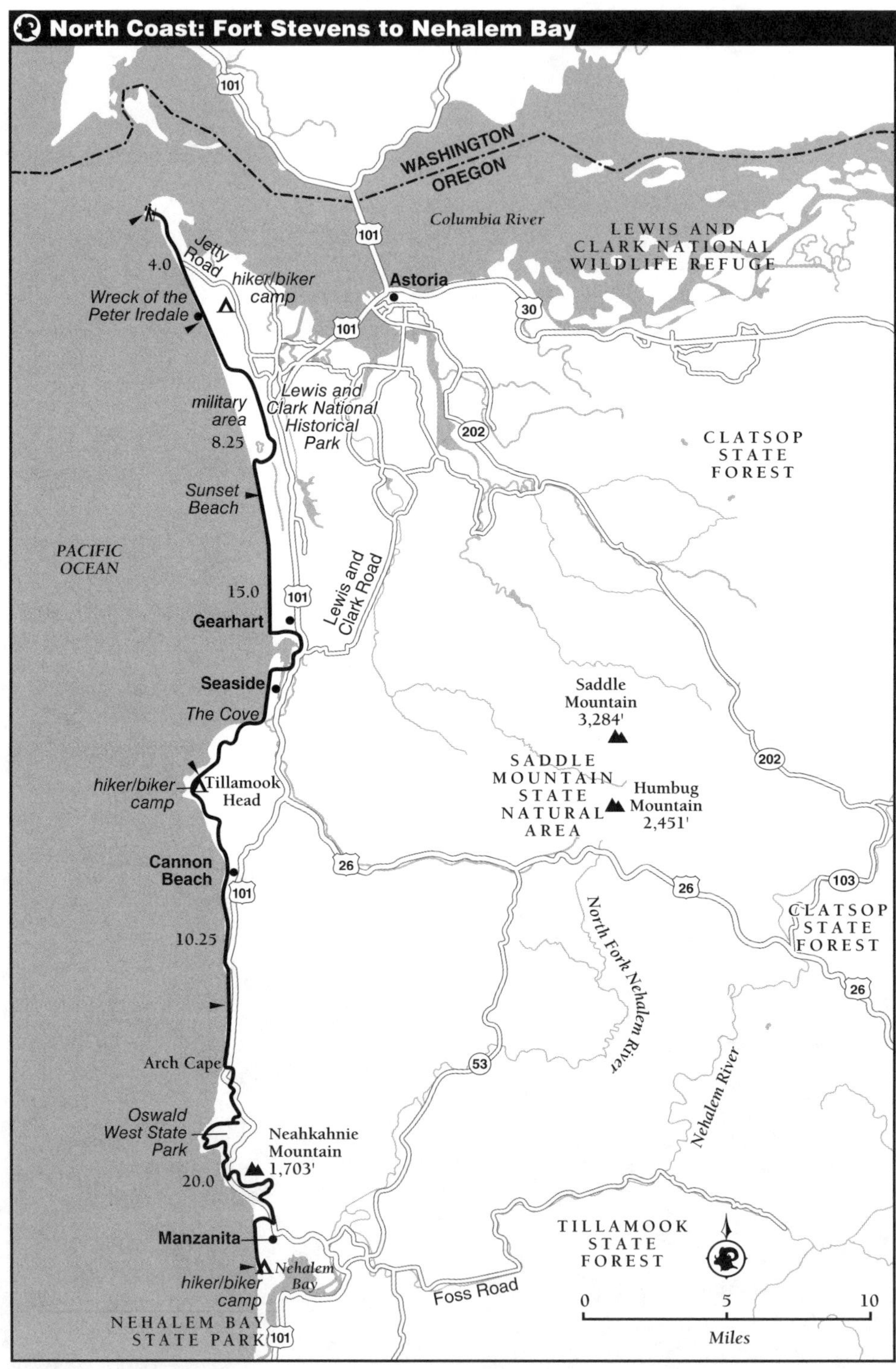
North Coast: Fort Stevens to Nehalem Bay
101
WASHINGTON
OREGON
Columbia River
LEWIS AND CLARK NATIONAL WILDLIFE REFUGE
101
Jetty Road
4.0
hiker/biker camp
Astoria
Wreck of the Peter Iredale
30
101
Lewis and Clark National Historical Park
military area
8.25
202
CLATSOP STATE FOREST
Sunset Beach
PACIFIC OCEAN
Lewis and Clark Road
15.0
101
Gearhart
Seaside
The Cove
Saddle Mountain 3,284'
SADDLE MOUNTAIN STATE NATURAL AREA
Humbug Mountain 2,451'
202
hiker/biker camp
Tillamook Head
Cannon Beach
26
101
26
103
CLATSOP STATE FOREST
10.25
North Fork Nehalem River
26
Arch Cape
53
Nehalem River
Oswald West State Park
Neahkahnie Mountain 1,703'
20.0
Manzanita
TILLAMOOK STATE FOREST
Nehalem Bay
hiker/biker camp
Foss Road
0
5
10
Miles
NEHALEM BAY STATE PARK
101

NORTH COAST: FORT STEVENS TO NEHALEM BAY

RATINGS: Scenery 8 **Solitude** 2 **Difficulty** 5

MILES: 58

ELEVATION GAIN: 6,240'

DAYS: 5

SHUTTLE MILEAGE: 42

MAPS: Green Trails *Oregon Coast North, Oregon Coast Trail, Astoria to Newport* (#356SX); oregoncoasttrail.org/maps

USUALLY OPEN: Year-round

BEST: May–September

PERMITS: None

RULES: No beach camping adjacent to state parks or within city limits. Stay out of marked nesting grounds of snowy plovers (March–September).

CONTACT: Fort Stevens State Park, 503-861-3170; Nehalem Bay State Park, 503-812-0650; Oregon Parks & Rec, 503-986-0707; stateparks.oregon.gov

SPECIAL ATTRACTIONS

Magnificent coastal scenery, open year-round

Above: Tillamook Head

CHALLENGES

Crowds, tides, limited trailhead parking, limited legal camping, some road walking

HOW TO GET THERE

For the north trailhead, from Portland, take US 26 west to US 101 North. Follow US 101 North for 13.5 miles, then turn left onto OR 104 North. In 0.3 mile turn left onto Columbia Beach Road and continue 4.5 miles, then turn left onto Jetty Road into Fort Stevens State Park and drive 4 miles to parking lot C.

To reach the south trailhead, return to US 101 South for 31 miles to Manzanita, then turn right onto Laneda Avenue and quickly left onto Classic Street for 1.5 miles, following signs to Nehalem Bay Campground, where the registration office can direct you to the hiker-biker campground and overflow parking area ($7 per vehicle per night).

GPS TRAILHEAD COORDINATES:

(Fort Stevens) N46° 13.612' W124° 0.847'
(Nehalem Bay) N45° 42.165' W123° 56.075'

INTRODUCTION

In the previous edition of this book, we made the tough decision not to include any backpacking trips along the Oregon Coast. At that time, the logistics of these trips had become challenging enough to discourage all but the most determined hiker. But since then, several equally determined folks have made substantial progress in getting around some of the trickier sections of the Oregon Coast Trail, a long-distance trek stretching 400 miles from the Columbia River to the California border. This trail has been hiked, with difficulty, since the 1980s, but it's getting less complicated all the time. There are still "critical gaps" in the trail, where hikers must trudge along US 101 or resort to non-hiking modes of transport to get across a bay or river, but the spectacular beauty of the Oregon Coast is worth the hassle.

In fact, some might argue that the challenges add to the fun. Backpacking along the Oregon Coast is unlike any other trip in this book. Let's be clear: This is not a wilderness trek. Most of the time, you're within a few miles of a mocha latte. On a clear day, kids might be flying kites right across your trail. And speaking of the "trail," it's often imaginary, drawn in sand. But if you're thinking, "Great, I love long walks on the beach," well, this isn't quite that, either. There is some beach walking, but there are also muddy trudges over forested headlands and a bit of navigating the streets of coastal towns. And while coffee shops are everywhere, legal camping is scarce.

Still, backpacking here is more feasible now than it has been for years, and much more satisfying than a day hike. This northern stretch of coast packs a lot of variety into a small area, from beaches and tidepools to dense forests and scenic overlooks, including notable points in the travels of Lewis and Clark. It's a good early- or late-season hike. May is best for flowers, but fall is less crowded. The hike is best done from north to south, so you'll have the wind at your back.

DESCRIPTION

The launch point for this hike is immediately thrilling, especially on a foggy morning. The trail starts along the South Jetty at the mouth of the Columbia River, a lofty vantage point from which to gaze either at the distant headlands you'll be climbing later or, depending on the weather, into an impenetrably thick gray cloud with occasional seagulls.

Start by passing two trailhead posts and heading south along the jetty, leaving behind a parking lot and now-closed observation deck. The jetty soon spits you out onto the first of many lovely beaches. Follow it 3 miles until you reach the ghostly wreck of the Peter Iredale, embedded in the sand. There's a public restroom and water here, and this is also the place to turn off if you plan on camping at the Fort Stevens State Park hiker-biker campground, a quarter mile inland.

Continue south along the beach for 2 miles until you reach the Camp Rilea military training area; if you're lucky you can just continue along the beach, but if there are training exercises going on, you may need to skirt around a 3-mile stretch of beach here using marked trails that head slightly inland. (Officers will let you know.) The detour adds just over 2 miles, partly along the Fort to Sea Trail, which follows in some of the many footsteps of the Lewis & Clark Expedition.

Back on the beach, you continue to make your way south; in 3 miles you reach Sunset Beach, with access to a public restroom. Although beach camping is officially discouraged here, people do it (try to be subtle and be aware there's no water source until Gearhart).

Five miles south of the beach access to Sunset Beach, turn inland to the town of Gearhart. Make your way through town, crossing Neacoxie Creek and walking south along US 101 for a short stretch into the town of Seaside, over Neawanna Creek and the Necanicum River. This is a good chance to resupply; you may also be able to find hiker-biker sites at one of the handful of commercial RV parks in Seaside.

At the south end of Seaside, you pass Seltzer Park (restroom and water available here), where you can watch surfers enjoying the Cove, then continue west along Sunset Boulevard until you reach a parking lot for the signed trail that climbs up and over Tillamook Head.

WARNING: This often-steep trail can be wet and squelchy at any time of year; the shoes that were perfect on the beach may not seem so great now, but then again, we've seen people tackle it in sandals. Just know that you'll likely have to step around muddy, slippery roots, over fallen logs, and across partially disintegrating boardwalks on this section.

The trail has been mostly flat until now, but here it begins a long climb through the second-growth forests of Ecola State Park up to the top of hulking Tillamook Head. It's usually cool, shaded, and even misty in these woods. You can catch occasional views over the ocean, but you mostly hear it rather than see it through the forest. The scenery soon improves again, though, as the trail closely follows the edge of Tillamook Head's dramatic cliffs. Several places provide breaks in the trees with sweeping views of cliffs and ocean. The highest of these is known as Clark's Point of View. In January 1806, Captain William Clark (of Lewis and Clark fame) stopped here with Sacagawea and other members of his party. The view, Clark wrote in his journal, encompassed "the grandest and most pleasing prospects which my eyes ever surveyed" (high praise considering all the wonders he had seen over the preceding two years).

The trail now drops half a mile in a series of switchbacks to a four-way junction. Turn right to reach a backpacker's camping area with a rough wooden shelter. (You'll need to bring your own water up here, but there is an outhouse.) Nearby is a spectacular viewpoint several hundred feet above the pounding surf. Not far off the coast, Tillamook Rock Lighthouse (fondly nicknamed Terrible Tilly) sits on a wind- and wave-swept offshore island. After dangerous and heroic construction efforts, this historic structure began operation in 1881 and continued its service until 1957, when it was abandoned.

TIP: A highly recommended book—fine reading material for this trip—is *Tillamook Light* by James Gibbs, a former lightkeeper on Tillamook Rock. His book masterfully mixes history with humorous anecdotes for a short but satisfying read.

Back at the four-way junction, turn south and steeply descend through a forest of ancient Sitka spruce trees.

After 1.6 miles you reach the Indian Beach Picnic Area at the end of the Ecola State Park access road (with restrooms and water). The old trail from here to Ecola Point Picnic

Manzanita Beach

Area washed out in 2017, and the new route takes you slightly farther inland, which means not as many good views along the way. But there are excellent viewpoints at either end, including from the Ecola Point Picnic Area (although the trail out to Ecola Point is permanently off-limits due to washouts). You'll share the view with lots of tourists, but it's still a worthwhile stop.

To continue your tour, pick up the Oregon Coast Trail near the picnic area's restroom and hike south. Cross a road leading to the park maintenance center, then top a small ridge where there is a superb viewpoint looking to the south. The trail drops a bit, then goes up and down for almost a mile before reaching the access path to Crescent Beach—well worth the side trip. The main trail goes straight from the junction and follows an often-muddy route that features several nice viewpoints.

The trail joins a road shortly before the park entrance gate and follows it to another road, which drops into the photogenic town of Cannon Beach. Here you have the option (unusual in the middle of a backpacking trip) to do some shopping, go to a nice restaurant, or spend the night in a luxury hotel.

TIP: Plan to hike the next several miles of beach at low tide. This will allow you to explore the many interesting tidepools near famous Haystack Rock. In addition, the beach is more solid on the hard-packed wet sand of low tide, making hiking much easier, and three of the headlands require medium-to-low tide to get around.

Walk south along the popular beach and slowly leave civilization behind as you pass first Cannon Beach and Haystack Rock, and then the resort community of Tolovana Beach (where there's a large parking lot with a public restroom). Silver Point and, 0.7 mile later, Humbug Point can both be rounded at any tide other than high tide. There's water and a restroom at Arcadia Beach, and it's possible to camp south of here (just not directly adjacent to the state recreation area).

WARNING: In winter, storms often erode the beach, making it difficult to walk this section at any time but very low tide.

Low tide is necessary to getting around historic Hug Point, where the route is briefly an old roadbed. In the days before US 101 was built, the beach was the road between Cannon Beach and Arch Cape, and Hug Point was a significant obstacle. A narrow roadway that was blasted into the rock here allowed vehicles to get around this point (one at a time) in between crashing waves. In addition to the historical interest, Hug Point features a scenic little waterfall, small caves, and picturesque sandstone cliffs.

From Hug Point, you continue south for 2 more miles of beach until you reach Arch Cape, and then you turn inland to US 101. Cross the highway onto East Shingle Mill Lane and walk a half mile. Turn right up a gravel road that becomes the Oregon Coast Trail and cross a suspension bridge over Arch Cape Creek. Climb the forested switchbacks to a ridge saddle and then drop to another crossing of busy US 101, picking up the OCT/Arch Cape–Cape Falcon Trail on the other side.

The trail parallels the highway for a short distance, crosses an access road to Cove Beach, and then begins to enter wilder country. Your path climbs in long switchbacks through viewless second-growth forests to a broad ridge and then turns west through an area with lots of downed trees, testimony to the coast's sometimes vicious winter storms.

As the trail drops from the ridge, it passes near several dramatic viewpoints. First, you'll be able to look north to Tillamook Head. After you round a ridge, there are views south to the cliffs of Cape Falcon. Wind-tortured snags add to the scenery—although this is no place to be when these trees are being tortured.

Turn right in a clearing to take the 0.2-mile spur trail between thick walls of salal to the noteworthy viewpoint near the end of Cape Falcon. Birders, especially, will enjoy surveying all the preening seabirds on the rocks below. The view southeast toward massive Neahkahnie Mountain, the next scenic highlight, is particularly impressive. The main trail continues through woods to a confusing set of trails near tiny Short Sand Beach, a surfer favorite. Keep right at all junctions.

To tackle the final obstacle, follow the scenic Coast Trail up three switchbacks and then along a view-packed route between US 101 on the left and the ocean's cliffs on the right. You cross the road at a large gravel parking area and begin the long climb of Neahkahnie Mountain. Views are intermittent but excellent on this heavily used forest trail. After 2 miles the trail breaks out into large sloping meadows near the top of Neahkahnie Mountain.

TIP: From late May into June, a beautiful variety of wildflowers covers the slopes here.

Short side trails reach the summit's dual viewpoints. Traverse a wooded slope for 0.5 mile, cross a jeep road, and drop steeply to the gravel road on the peak's south flank.

From the South Trailhead of Neahkahnie Mountain, continue south along US 101 for 1.3 miles to just outside the lively little town of Manzanita. Turn right (west) onto Nehalem Road to the beach and head south 2.5 miles along Manzanita's very pretty beach to the Nehalem Bay hiker-biker camp and the end of your trip.

POSSIBLE ITINERARY

	CAMP	MILES	ELEVATION GAIN
Day 1	Fort Stevens hiker-biker camp	4.0	100'
Day 2	Sunset Beach area	8.25	280'
Day 3	Tillamook Head hiker camp	15.0	1,500'
Day 4	South of Humbug Point	10.25	860'
Day 5	Out/Nehalem Bay State Park hiker-biker camp	20.0	3,500'

Previous page: Arcadia Beach; North Coast (Trip 1, page 17)

Above left: Zane Grey Cabin; Rogue River Trail (Trip 3, page 31)

Left: View of Drake Peak from the Fremont National Recreation Trail: Southern Segment (Trip 29, page 188)

Above: Hunts Creek Trail; Jefferson Park Trek (Trip 8, page 63)

Right: Whitebark pine; Timberline Trail Loop (Trip 6, page 50)

Above: Wildflowers on Steens Mountain Gorges Loop (Trip 27, page 177)

Left: Wildflowers on Wallowa River Loop (Trip 21, page 137)

Right: Paintbrush along the trail to Eagle Lake; Southern Wallowas Traverse (Trip 22, page 142)

Above left: View from Grayback Meadow; Siskiyou–Boundary Trail (Trip 4, page 37)

Left: Punchbowl Falls; Eagle Creek Loop (Trip 5, page 44)

Above: Aneroid Lake; Wallowa River Loop (Trip 21, page 137)

Right: Footbridge along Separation Creek Loop (Trip 11, page 81)

Above: Cape Blanco State Park; South Coast (Trip 2, page 23)

Left: View from Hells Canyon Bench High Trail (Trip 26, page 170)

2

SOUTH COAST: BANDON TO PORT ORFORD

RATINGS: Scenery 8 **Solitude** 6 **Difficulty** 4
MILES: 30
ELEVATION GAIN: 600'
DAYS: 3–4
SHUTTLE MILEAGE: 27
MAPS: Green Trails *Oregon Coast South, Oregon Coast Trail, Bandon to Brookings* (#656SX)
USUALLY OPEN: Year-round
BEST: April–May and September–October
PERMITS: None
RULES: No beach camping in state parks or within Bandon city limits. Stay out of marked nesting grounds of snowy plovers (March–September).
CONTACT: Cape Blanco State Park, 541-332-6774; BLM Coos Bay District, 541-756-0100; Boice Cope Park Campground, 541-247-3386

SPECIAL ATTRACTIONS

Coastal scenery, solitude, Cape Blanco Lighthouse, wildlife

Above: The Sixes River just before it meets the ocean

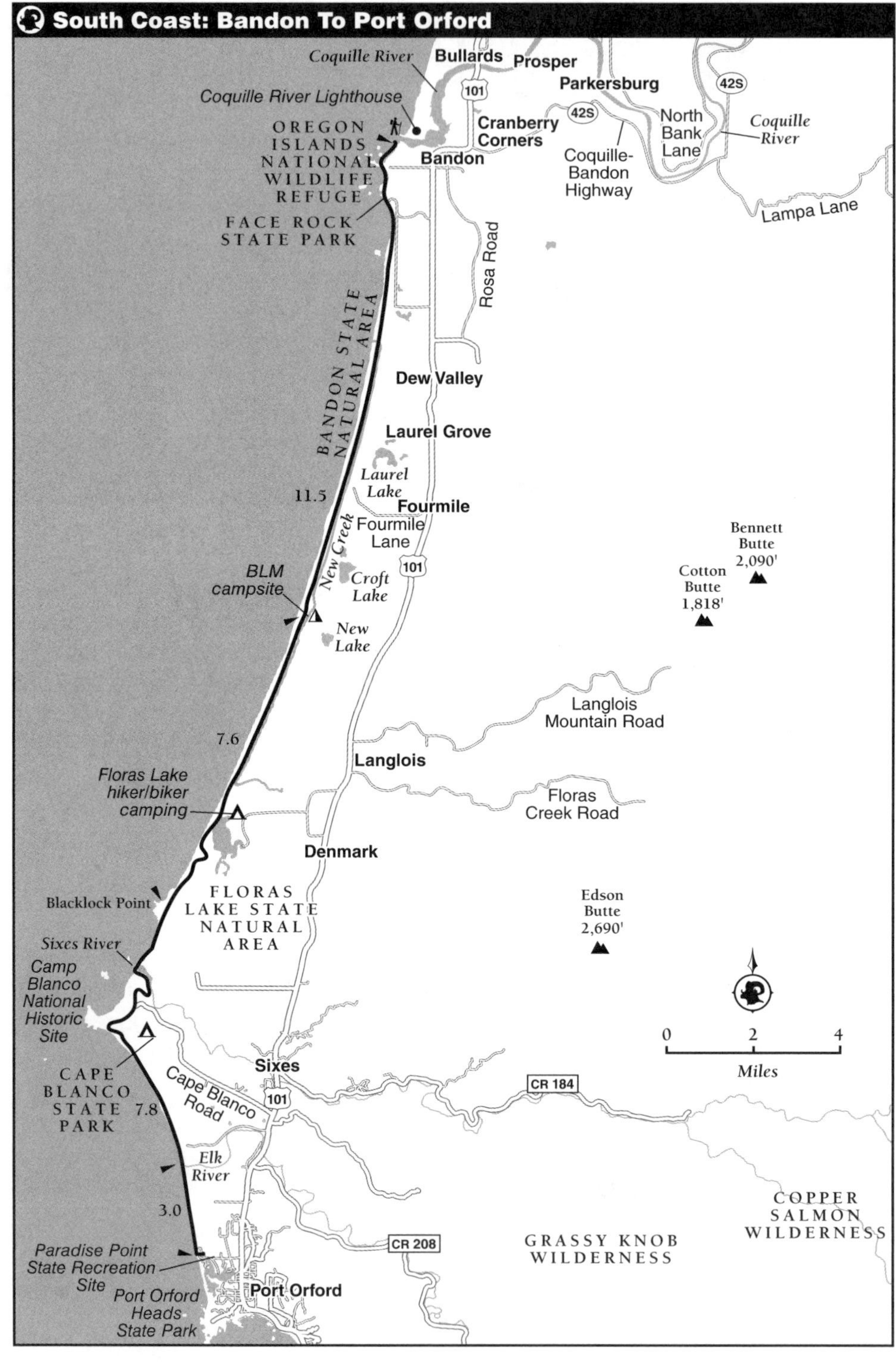
South Coast: Bandon To Port Orford
Coquille River
Bullards
Prosper
Parkersburg
Coquille River Lighthouse
101
42S
OREGON ISLANDS NATIONAL WILDLIFE REFUGE
Cranberry Corners
North Bank Lane
Coquille River
Bandon
Coquille-Bandon Highway
Lampa Lane
FACE ROCK STATE PARK
Rosa Road
BANDON STATE NATURAL AREA
Dew Valley
Laurel Grove
Laurel Lake
11.5
Fourmile
New Creek
Fourmile Lane
Bennett Butte 2,090'
BLM campsite
Croft Lake
Cotton Butte 1,818'
New Lake
Langlois Mountain Road
7.6
Langlois
Floras Lake hiker/biker camping
Floras Creek Road
Denmark
Blacklock Point
FLORAS LAKE STATE NATURAL AREA
Edson Butte 2,690'
Sixes River
Camp Blanco National Historic Site
0 2 4
Miles
CAPE BLANCO STATE PARK
7.8
Sixes
Cape Blanco Road
CR 184
Elk River
3.0
COPPER SALMON WILDERNESS
Paradise Point State Recreation Site
CR 208
GRASSY KNOB WILDERNESS
Port Orford
Port Orford Heads State Park

CHALLENGES

Tides, frequent storms, hazardous stream crossings

HOW TO GET THERE

To reach the hike's south end, leave US 101 just north of Port Orford on the marked road to Paradise Point. The road dead-ends at a gravel parking lot with beach access.

The north trailhead is reached by following First Street through the charming town of Bandon and then Jetty Street to its end beside the south jetty of the Coquille River. Overnight parking is no longer allowed at the northern trailhead and is not easy to find anywhere within less than a mile. Plan to be dropped off here, and leave a car at the southern trailhead.

TIP: Regular bus service between the two cities allows you to do the trip without a car shuttle. Find schedules for the Coastal Express on the Curry Public Transit website (currypublictransit.org/coastal-express) or call (541) 412-8806 or (800) 921-2871.

GPS TRAILHEAD COORDINATES:

(Paradise Point) N42° 45.695' W124° 31.023'

(South Jetty) N43° 07.303' W124° 25.668'

INTRODUCTION

If you're familiar with the popular north coast of Oregon, prepare yourself. The south coast—generally meaning everything south of the town of Reedsport and the Umpqua River—is a different world. It's less touristy, more rugged, and usually warmer but also (even) windier. On the sandy beaches between Bandon and Port Orford, it feels extremely quiet and remote. This hike follows the state's only true wilderness beach and deserves the attention of backpackers who love coastal scenery, wildlife, and wild surf.

WARNING: Unless you are a strong hiker with experience in stream crossings, this trip is best done in late summer or fall. Crossing the Sixes and Elk Rivers may be impossible early in the year.

We recommend hiking north to south because that usually means the wind is at your back. If you're hiking outside of summer, check the forecast, as this can vary in the off-season.

NOTE: To protect a nesting population of threatened snowy plovers, restrictions are in effect from March 15 to September 15. Look for (and respect) signs requiring hikers to walk on wet sand only and have dogs leashed at all times; camping is strictly prohibited in the protected zones. If this seems like a hassle, look up a photo of a snowy plover chick and just try not to melt.

DESCRIPTION

Start the hike by admiring the view of the squat little Coquille River Lighthouse across the river. Then turn south and onto the beach, where you're likely to walk past dozens of bucket-holding rock-hunters for a hundred yards or so before the surface turns to firmer sand.

For the first few miles, your entertainment consists of otherworldly rock formations jutting out of the sand at every turn. Wonky pyramids, pinnacles, mussel-encrusted blobs, and haunted caves keep the scenery exciting. Look for vivid sea stars and other creatures clinging to the lower parts of these sculptures, waiting for the tide to come in. Table Rock is among the largest of the sea stacks here, and like the others, it supports a large population of nesting seabirds (numbers peak in May and June).

Cape Blanco Lighthouse

TIP: Hike this first 3 miles at low tide, when the rocks are more accessible and picturesque. Avoid high tide, as the waves will force you to walk higher up the beach, where the loose surface makes progress difficult.

The sea stacks and pinnacles become more numerous and interesting as you approach Grave Point and Face Rock. A staircase connects to a parking lot opposite Face Rock, so the beach here is often crowded. The crowds thin considerably as you continue south another 1.9 miles to a scenic little cove called Devil's Kitchen (restrooms and water available). South of Devil's Kitchen, there is no easy road access for many miles, so the beach is lonesome. To the east is a land of marshes and dunes that blooms profusely with yellow gorse in April. The beach is wide, smooth, and lovely all the way to Fourmile Creek. The crossing of Fourmile Creek is easy late in the season but potentially hazardous after heavy winter or spring rains.

TIP: Trekking poles help with this and other stream crossings.

Not far inland, on the north side of the creek, is Lower Fourmile Creek Road. If the crossing is not feasible, you can use this road as an exit point.

The next few miles are basically more of the same—a wide, lovely, lonesome beach with nearby marshes and dunes. An added attraction/challenge is the New River—a slow-moving stream popular with both canoeists and wildlife. This "river" parallels the ocean for several miles, so once you cross it (again, best done at low tide), you are actually walking along a sand spit.

Partway down the spit, about 4 miles north of Floras Creek, is a primitive camping spot provided by the BLM; look for a sign posted in the dunes alongside the New River.

WARNING: Major winter storms sometimes break through this spit, creating new river "mouths" for hikers to negotiate.

About 7 miles south of Fourmile Creek you reach the developments near Floras Lake, over a low rise and a short distance inland. It's worth climbing the foredune to take a peek at the lake. You might see windsurfers practicing, and the campground is busy in summer, but it's hard to imagine that this quiet spot was almost turned into a high-end resort town in the 1900s, complete with a grand hotel and a shipping channel blasted through the dunes. The plan was abandoned, and these days the most excitement you're likely to find here comes from spotting interesting shorebirds.

TIP: If you're thinking about spending the night at Boice Cope Park Campground, reservations are recommended, although the park does have space for a few drop-in hiker-biker tents.

Two trails go inland from the southwest side of Floras Lake. The first starts very close to the lake's shore; the second (your route) begins farther south after you pass a pond and reach a small cove.

South of Floras Lake the shoreline is characterized by bluffs and high cliffs. If the tide is moderate to low, take the time for a side trip down this beach. After 1.2 miles the beach ends near the base of a twisting waterfall. If there is a minus tide, it is possible to go around the base of Battleship Bow—as these cliffs at the north end of Blacklock Point are called—by scrambling over the beach's slippery boulders. The trail on the cliffs above, however, is easier and more attractive.

Taking the second inland trail from Floras Lake leads to a small creek with nearby meadows, trees, and a very attractive campsite. The poorly marked trail continues, mostly in forest, to a junction marked by a gray post. To the left is an exit to the Cape Blanco Airport. Your route turns right and alternates between forests and brush-covered meadows. Several short spur trails access a series of wonderful cliff-edge viewpoints. All of these are worth visiting, particularly the one featuring an excellent side view of the tall waterfall at Battleship Bow. One mile from the last junction is the next major junction. To the right is a not-to-be-missed 0.5-mile side trip to the meadowy headland of Blacklock Point. Offshore rocks and spring wildflowers add to the scene, which includes colorful sandstone soils and cliffs near the edge of the headland. Plan on spending at least an hour here exploring and just enjoying the view.

To continue your tour, drop down to the beach on the south side of Blacklock Point and travel another 1.3 miles to the Sixes River. Frequent changes in the river's course have made this crossing sometimes deep and potentially difficult. Unless you can find a convenient log jam (as often happens), plan on a tough crossing even in the low water of summer. Ask locals about conditions or scout it out from the nearby road in Cape Blanco State Park before you start your trip.

TIP: A low-tide crossing is better because the river's water fans out across the beach, and the deeper channel is only a couple of steps wide.

Leaving behind this obstacle, the next goal is obvious and enticing. The massive form of Cape Blanco juts out into the Pacific in open defiance of the strong waves and fierce winds that routinely pound this area. Picturesque Cape Blanco Lighthouse sends its flashing warning in all directions. The beach walk to this landmark is scenic and enjoyable.

TIP: Low tide makes the walk easier.

After 1.5 miles, just before the beach comes to an end, turn onto a trail that climbs the rolling meadow slopes to a road.

TIP: Don't miss the side trip west along this road to the Cape Blanco Lighthouse. Excellent guided tours are available most of the year.

From the lighthouse, you have two options. The first is to go back to the road and follow a cliff-top trail through meadows and past viewpoints before dropping to the beach. This route passes near the park's pleasant car campground, which is a good choice for the night. The second option is more private and interesting: Drop down the steep and trailless meadow slopes south of the lighthouse to reach a narrow beach. Walk this strip of sand and cobblestones past driftwood logs and offshore rocks.

WARNING: This beach may be impassable at high tide and should not be attempted if there is a storm coming in. The wind and waves here are legendary.

After 2.6 miles the beach ends at Elk River, the trip's final major obstacle. In winter or early spring, this stream is uncrossable, and it can be an adventure in any season after rain. Excellent camps can be made near the river. The final segment of beach stretches 3 miles

The Wizard Hat is one of many rock formations on the beach near Bandon.

south from Elk River to Paradise Point—the south terminus of your wonderfully wild coastal adventure.

POSSIBLE ITINERARY

	CAMP	MILES	ELEVATION GAIN
Day 1	BLM camp near New Lake	11.5	0'
Day 2	Blacklock Point	7.6	200'
Day 3	Elk River (with side trip to Blacklock Point)	7.8	400'
Day 4	Out	3.0	0'

Rogue River Trail

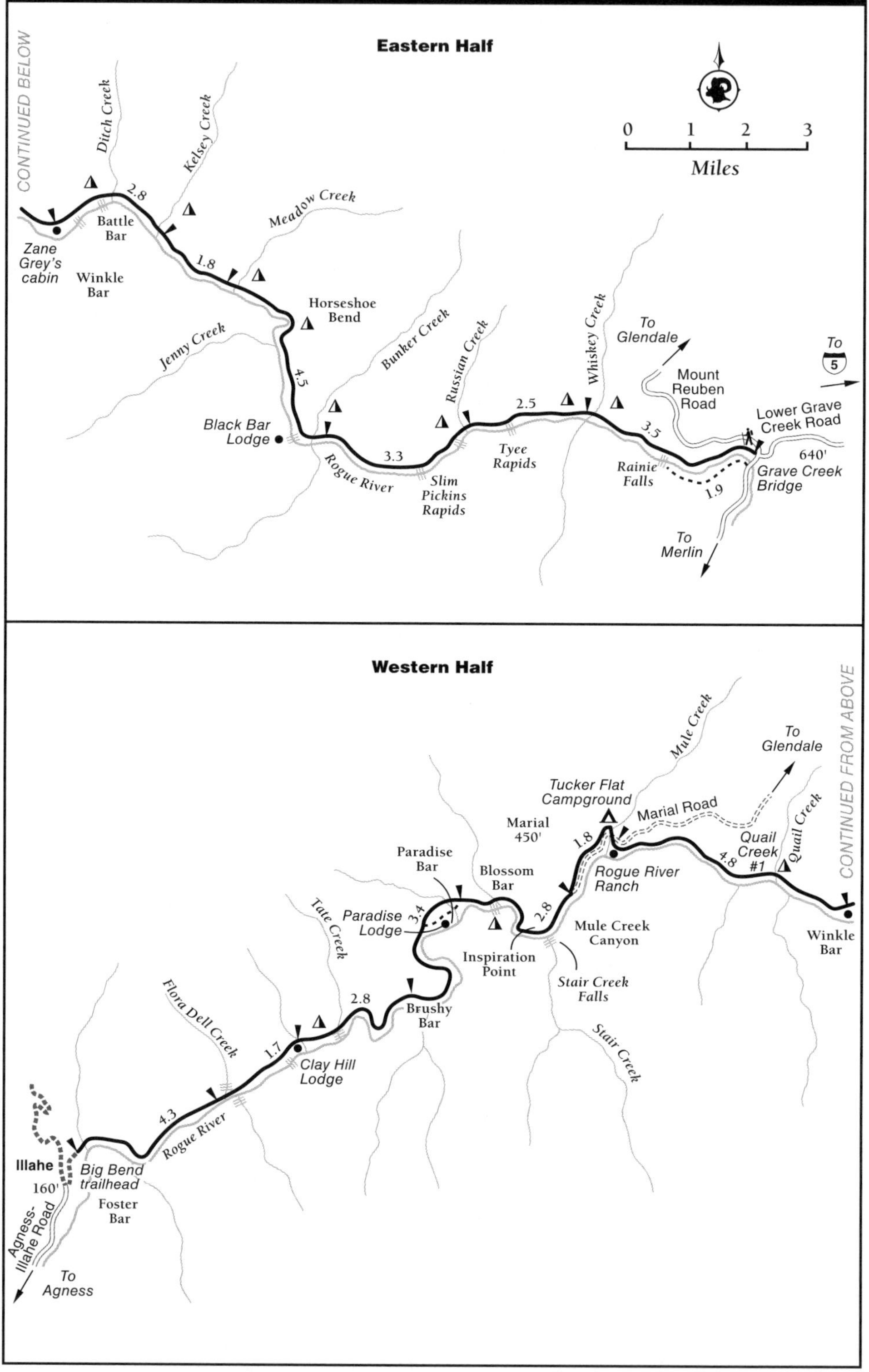

Eastern Half

CONTINUED BELOW
0 1 2 3
Miles
Ditch Creek
Kelsey Creek
Meadow Creek
2.8
Battle Bar
Zane Grey's cabin
Winkle Bar
1.8
Horseshoe Bend
Jenny Creek
4.5
Bunker Creek
Russian Creek
Whiskey Creek
To Glendale
To 5
Mount Reuben Road
Black Bar Lodge
3.3
Rogue River
Slim Pickins Rapids
2.5
Tyee Rapids
3.5
Rainie Falls
1.9
Lower Grave Creek Road
640'
Grave Creek Bridge
To Merlin

Western Half

CONTINUED FROM ABOVE
Mule Creek
To Glendale
Tucker Flat Campground
Marial Road
Marial 450'
1.8
Quail Creek
4.8
Quail Creek #1
Rogue River Ranch
Winkle Bar
Paradise Bar
Blossom Bar
Paradise Lodge
3.4
2.8
Mule Creek Canyon
Tate Creek
Inspiration Point
Stair Creek Falls
Stair Creek
2.8
Brushy Bar
Flora Dell Creek
1.7
Clay Hill Lodge
4.3
Rogue River
Illahe
160'
Big Bend trailhead
Foster Bar
Agness-Illahe Road
To Agness

3

ROGUE RIVER TRAIL

RATINGS: **Scenery** 9 **Solitude** 5 **Difficulty** 4
MILES: 40
ELEVATION GAIN: 4,500'
DAYS: 4–5
SHUTTLE MILEAGE: 49
MAPS: USFS *Rogue River National Forest Oregon* and *Powers and Gold Beach Ranger Districts;* USGS *Mount Reuben* and *Bunker Creek*
USUALLY OPEN: Year-round most years
BEST: Late April–May and late October–early November
PERMITS: None
RULES: Fires within 400 feet of the river must use a firepan. Check for current fire regulations with the Smullin Visitor Center at Rand, 541-479-3735, or the Gold Beach Ranger District, 541-247-3600, before you start your trip. Fireworks and use of firearms are prohibited in or near recreation areas. No pack stock, motorbikes, or trail bikes allowed.
CONTACT: Grants Pass Office, Bureau of Land Management, 541-471-6500, blm.gov/office/grants-pass-interagency-office; Gold Beach Ranger District, Rogue River–Siskiyou National Forest, 541-247-3600, fs.usda.gov/rogue-siskiyou

Above: The Rogue River as seen from the trail

SPECIAL ATTRACTIONS

Outstanding river and canyon scenery, whitewater rafters to watch, waterfalls, wildlife, fall colors

CHALLENGES

Profuse poison oak, rattlesnakes, ticks, summer heat, camp-raiding black bears, long car shuttle

HOW TO GET THERE

To reach the Grave Creek (upstream) trailhead from Portland, take I-5 south to Exit 76 onto Old State Hwy 99 and go 0.5 mile. Turn north (right) onto Front Street; Front Street veers west (left) and becomes Lower Wolf Creek Road in 0.1 mile. Drive 5.6 miles on Lower Wolf Creek Road, then continue straight onto Lower Grave Creek Road. Go 8.9 twisty miles west to the Grave Creek Bridge; just before you cross the bridge turn right. (If you're coming from Grants Pass, take I-5 north to Merlin, Exit 61, turn left onto Merlin Road and follow it for 3.6 miles. Make another left turn onto Galice Road and drive until you reach Grave Creek Bridge.) A sign indicates the boat ramp parking lot, where you'll find the trailhead and a pit toilet.

Note: This lot is day-use only; no overnight parking is allowed. You can park overnight along the main road above the boat ramp, but rangers warn of rockslides and vandalism. Your best bet is to hire one of the many shuttle services to take your car from here to the Foster Bar trail exit. This option saves you hours of driving on twisty, sketchy back roads; the shortest route between the trailheads is via Bear Camp Road, which is only 49 miles but a 2-hour drive.

To reach the lower (downstream) trailhead from Gold Beach along US 101, drive northeast on County Road 595 (variously Jerrys Flat Road and Rogue River Road) for 9.8 miles. Continue straight on what is now Agness Road/Forest Service Road 33 for 20.9 miles. Turn right onto CR 375 just after the bridge over the river and drive 3.5 miles to the trailhead (about half a mile north of the Foster Bar boat launch and campground). Overnight parking is free at the trailhead and the boat launch.

Free parking is also available at the Marial Trailhead, roughly halfway along the trail, reached by the very rough, winding Marial Road from Grave Creek.

GPS TRAILHEAD COORDINATES:

(Grave Creek) N42° 38.928' W123° 35.085'
(Foster Bar) N42° 38.306' W124° 03.344'

INTRODUCTION

Southern Oregon's Rogue River has earned a special place in the hearts of whitewater rafters. The 40-mile float trip from Grave Creek to Illahe/Foster Bar is one of the most popular in the country, and it's easy to understand why. This wild canyon provides continuously spectacular scenery, waterfalls, unusually abundant wildlife, and plenty of thrilling rapids. The Bureau of Land Management (BLM) has a lottery system in place to regulate the number of people on the river. For backpackers there is an equally scenic way to see this roadless canyon. The Rogue River Trail is seldom crowded and requires no permits. The route parallels the north bank of the river for 40 miles, providing bird's-eye views over many of the rapids. It is unquestionably one of Oregon's most exciting long backpacking trips.

WARNINGS: While the hike is undeniably outstanding, there are more than a few difficulties to keep in mind. Refer to pages 9–11 for more information about poison oak, ticks, rattlesnakes, and bears.

Poison oak is profuse along the trail, especially the last few miles toward Foster Bar, where it can be impossible to avoid. Ticks and rattlesnakes are also common. Black bears (*Ursus americanus*) have learned to raid the camps of river rafters for food. They are more of a problem here than anywhere else in the state. Several of the campsites have bear boxes or electric fences; take advantage of these and consider using a bear canister or at least a bear-proof food bag on your hike.

The Rogue River flows through a wild and scenic canyon.

Avoid this trail in midsummer, when the heat can reach dangerous levels. Most of the trail is on sunny south-facing slopes, so bring a hat and sunscreen any time of year.

Probably the best way to see and enjoy the canyon is to hike upstream from the Foster Bar trailhead near Illahe to the Grave Creek trailhead, then float down the river back to your car. Unless you have a pack raft, paddling skills, and luck with permits, though, the logistics of this plan are rather complicated. For hikers, the simplest option is to arrange for a shuttle service to move your car to the trail exit. If doing your own car shuttle, plan on at least 2–4 hours to drive between the two trailheads, depending on which route is open.

DESCRIPTION

From the Grave Creek trailhead, the hiker-only trail starts with an easy stroll over mostly open slopes well above the river. Twisted oak trees provide frames for canyon photographs. You pass frothing Grave Creek Rapids and the remains of a footbridge that was washed out by a flood in 1927. At the 1.9-mile mark, you reach the Class V rapids of Rainie Falls, although it's easier to hear than see them from this angle. Many rafters avoid running this dangerous section by using ropes to walk their boats over a fish-diversion channel. (A short side path leads down to river level, although the best views are from the 2-mile Rainie Falls trail along the south bank.) The main trail continues downstream, passes a nice sandy beach (a popular campsite for boaters), and then goes inland to the footbridge over Whiskey Creek. A short spur trail to the right leads to a historical cluster of mining machinery and a cabin built around 1880—evidence of the extensive gold mining activity that took place along the river at the time, and well worth exploring. There are good camps near here for hikers setting a leisurely pace. The best camps are on a bench 0.4 mile west of Whiskey Creek.

Mule Creek, near the halfway point of the Rogue River hike

To continue your tour, keep going west along the well-graded up-and-down trail, generally staying on slopes 50–100 feet above the river. Pass the Russian Creek camps 2.5 miles from Whiskey Creek and then Slim Pickins Rapids in a narrow section of the canyon. After crossing Bunker Creek on a large bridge (good camping here) and passing Black Bar Lodge on the other side of the river, the trail begins to climb and enters a thicker forest of firs and maples on its way to Horseshoe Bend, where there are nice camps and a good view of this large loop in the river. Good camps at Meadow Creek tempt hikers, but the ones just before the bridge over Kelsey Creek are even better. After passing Ditch Creek (a small camp here) and Battle Bar, the trail traverses an open grassy bench at Winkle Bar. Here you can take a peek into a log fishing cabin and a few outbuildings once owned by Zane Grey (1872–1939), the famous Western author. The cabin, listed on the National Register of Historic Places, is managed by the BLM, but hikers are asked to refrain from camping or backpacking there.

Near Quail Creek (nice campsite here) the trail returns to river level at a sandy beach. The path now climbs back up the slope to detour around a slide and then passes through a 1970 burn area before reaching Rogue River Ranch, 23 miles from Grave Creek. This historic home, located in a pretty valley and now a museum (open May–October), is listed on the National Register of Historic Places. It is accessible by car via Marial Road, so don't expect to be lonesome.

TIP: Be sure to schedule some time to tour the restored ranch and nearby exhibits, which include a blacksmith shop and tack house.

The Rogue River "Trail" now follows roads for about 2 miles as it climbs to Marial Road, crosses a bridge over Mule Creek near the primitive six-spot Tucker Flat car campground, and then follows the deteriorating dirt road to its end, where the trail resumes.

The lower canyon section from Marial to Illahe is even more dramatic and interesting than the upper canyon. In addition to the improved scenery, two trailside lodges welcome hungry hikers.

WARNING: Jet boats use this section of the river (at least as far up as Blossom Bar), so hikers can expect the tranquility to be interrupted occasionally by the roar of powerboats.

You reach one of the major highlights of the lower river not long after the Marial Trailhead. Beyond a short stretch through forests, you break out and follow a trail that has been blasted into the cliffs above very narrow Mule Creek Canyon. At aptly named Inspiration Point, savor a breathtaking view of this slot canyon. Adding even more to an already tremendous scene is Stair Creek Falls, dropping into the river across from you. After rounding this dramatic section, the trail reenters forests and then drops a bit to Blossom Bar.

TIP: Blossom Bar rapids are one of the most challenging and exciting sections of the river for rafters. It's great fun to watch them run the whitewater. There are nice camps with a bear box near Blossom Bar Creek.

Continuing the trip, you soon reach Paradise Lodge on a large meadowy flat above the river. From May to early November, hikers can stop for lunch and even spend the night—but you'll need to make reservations months in advance (541-842-2822 or paradise-lodge.com). Jet boats also make scheduled stops here. If you choose not to visit Paradise Lodge, the official trail detours around the meadow, staying in the perimeter forest.

TIP: Watch and listen for wild turkeys in this area.

After Paradise Lodge the trail follows the river around a prominent bend with the option to cut across a ridge called Devils Backbone, a steep "shortcut" trail that provides good canyon views and rejoins the main trail at Brushy Bar. You then cross Brushy Bar—a forested flat that includes a ranger cabin, a creek, and several good campsites.

WARNING: Black bears are numerous in this area.

From Brushy Bar the trail climbs to a historic marker noting CAPTAIN TICHENOR'S DEFEAT. In 1856 Takelma Indians overwhelmed a group of Army soldiers under the captain's command by simply rolling rocks down the steep slopes onto the troops. Follow the trail as it drops to Solitude Bar, another good place for viewing rafters, and then continues to the bridge over Tate Creek. Just below the bridge is a lovely waterfall. You will find good camps here and 0.1 mile farther at Camp Tacoma. For more luxurious accommodations, try Clay Hill Lodge (reservations required: 503-859-3772; clayhilllodge.com) about 0.5 mile ahead.

The trail crosses a long, sparsely forested section with plenty of river views on its way to Flora Dell Creek. Twenty-foot-high Flora Dell Falls has created an idyllic little fern-lined grotto and swimming hole just above the trail. Plan on spending extra time here to cool off and enjoy the scenery. The falls is a common day-hike goal for people coming upriver from the Foster Bar trailhead.

The final stretch of trail remains very scenic as it crosses open slopes with nice river views, especially of Big Bend. The trail climbs some 350 feet to make a detour around a landslide, but otherwise the hiking is easy. Impressive old-growth forests and several splashing side creeks add to the scenery. The last 0.5 mile passes an old apple orchard near the former Billings homestead. You may have to walk down the road a bit to reach the Foster Bar boat ramp, where commercial float-trip operators take out their rafts for the shuttle back to Grave Creek.

POSSIBLE ITINERARY

	CAMP	MILES	ELEVATION GAIN
Day 1	Russian Creek	6.0	500'
Day 2	Battle Bar/Ditch Creek	10.8	1,500'
Day 3	Blossom Bar	10.3	1,600'
Day 4	Out	12.9	900'

4

SISKIYOU–BOUNDARY TRAIL

RATINGS: Scenery 8 **Solitude** 7 **Difficulty** 7
MILES: 36 (41)
ELEVATION GAIN: 9,100' (10,500')
DAYS: 4 (4–5)
SHUTTLE MILEAGE: 25
MAPS: USFS *Red Buttes Wilderness;* USGS *Grayback Mountain*
USUALLY OPEN: Mid-June–October
BEST: Late June–mid-July, September
PERMITS: None
RULES: Maximum group size of 8 people/12 stock; no camping within 100 feet of lakes; no camping or fires within the boundaries of the Azalea Lake Loop Trail
CONTACT: Siskiyou Mountains Ranger District, Rogue River–Siskiyou National Forest, 541-899-3800, fs.usda.gov/rogue-siskiyou

SPECIAL ATTRACTIONS

Solitude, expansive views, wildlife, unusual geology and botany

CHALLENGES

Black bears are common (hang all food and avoid areas with recent signs of bears); ticks; heat and exposure

Above: Don't forget to look up! I spotted these owls in the woods near Grayback Mountain.

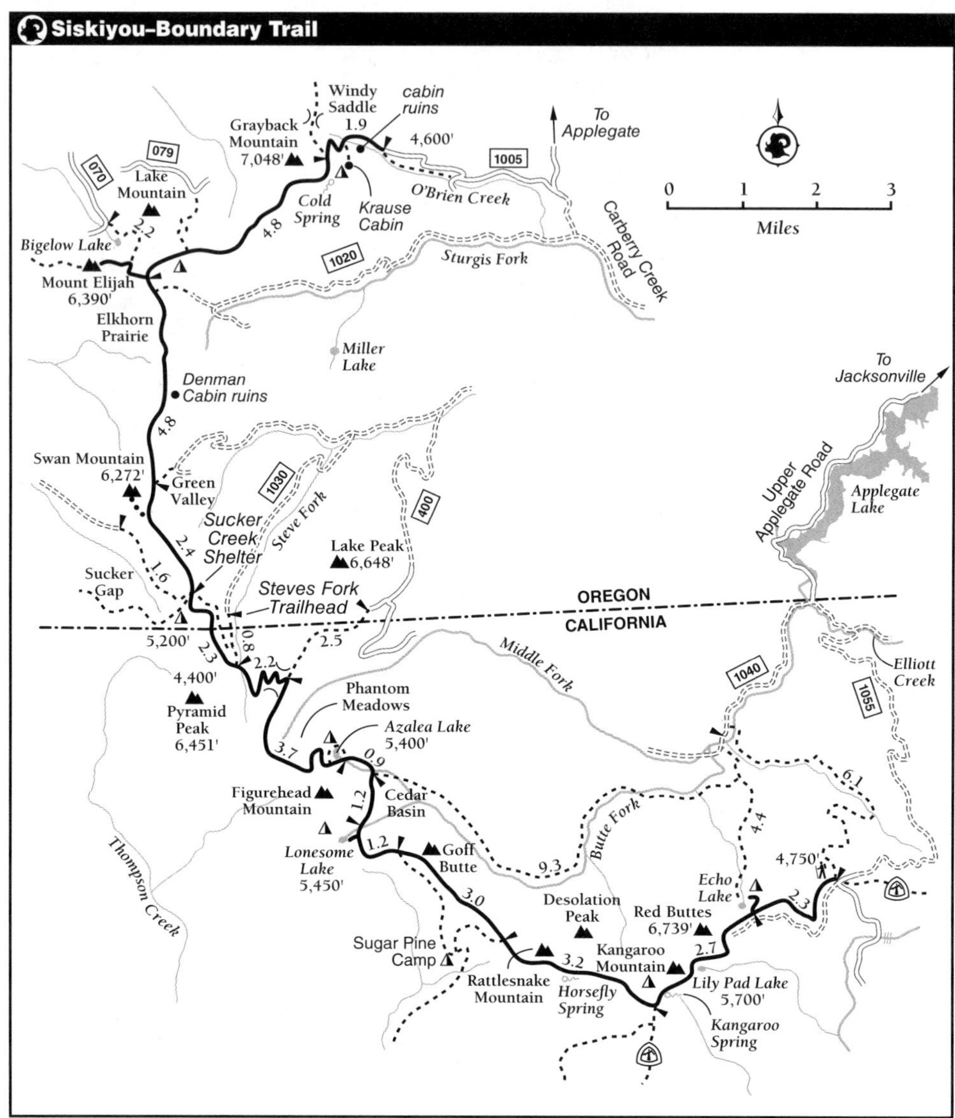

HOW TO GET THERE

To reach the east trailhead from I-5, take Exit 30 in Medford, and head west on OR 62, which becomes OR 238. In 5.5 miles turn right in Jacksonville to remain on OR 238; continue 7.8 miles to Ruch. Turn left (south) onto Upper Applegate Road and follow the paved road 18.8 miles to Applegate Lake and a junction at the south end of the lake. Turn left and 1.3 miles later keep straight on gravel Forest Service Road 1050, which goes up Elliott Creek. At a fork in 0.8 mile, turn right onto FS 1055, which climbs 9.5 miles all the way to the Pacific Crest Trail crossing at Cook and Green Pass.

To reach the Upper O'Brien Creek trailhead, the recommended exit point, follow the directions above to the south end of Applegate Lake and turn right (northwest) onto

Carberry Creek Road. Follow this paved and gravel road for about 9 miles to a pass. (It's worth calling ahead to check the status of this road, which occasionally washes out; if in doubt, take OR 238 from Ruch west for 7 miles, then go south on Thompson Creek Road for 11 miles to FS 1005.) Turn west onto FS 1005 for 4 sometimes rocky miles to the hiker's trailhead at road-end. (You'll drive right past the Lower O'Brien Creek trailhead, a good alternative exit point for low-clearance vehicles—it adds 1 steep mile to the hike.)

GPS TRAILHEAD COORDINATES:

(Cook and Green Pass) N41° 50.511' W123° 08.705'

(O'Brien Creek) N42° 06.641' W123° 17.243'

INTRODUCTION

The Siskiyou Mountains are unique. Nowhere else in the world is there a similar combination of converging climatic zones, merging geographic regions, and rare soils. The unusual east-west orientation of the range also helps to create a peculiar pattern of rainfall and ecologic zones. The result is one of the most diverse plant communities on the continent. There are both dry-zone plants and rainforest ferns; odd-looking endemic species live beside familiar favorites; alpine wildflowers grow next to sagebrush; and more species of conifers live here than almost anywhere else on the planet.

But this area has more to offer than just unique flora. There is also a fascinating and highly scenic assortment of rocks. Shining white marble intrusions mix with gray granite and green-black serpentinite, while in other places reddish-orange peridotite turns whole mountains its own special color. Small lakes and frequent vistas also enchant visitors. Even the wildlife seems to agree about the attributes of these mountains, as they live here in abundance.

As the observant reader will note, a large part of the suggested route actually lies in California. The trip has been included here in a book of Oregon backpacking trips for two reasons: First, it really is too good to leave out, and second, from a practical standpoint, this truly is an Oregon hike. Road access is almost exclusively from the Oregon side, and the short car shuttle is almost entirely in Oregon. In addition, the nearest population center is Oregon's Rogue River Valley, where the Siskiyous are familiar landmarks. The hike is equally attractive in either direction but is described here from east to west, as this involves less elevation gain.

DESCRIPTION

From Cook and Green Pass, your route, the Pacific Crest Trail (PCT), heads southwest on a south-facing slope above a jeep road. In general, south-facing slopes in these mountains tend to have only scattered trees but can be choked with heavy brush. North-facing slopes have thicker forests with much less undergrowth. Excellent views extend toward the mountainous country to the south—but as usual, the trade-off for epic views is a lot of exposure, so avoid this stretch of trail during the hottest part of the day. You'll also see plenty of evidence along the trail of the wildfires that swept through in 2012, 2017, and 2020.

At a pass covered with manzanita bushes is a junction, and to the right is a steep but worthwhile 0.5-mile downhill side trip to Echo Lake. In fact, this entire route offers worthwhile side trips every couple of miles, so be sure to allow yourself enough extra time to investigate as many as you like.

The PCT continues to gradually climb west, crosses the end of the jeep road, and contours around a ridge to Lily Pad Lake. Grazing cattle and exposed terrain make this otherwise attractive pool unsuited for camping. Instead, continue hiking toward the scenic basin holding Kangaroo Spring. The massive double summit of Red Buttes dominates the skyline; on a clear day you can sometimes make out Mount Shasta to the south. Rare Brewer's weeping spruce is found near the PCT as you hike. The hulking form of reddish-colored Kangaroo Mountain serves as the backdrop for the lush meadow at Kangaroo Spring, which features a small pond and good camps.

TIP: The next several trail miles have little or no water. Fill your bottles here.

As you climb away from Kangaroo Spring, the trail passes a particularly good example of white marble intermixed with the other assorted rocks of these mountains. At a ridgetop junction, the PCT heads south on its way to Devils Peak and the Klamath River canyon. Your route, however, turns right and contours across the south side of the main ridge for the next few miles. The trail passes beneath or beside ominously named places such as Desolation Peak, Horsefly Spring, and Rattlesnake Mountain (none of which lives up to its name) before dropping to a saddle and a junction. The trail to the left goes down to Sugar Pine Camp. The more scenic alternative stays with the Boundary Trail as it closely follows the up-and-down ridgetop to Goff Butte. You pass on the south side of this peak and then climb over another high point in the ridge. Now drop to a small creek and look for the possibly unsigned junction with the trail to Lonesome Lake. The short side trip to this irregularly shaped pool is highly recommended due to its scenic setting, nice camps, and the reasonable chance of solitude.

To continue your tour, return to the main trail and follow it along the lake's outlet creek. The path goes up and down along the side of a mostly wooded ridge. You reach a marshy area with a nice view up to Figurehead Mountain and then drop to a junction in Cedar Basin. A fine collection of old-growth incense cedars accounts for the name of this place. The basin also has good camps, a wildflower meadow, and a small stream.

Columbia windflower along the O'Brien Creek Trail

Turn left at the junction in Cedar Basin and climb beside the creek to shallow but good-sized Azalea Lake. A trail circles this fairly popular lake, passing designated camping areas for both horses and hikers. Craggy Figurehead Mountain looms above the southern shore. Mid-June–July the air is filled with the sweet, pungent aroma of

Columbine in the meadow below Grayback Mountain

blooming mountain azalea—one of nature's most powerful and lovely perfumes. Of course, the colorful flowers also provide a treat for the eyes. A well-timed visit makes it clear that Azalea Lake has earned its name.

As you switchback out of this basin, the trail ascends through an open forest of lodgepole pine (unusual for these mountains) to a pass. The route then cuts across a rocky, view-packed slope to a saddle, where knobcone pine and Brewer's weeping spruce dominate. You loop north around the basin that holds Phantom Meadows and gradually descend a brushy sidehill with numerous views. Turn left at a junction and make a quick climb to a saddle with an excellent perspective of Pyramid Peak to the west before descending a series of long switchbacks into Steve Fork Canyon.

Just after crossing the creek, reach a junction. (If you turned right here, you'd get to the Steve Fork Trailhead, a possible exit and the usual starting point for day hikers to Azalea Lake.) Turn left, make a switchback, and then begin a long, gradual, and usually dry climb northwest. Shortly after crossing a creekbed, you'll pass into Oregon (the occasion apparently not worthy of a sign).

TIP: At a sharp right turn about 2 miles from Steve Fork Creek, look for a short, unsigned, unmaintained path that leads west to a scenic lake in a cliff-walled little basin–well worth a visit.

The trail then climbs to a four-way junction at grassy Sucker Gap. The Boundary Trail turns to the right, but you first veer left for about 100 yards and then scramble down a steep trail to the lovely meadow beside Sucker Creek shelter. This meadow features a spring, lots of wildflowers, old-growth cedar trees, and welcome campsites. What may or may not be welcome are the black bears that seem to favor this basin. Hang all food, and camp away from the shelter, where bruins have become accustomed to finding bits of food. Deer are also common.

To continue your tour on the Boundary Trail, return to Sucker Gap and head north. The well-graded trail gradually climbs along the west side of a wooded ridge, skirting the edge of the 2020 Slater fire, and eventually reaching a saddle with good views.

TIP: For an outstanding side trip, climb cross-country 0.5 mile northwest along a narrow brushy ridge to the top of Swan Mountain. It requires scrambling, but you might be able to find pieces of an old trail through the brush. At 6,272 feet, Swan Mountain provides an exceptional vantage point, particularly of the Oregon part of this range and the distant Cascade peaks to the east. To the north, you can pick out Craggy

Mountain, Mount Elijah, Lake Mountain, and Grayback Mountain—the string of scenic peaks that will occupy your attention for the next several miles.

From the saddle, follow the main trail north as it slowly descends the east side of a ridge. You pass an unmarked junction in a sloping meadow, appropriately called Green Valley, and then climb back to another saddle. Now the trail loops around the west side of a hill and reaches a pass on the south flank of aptly named Craggy Mountain.

TIP: It is possible to scramble to the top of this peak, but the going is much steeper and more difficult than the route up Swan Mountain.

Continuing to alternate between the east and west sides of the ridge, the trail leads around the east side of Craggy Mountain, passes below the remains of Denman Cabin, and then crosses a saddle back to the west. Shortly after the saddle, two springs just below the trail provide water. As you continue north, the path alternates between forest and open areas with nice views and lots of wildflowers.

Your trail now returns to the ridgecrest and crosses spacious Elkhorn Prairie. From this sloping meadow, the trail descends to a junction in a forested saddle and then climbs briefly to a second junction. There is a nice, sheltered campsite at this junction, with water from a spring 0.2 mile northeast along the Boundary Trail.

TIP: A worthwhile side trip goes left (west) from here to the top of Mount Elijah, overlooking the Oregon Caves area. From partway along this side trail, you can also take a trail down to the wildflower meadow holding Bigelow Lake.

The main trail turns right at the junction, cuts across the south face of Lake Mountain, and then traces a tiring up-and-down course along the ridge to the northeast. Water is limited or nonexistent, but there are some nice views.

At a forested saddle on the south side of hulking Grayback Mountain (the tallest peak along this ridge), the trail turns east and loops around the south side of this lofty summit. You round a ridge and pass just below the wooded area holding Cold Spring (good camps). The trail then goes north across a large sloping meadow with several springs, wildflowers, and a sweeping look up at Grayback Mountain.

TIP: Determined scramblers can reach the summit of this peak with its expected great

Inside the Grayback Snow Survey Cabin

Grayback Snow Survey Cabin

vistas by making their way up the steep meadow and then climbing a rocky ridge. An easier but longer approach first follows the moderately steep Boundary Trail north for 0.5 mile to Windy Gap, with its own exceptional views, then bushwhacking off-trail up Grayback's north ridge.

To complete your tour, turn right at a junction with the O'Brien Creek Trail and descend a series of switchbacks to a junction just before the trail crosses O'Brien Creek. Be sure to make a quick side trip to the right from here to visit the Grayback Snow Survey Cabin (1944) and the site of the historic Krause Cabin—though all that's left after the cabin burned down is a rusted stovepipe, a snow-measuring stick, and gorgeous views from the sloping wildflower meadow.

Back on the main trail, cross O'Brien Creek and complete the hike with a steep descent through a forested area to either the upper or the lower trailhead and your waiting car.

SHORTER LOOP OPTION: You can sample the best of this area with a 15-mile loop along the Cook and Green Trail (USFS #959), the PCT, and Horse Camp Trail (USFS #958). Doing the loop clockwise means a gradual 11-mile climb and a steep 4-mile descent (of 3,600 feet). Note that parts of the loop are not always consistently maintained.

POSSIBLE ITINERARY

	CAMP	MILES	ELEVATION GAIN
Day 1	Kangaroo Spring (with side trip to Echo Lake)	5.6	1,600'
Day 2	Azalea Lake (with side trip to (Lonesome Lake)	9.9	2,200'
Day 3	Sucker Gap	8.4	1,600'
Day 4	Bigelow Lake junction (with side trips up Swan Mountain and Mount Elijah)	9.9	2,300'
Day 5	Out	6.7	1,400'

5

EAGLE CREEK LOOP

RATINGS: **Scenery** 6 **Solitude** 4 **Difficulty** 6
MILES: 31
ELEVATION GAIN: 5,100'
DAYS: 3–4
SHUTTLE MILEAGE: NA
MAP: Green Trails *Columbia River Gorge West (#428S)*
USUALLY OPEN: mid-May–November
BEST: Late May–June and mid–late October
PERMIT: Northwest Forest Pass required at trailhead
RULES: Campfires prohibited June 1–September 15; no fires within 100 feet of the trail rest of year; no overnight camping below High Bridge on Eagle Creek Trail; camp only in designated sites at Wahtum Lake
CONTACT: Columbia River Gorge National Scenic Area, 541-308-1700, fs.usda.gov/r06/columbiarivergorge

SPECIAL ATTRACTIONS

Spectacular waterfalls, easy road access

CHALLENGES

Recent fire damage, nearby trail closures, crowded in places, poison oak at lower elevations

Above: Twister Falls

HOW TO GET THERE

From I-84 eastbound take Exit 41/Eagle Creek, turn right, and drive 0.6 mile along Eagle Creek to the parking area and trailhead at road's end.

NOTE: The Eagle Creek Trailhead is very busy, and parking can fill up early, especially on weekends. If the trailhead lot is full, turn around and park in the large lot near the restroom and fish hatchery; some recommend parking here anyway for overnight trips to increase security. This adds about 0.5 mile of walking to the start of the hike.

GPS TRAILHEAD COORDINATES:
N45° 38.212' W121° 55.173'

INTRODUCTION

The novelty of walking through a tunnel behind a cascading waterfall is only one of many reasons the Eagle Creek Trail is among the most popular in the state. In addition to Tunnel Falls, a dozen other waterfalls are visible within about a 5-mile stretch of the trail. It's also conveniently close to Portland and very easy to drive to, with the trailhead right off a major highway (no four-wheel drive required!). On top of all that, it's an exciting trail, especially in the places where it hugs the jagged rock walls high above Eagle Creek. At certain points, the trail is so narrow and the cliffs so steep that there are cables bolted to the wall to provide a handhold. Though it might not be ideal for hikers with vertigo, this trip is an excellent way to get a taste of the Columbia River Gorge ecosystem.

The landscape, however, is not what it was a couple of decades ago. This part of the gorge has been ravaged by substantial wildfires at least a couple of times in recent years—most notably in 2017, when the devastating Eagle Creek Fire burned through almost 50,000 acres and closed the area for several seasons. In fact, many trails in the burned area remain closed indefinitely. In 2024, the PCT section of this loop was temporarily off-limits while firefighters dealt with the (much smaller) Whisky Creek Fire. This is a trip that will make you appreciate the resilience of the wilderness and the hard work of land stewards and trail builders. As always, check the status of any trails locally before planning and starting your trip—as you'll witness, even forests as lush as these experience drought and are susceptible to fires.

DESCRIPTION

From the trailhead, you climb gradually, heading southeast, beside and above pretty Eagle Creek on a sometimes rocky but well-used trail. Scorched and blackened trees from the 2017 fire abound, but there's still plenty of tree cover and the undergrowth is lush. About 1.5 miles in, you'll catch a glimpse of the first of many waterfalls, Sorenson and Metlako Falls. Half a mile farther up the trail, you reach another big highlight of the trip: Punchbowl Falls. The trail has been widened and shored up to create a viewing area above the falls, but before you reach it, look for the short (0.2-mile) side trail that drops down to the right. It leads to the pool and a lower set of falls, a popular site for a quick dip or a selfie. (Landslides and logjams in the wake of the fires have changed the access route here, so getting a postcard view of Punchbowl Falls from below requires determined scrambling.)

WARNING: Look out for poison oak here and throughout the lower canyon.

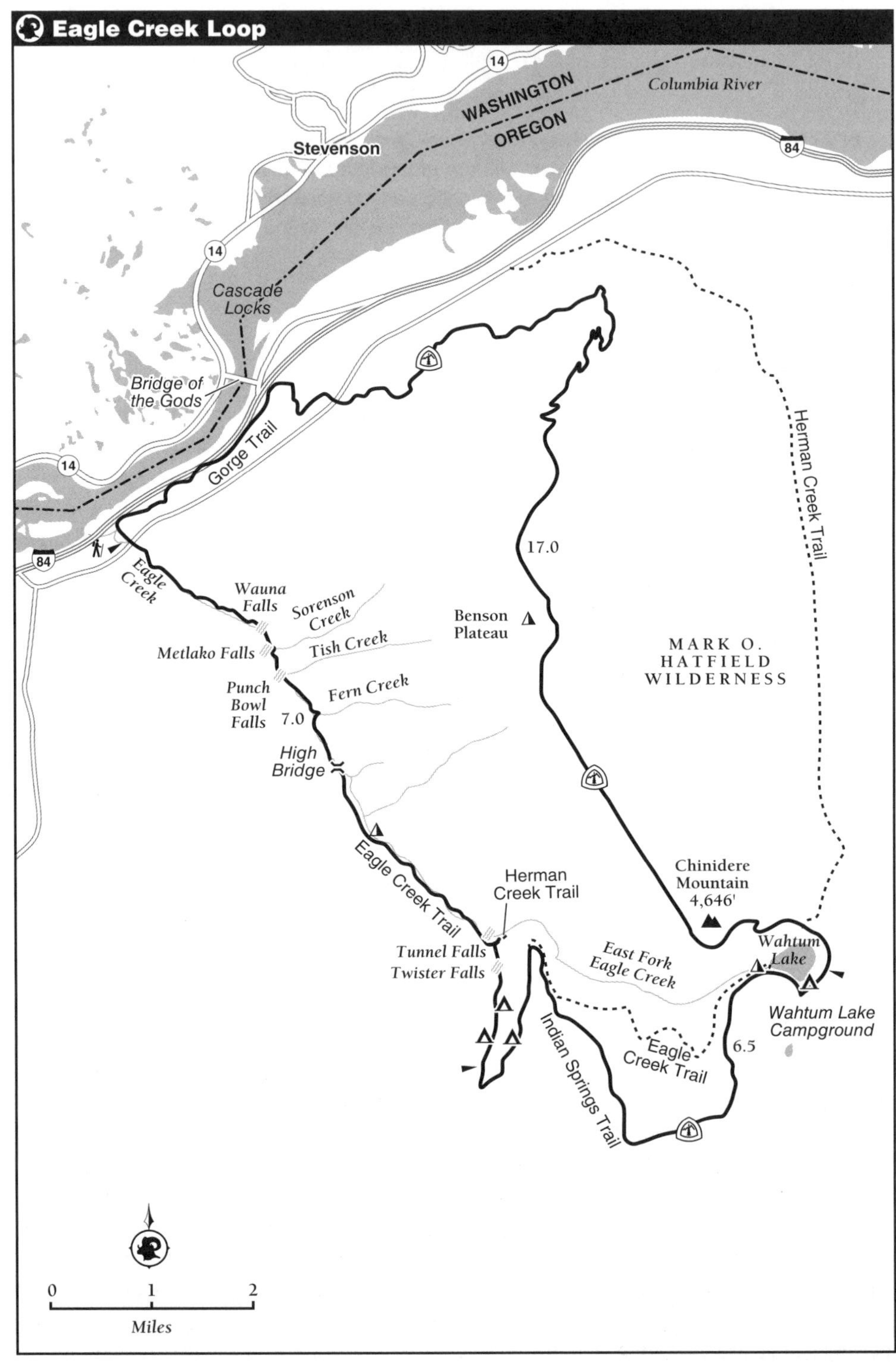
Eagle Creek Loop
14
WASHINGTON
OREGON
Columbia River
Stevenson
84
14
Cascade Locks
Bridge of the Gods
Gorge Trail
14
84
Eagle Creek
Wauna Falls
Sorenson Creek
Metlako Falls
Tish Creek
Punch Bowl Falls
Fern Creek
7.0
High Bridge
17.0
Benson Plateau
MARK O. HATFIELD WILDERNESS
Herman Creek Trail
Eagle Creek Trail
Herman Creek Trail
Chinidere Mountain 4,646'
Tunnel Falls
Twister Falls
East Fork Eagle Creek
Wahtum Lake
Wahtum Lake Campground
Indian Springs Trail
Eagle Creek Trail
6.5
0
1
2
Miles

Continuing up the trail you'll see delicate Loowit Falls plunging into a perfect mini pool on the opposite side of the creek. At just over 3 miles, you reach the aptly named High Bridge. Take a deep breath: The view from the bridge over the deep slot canyon below is another of the arresting sights on this trail. Not only can you see straight down the shadowy gorge below, but standing on the bridge also gives you a nice view up the creek where the sheer walls widen out. Reassuringly, this is a new bridge airlifted in in 2019 after the original one burned.

Next up after you cross the bridge is double-tiered Skoonichuck Falls, then Four and a Half Mile Bridge, which has easy access to the water—a nice spot for a break and refilling bottles. You'll then pass Wy'east Camp, where several sites are closed for restoration (look for posted signs). Soon after, you cross into the Mark O. Hatfield Wilderness area. You might spot a junction with the Eagle Benson Trail, but the trail has been unmaintained and effectively closed since the 2017 fire.

From the junction, it's 0.8 mile to Tunnel Falls and the most dramatic section of the trail. It's another very high, very narrow stretch of trail with cables as handrails—small comfort if you meet anyone going the other direction, which is all but assured in this popular spot.

WARNING: If you hike with a pet, this trail is a particularly bad place to violate the leash law.

The falls gets its name because the trail goes through a human-made tunnel created around 1917 in the basalt cliffs behind the falling water. As the falls roars in your ears, take a moment to admire the work (and audacity!) of those long-ago trail builders. Then venture ahead into what looks like the mouth of a mossy cave, and on out the other side. In spring you can expect to get a bit of a shower as you round this exciting section. Tunnel Falls is the usual turnaround point for strong day hikers coming up the Eagle Creek Trail. With luck, you'll enjoy more solitude as you continue up the canyon.

Just as you're recovering from Tunnel Falls, you reach the fascinating Twister Falls, where two strands of water cross over each other on the way down. At the top of Twister Falls is a series of clear, shallow, rock-bottomed pools that practically beg you to jump in on a hot day. A little over half a mile farther are the handful of sites that make up Seven and a Half Mile Camp.

Leaving camp, the trail gets steeper and in places a little overgrown. You'll cross two side creeks and then turn hard left (north) at a junction with the little-used Eagle Tanner Trail. Continue for 1.5 miles to a point and a hard-right switchback, with excellent views to reward your climb. You pass a junction with the Indian Springs Trail and soon leave behind the Eagle Creek burn area (for now).

At the Eagle Creek–Chinidere Cutoff Trail junction, you can turn left to reach some campsites across the East Fork Eagle Creek beside the outlet of large, tranquil Wahtum Lake, or you can continue straight to a junction with the PCT toward designated campsites on the south side of the lake.

TIP: Those interested in rare plants will want to keep an eye out for cutleaf bugbane *(Actaea laciniata),* with its 5-foot-tall stalks holding plumes of small white flowers.

Hikers contemplating Tunnel Falls

When you leave Wahtum Lake, just after the cutoff trail meets the PCT, don't miss the moderately steep but short Chinidere Mountain Trail (0.4 mile) up to a viewpoint. If it's a clear day, you can see down to Wahtum Lake, as well as Mount Defiance and Larch Mountain, and even possibly Mounts Jefferson and Rainier in the distance.

Back at the main trail, continue along the PCT northwest toward Benson Plateau. The trail hugs the edge of the Eagle Creek Fire area. The fire created a mosaic pattern of lightly burned, badly burned, and basically untouched areas. Just under 3 miles from the Chinidere junction, you'll reach a junction with the Eagle Benson Trail leading off to the left, the opposite end of which you passed on the Eagle Creek Trail. Continue straight onto the plateau. The top of the plateau was mostly spared in the fire, and if you have an extra day or two you might find a tempting campsite here (there's a nice one right in the middle of the plateau, where Ruckel Creek begins). Otherwise, it's a bit of a long hike out, though mostly downhill.

Before the Eagle Creek Fire, you would have been able to head west from Benson Plateau along Ruckel Creek and back to your car. But those trails and the whole Ruckel Creek area have been inaccessible since 2017 and do not appear to be reopening anytime soon. Instead, your route follows the PCT north toward Teakettle Spring, a usually reliable water source. The next stretch offers many switchbacks and nice open views as you zigzag toward an overlook of Herman Creek. The trail rounds this point and turns left (west), and you make the long traverse toward Cascade Locks. Take advantage of the restrooms and water at the Bridge of the Gods Trailhead, which marks this end of the Oregon section of the PCT. Then follow the well-graded, partly paved Gorge Trail #400 for the final 2.6 miles back to your car.

LONGER LOOP OPTIONS: To extend your trip, you could take the Rainy-Wahtum Trail #409 from Wahtum Lake north to Rainy Lake (campground and road access), explore North Lake, then return to the trailhead via Gorton Creek or Nick Eaton Trails. Another option is to return from Wahtum Lake via the Herman Creek Trail, although at the time of this writing, the Herman Creek Trail is directly in the middle of the Whisky Creek Fire zone, so hikers would need to confirm trail status before considering this option. For any of the above options, you can also set up a very short car shuttle by leaving a vehicle at the Herman Creek Trailhead.

POSSIBLE ITINERARY

	CAMP	MILES	ELEVATION GAIN
Day 1	7½ Mile Camp	7.0	1,400'
Day 2	Wahtum Lake	6.5	2,500'
Day 3	PCT to exit	17.0	1,200'

6

TIMBERLINE TRAIL LOOP

RATINGS: Scenery 10 **Solitude** 2 **Difficulty** 8
MILES: 42 (52)
ELEVATION GAIN: 9,600' (13,000')
DAYS: 3–5 (5–7)
SHUTTLE MILEAGE: NA
MAPS: Green Trails *Government Camp (#461)* and *Mount Hood (#462)*
USUALLY OPEN: July–October
BEST: Mid-August–mid-September
PERMITS: Free, self-issued wilderness permit required May 15–October 15 at some trailheads. Northwest Forest Pass required to park at Cloud Cap, Elk Meadows, Ramona Falls, Paradise Park, Tilly Jane, and Top Spur trailheads.
RULES: No horses except on the Pacific Crest Trail; no campfires within 500 feet of Ramona Falls and McNeil Point, within the tree-covered islands in Elk Cove and Elk Meadows, or within Paradise Park; no camping in any meadow, within the tree-covered islands in Elk Cove and Elk Meadows, or within 500 feet of Ramona Falls
CONTACT: Hood River Ranger District, Mount Hood National Forest, 541-352-6002; Zigzag Ranger District, Mount Hood National Forest, 503-622-3191, fs.usda.gov/mthood

Above: View of Mount Hood from Elk Meadow

SPECIAL ATTRACTIONS

Great mountain scenery, wildflowers, bragging rights

CHALLENGES

Crowded in places, potentially dangerous water crossings

HOW TO GET THERE

From Portland, take I-84 east for 12 miles to Exit 16. Stay on NE Hogan Drive, following signs to Mount Hood/238th Drive for 3 miles. Turn left onto NE Burnside Road/US 26. Go 39.5 miles to Government Camp and turn left onto Timberline Highway. Go 5.5 miles to Timberline Lodge.

TIP: Spacious is hardly an adequate word to describe the acres of parking here. Don't forget to take a photo of where you parked, or you might face hours of embarrassment trying to locate your vehicle when you return.

GPS TRAILHEAD COORDINATES:
N45° 19.870' W121° 42.678'

INTRODUCTION

After the PCT, the Timberline Trail circling Mount Hood is probably the most famous footpath in the state. There's an undeniable allure to the idea of walking all the way around this peak that so defines the local landscape. But it's not just locals who appreciate this spectacular route; it draws people from all over the country and the world. Even before the official trail was built by Civilian Conservation Corps workers in the 1930s, this round-the-mountain tour had many admirers—and justifiably so. The mountain views are stunning, wildflowers carpet the meadows in spring, and exceptional side trips abound.

Yes, that means the trail can be busy in places. Part of the beauty of the Timberline Trail is that you can access it from many different corners, on all sides of the mountain. For that reason, you'll run into a lot of day hikers near each trailhead. But the terrain is challenging enough to keep the crowds thinned out, and campsites are plentiful.

Because this is a storied hike around an iconic mountain, it makes sense that most backpackers start at Timberline Lodge, an appropriately impressive landmark. (Be sure to pop in and admire the outsized architecture and decor, either before or after your trip.) The route below is described clockwise, although the trip is equally scenic in either direction and can be started from any of several trailheads along the route.

DESCRIPTION

From the back side of Timberline Lodge, follow a paved route signed TIMBERLINE TRAIL to a junction with the Pacific Crest Trail (PCT) and turn left. The scenic path gradually loses elevation through flowery meadows and then crosses Little Zigzag Canyon. Keep right at the Hidden Lake Trail junction and continue losing elevation. The trail rounds a narrow ridge, where you will enjoy a fine view of Zigzag Canyon before dropping in long switchbacks to its bottom.

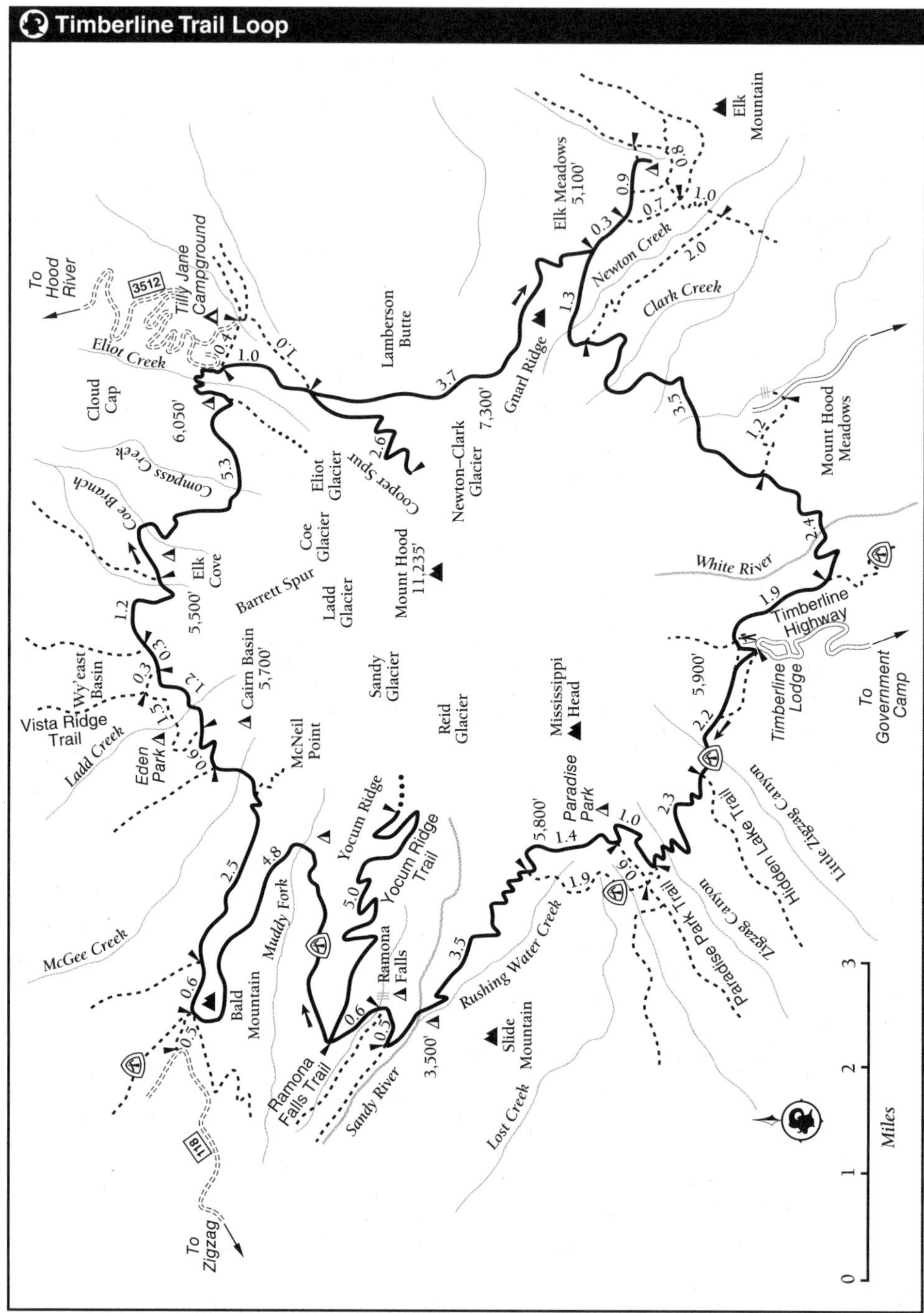

Climb back up the west side of this gorge to a junction. The horse route below Paradise Park goes left, while the more scenic hiker's trail goes right and continues its long climb out of Zigzag Canyon.

In a sloping meadow covered with blossoms, you will find a junction with the Paradise Park Trail. Keep right to reach the remains of an old trail shelter, near many good but heavily used camps (please use a designated site). Although the camps are pleasant, trees and a small ridge block the sight of Mount Hood from here. You'll get better vistas as you continue hiking northwest on the up-and-down route for another 0.6 mile, with flowers and unrestricted views, before dropping back down to a reunion with the horse trail.

Brace your knees for a long series of downhill switchbacks as the trail descends 2,200 feet on its way into the Sandy River canyon. Along the way are excellent views of the eroding cliffs of Slide Mountain.

TIP: Shortly before crossing the Sandy River is a nice, uncrowded camp beside Rushing Water Creek on the left. (Be sure to camp at least 200 feet from the creek.)

You cross the Sandy River—scout around for makeshift log bridges or cairns showing the best place to cross; as with all the river crossings, it might not be exactly where the line on the map goes, and you'll need to be cautious and use good judgment. Climb a bench on the far side to a junction with the popular Ramona Falls Trail coming in from the west. Make a sharp right turn and climb gradually 0.5 mile to Ramona Falls—a lovely curtain of water that cascades over a basalt cliff. Camps must be made at least 500 feet from the falls. A designated camping area is located to the south.

If the weather is good, we strongly recommend that you spend an extra day here with a long side trip up Yocum Ridge. The ridge trail (#771) leaves the Timberline Trail at a ridgecrest 0.6 mile northwest of Ramona Falls and makes a long but moderately graded climb through mostly viewless forests (expect to navigate quite a few blown-down trees). Eventually, the trail breaks out into wildflower meadows with a terrific perspective of Reid Glacier. By continuing another mile and scrambling up a ridge, you can also get up close and personal with the Sandy Glacier—see if you can spot the glacial caves!

Back on the main circuit, from the junction with the Yocum Ridge Trail, you have a choice to make. The section of the Timberline Trail that goes from the Yocum Ridge junction to the Muddy Fork River was ravaged in 2020 during a windstorm that caused a huge amount of blowdown. A lot of work has been done since then, but this stretch may or may not be passable, depending on whom you ask and when. (The blowdown has also worsened erosion and made snowfields more treacherous in this area.) So call the forest service for conditions before you decide. The alternate route is to return to Ramona Falls from the Yocum Ridge junction, then turn right onto the Ramona Falls Loop Trail (#797) for 1.8 miles to where it meets the PCT. Turn right (north) and follow the PCT about 3 miles toward Bald Mountain, where it rejoins the Timberline Trail.

TIP: Even if you've taken the Ramona Falls/PCT alternate route around the blowdown to get here, don't miss the viewpoint on the south side of Bald Mountain. To reach It, turn hard right at the PCT-Timberline junction for 0.5 mile. The scene as you look back to Mount Hood from the steeply sloping wildflower meadows below Bald Mountain is outstanding. If you don't want to backtrack to the junction, there's a very short (signed) cutoff trail another half mile east that will get you back to heading clockwise on the Timberline Trail; if you came up to Bald Mountain the traditional route, you will have passed it.

Back at the major junction in the forest, the PCT heads off to the northwest, but our trail (Timberline Trail) turns to the right (east). You hike through a viewless forest, pass a trail junction (the other end of that short cutoff trail), and then begin a steady climb along a ridge. Eventually the trail breaks out into ridgetop meadows with flowers and terrific vistas of Mount Hood. Make four switchbacks and encounter an unmarked but obvious side trail that climbs very steeply over loose rocks and roots to McNeil Point (a tiring but worthwhile side trip).

Stick with the Timberline Trail and cross a basin with two small ponds.

TIP: Photographers will want to climb the small hill south of these ponds to a fine photo opportunity of the top third of Mount Hood.

The route climbs briefly over a ridge and then contours to the excellent camps in scenic Cairn Basin. This area still shows signs of the massive Dollar Lake Fire of 2011, but it's a great place to witness the slow but determined recovery in the aftermath of an alpine wildfire. There's also a sturdy stone shelter at Cairn Basin, built in 1934 and good mostly for photos, rather than a home for the night, unless the weather is truly vile. If the Cairn Basin camps are full, Eden Park on a nearby loop trail also has nice camps.

If you're camped at Cairn Basin and have time for some exploring, there are several options. You can make a lovely loop trip by dropping to the wildflower gardens of Eden Park, going east to Wy'east Basin, and returning to Cairn Basin via the Timberline Trail.

WARNING: The loop requires two crossings of Ladd Creek, which is not always easy.

Ambitious hikers should also consider making the trailless scramble up Barrett Spur. Take a user trail south from the Timberline Trail in Wy'east Basin near the junction with the Vista Ridge Trail and climb through meadows and over rocky slopes for about 1.5 miles to the summit viewpoint. The jumbled ice masses of Ladd and Coe Glaciers are especially impressive.

The main Timberline Trail goes through continuously spectacular terrain on an up-and-down course to the east. Shortly before it drops down a sidehill ridge, an unmarked side trail goes right to tiny Dollar Lake, which has camps but only limited views. Just ahead is Elk Cove, one of the mountain's most beautiful spots. The cove has a particularly striking view of the north face of Mount Hood and the white mass of Coe Glacier. Wildflowers carpet the meadow, and a clear brook provides water. Camps here must be made in the trees below the fragile meadow.

The magnificent circle route continues with a loss of elevation to the sometimes-difficult crossing of Coe Branch above two towering waterfalls (which you can hear but not see) and then climbs back to higher-elevation meadows. Look for frequent views north of Mount Adams and Mount Rainier. At the crossing of Compass Creek, you'll spot two waterfalls—a short one near the trail and a taller one a bit farther downstream.

TIP: From a ridge just west of Eliot Creek, an unmarked path climbs the moraine beside Eliot Glacier to some great observation points above the ice.

The crossing at Eliot Creek/Elliot Branch is notoriously difficult. After a 2006 flood washed out the bridge, this section of trail was officially closed for years until being rerouted in 2016 downstream of the original crossing. There's still no bridge, and no plans for one, so your best bet is to scout around for the safest crossing you can find given the ever-changing conditions and path of the river. (This is true for all the crossings on the trail.) Recently there have been logjam bridges and sometimes a helpful rope that make getting across the Elliot Branch a little easier.

After crossing, you climb a bit to the road and campground at Cloud Cap. It's a good place to take a break and fill up on drinking water from a tap.

The old inn at Cloud Cap is not open to the public; it's maintained by the Crag Rats, a volunteer search-and-rescue group. This is a popular trailhead with a campground to accommodate both car campers and backpackers. Tilly Jane Campground, 0.5 mile east, is another option for spending the night. Note that between here and Newton Creek it can be tough to find water sources, especially later in the fall.

From Cloud Cap, the Timberline Trail turns sharply southward, and skyward, as it climbs toward the highest part of the circuit. After 1 mile is a junction near a shelter, another of the stone huts built in 1934.

White River with Mount Hood in the background

TIP: An outstanding side trip from here climbs southwest in long switchbacks over talus slopes and snowfields to the viewpoint atop Cooper Spur. Before taking this side trip, keep in mind that it involves a round-trip distance of 5.2 miles and an elevation gain of 1,900 feet.

The main trail goes south, climbing above timberline and crossing steep snowfields.

WARNING: These snowfields are dangerously icy on cold mornings.

Expect plenty of wind near the trail's high point on Gnarl Ridge before beginning a long descent into more friendly terrain. Above Lamberson Butte, there are some great views across Newton Creek Canyon and up to Mount Hood. The massive Newton-Clark Glacier fills most of the mountain's east face.

The trail continues its long descent back into forests and meadows to a junction with the trail dropping to Elk Meadows. This large, popular meadow is well worth the 700-foot elevation loss and gain to make a visit. Highlights include an old shelter, excellent camps, marvelous views back up to Mount Hood, and a notorious population of gray jays that will happily eat from your hand (or steal your unguarded breakfast). To reduce damage here, the U.S. Forest Service asks that you camp in the trees around the perimeter of the meadow.

Back on the Timberline Trail, the route travels down a hillside to Newton Creek, which you can sometimes hop across, but a wet crossing is usually required. Pass a trail junction and then contour around a ridge before coming to Clark Creek, an easier crossing, and then a couple of small waterfalls right on the trail. The tour now passes through a few scenic wildflower meadows in the aptly named Mount Hood Meadows ski area. You cross a few roads and walk beneath some chairlifts, then reach a junction with the Umbrella Falls Trail; bear right to stay on Timberline.

Leave the ski area and start a long 1,000-foot descent into the bouldery wasteland of the White River valley. This stream has no bridge and is the last potentially difficult crossing, with steep, unstable banks. The trail crosses this valley and then climbs a long switchback up the far side back into meadows. In a particularly nice meadow, there is a junction with the PCT. Turn right and climb the final sandy 2 miles back to your car (somewhere in that huge parking lot).

POSSIBLE ITINERARY

	CAMP	MILES	ELEVATION GAIN
Day 1	Ramona Falls	11.0	1,400'
Day 2	Day trip up Yocum Ridge (return to Ramona Falls)	10.0	3,400'
Day 3	Elk Cove	12.0	3,000'
Day 4	Newton Creek	12.0	1,800'
Day 5	Out	7.0	3,400'

7

SALMON RIVER TRAIL

RATINGS: Scenery 6 **Solitude** 5 **Difficulty** 4
MILES: 16
ELEVATION GAIN: 4,000'
DAYS: 2–3
SHUTTLE MILEAGE: NA
MAP: Green Trails *Government Camp (#461)* and *High Rock (#493)*
USUALLY OPEN: March–November for riverside section; May–October for full loop
BEST: June–October
PERMITS: Free self-issued wilderness permits required where available at kiosks; Northwest Forest Pass required at trailhead
RULES: Wilderness rules apply
CONTACT: Zigzag Ranger District, Mount Hood National Forest, 503-622-3191, fs.usda.gov/mthood

SPECIAL ATTRACTIONS

Shady riverside hiking, lush forest, wildflowers, easy access

CHALLENGES

Washouts, trail overgrown in places

Above: Lush green forest near Rolling Riffle Camp

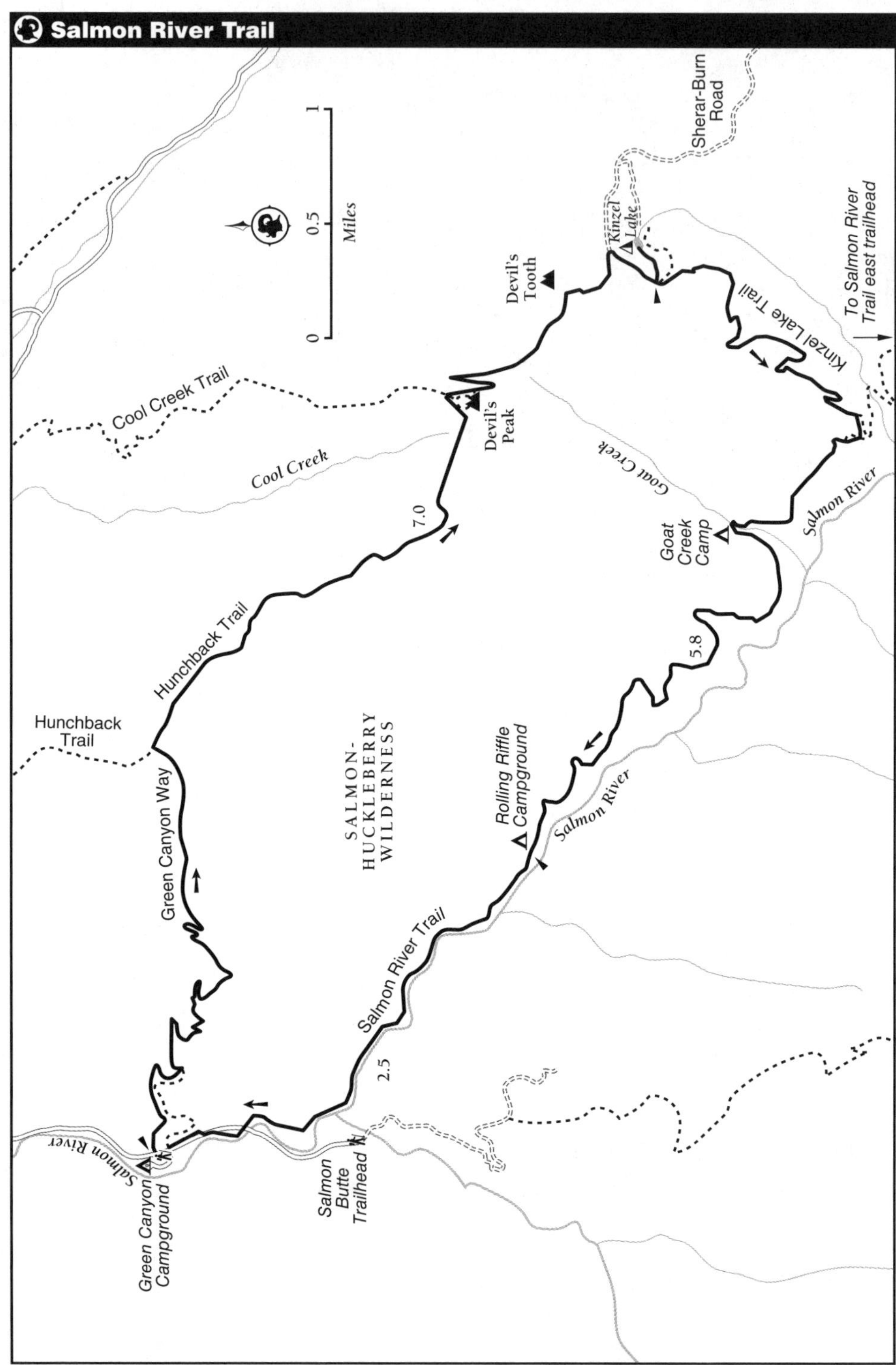
Salmon River Trail
Sherar-Burn Road
Kinzel Lake
Devil's Tooth
0 0.5 1
Miles
To Salmon River Trail east trailhead
Kinzel Lake Trail
Cool Creek Trail
Devil's Peak
Goat Creek
Cool Creek
Salmon River
7.0
Goat Creek Camp
Hunchback Trail
5.8
Hunchback Trail
SALMON-HUCKLEBERRY WILDERNESS
Rolling Riffle Campground
Salmon River
Green Canyon Way
Salmon River Trail
2.5
Salmon River
Salmon Butte Trailhead
Green Canyon Campground

HOW TO GET THERE

From Portland, take US 26 east for about 47 miles; along the way you will pass through the town of Sandy. Turn right (south) onto Salmon River Road. Follow this paved road 5 miles to the trailhead.

GPS TRAILHEAD COORDINATES:
N45° 16.669' W121° 56.387'

INTRODUCTION

On a hot summer day, this mellow riverside trail through shady old-growth forest and patches of wildflowers is just the ticket. The Salmon River carves a wooded canyon through the middle of the 62,000-acre Salmon-Huckleberry Wilderness, just southwest of Mount Hood. The trail that parallels the river is relatively flat, dotted with excellent campsites, and well maintained for most of its length; the rest of the recommended loop includes some steeper climbing and descending, as well as rougher trail and varied terrain. The trailhead is easy to reach from Portland and likely to be snow-free much earlier and later than any of the nearby higher-elevation trails. Anglers will appreciate the river's population of steelhead, chinook, and coho salmon, and everyone loves a riverside campsite. The surrounding forest of Douglas fir, western hemlock, and western red cedar blankets rugged volcanic ridges and outcrops that offer occasional viewpoints. And if you hike the river trail as part of a loop to tiny Kinzel Lake and the interesting fire lookout tower at Devil's Peak, you can revel in the deep, dark woods without sacrificing epic views of distant mountain peaks. (You can also do a simple out-and-back along the Salmon River and avoid nearly all the steep ups and downs as well as sun exposure.) The Salmon River Canyon also escaped the destructive effects of massive wildfires that swept through other parts of the Mount Hood National Forest in 2020–2021 and made many nearby trails, such as Bull of the Woods, virtually impossible to backpack.

DESCRIPTION

This loop can be completed in either direction—it really comes down to a choice between your lungs and your knees. Doing the hike clockwise means climbing up the steepest section first. Going counterclockwise means you will be hiking down that section, while also navigating blown-down trees and rocky terrain on a narrow trail. Your author's knees are extremely well broken-in at this point, and most people find that climbing around blowdown is easier going uphill than downhill, so we recommend tackling this route clockwise, as described here.

TIP: One other factor to consider as you plan is that there aren't many water sources between the Green Canyon trailhead and Kinzel Lake, so some prefer to go counterclockwise to avoid carrying lots of water up the steepest ascent. (But even so: the knees.)

From the Green Canyon Campground parking area, head east along Green Canyon Way (#793A), a mostly shaded trail that zigzags steeply uphill, gaining 2,400' elevation in just over 3 miles. The understory features a mix of ferns and rhododendron, maple, oxalis, and fir, and grassy patches dotted with wildflowers to keep things interesting as you switchback up toward the top of the ridge.

Near the crest of the ridge, you turn right at a junction with the Hunchback Trail (#793). This 9-mile trail starts at the Zigzag Ranger Station north of the junction and is considered a tough training hike, but by the time you intersect it, most of the climbing has already been done. That's not to say you've reached level ground, but there's only a gentle 1,000 feet of elevation gain between here and Devil's Peak. It's a long series of gentle ups and downs that more or less follows the rocky spine of Hunchback Ridge for 2.4 miles, on a trail that can be rugged, narrow, and cluttered with blown-down trees. Depending on the season, you'll see a range of wildflowers, including tiger lily, beargrass, paintbrush, lupine, cinquefoil, and maybe the elusive mariposa lily, as well as thimbleberries and fir trees.

A pool near the Salmon River Trailhead

WARNING: In a few places, huge fallen trees on steep terrain have created sketchy spots that call for patience and caution.

Just before a junction with the Cool Creek Trail, there's a sign indicating WATER, pointing you toward a campsite with a spring, but it's not always flowing, especially late in the season, and the path to it requires scrambling down a steep slope.

Continue southeast, keeping right at the Cool Creek junction, to reach the Devil's Peak fire lookout. Though it's now closed to the public, the lookout and the viewpoints around it provide impressive views, including Mount Jefferson and Three Fingered Jack to the south and Mount Hood to the north.

Descending from Devil's Peak, you switchback through a forest of Douglas fir and hemlock for 1.2 miles, then emerge onto a dirt road, where a sign on your right indicates the trail to Kinzel Lake and its primitive campground. The shallow, pretty lake sits at the western edge of the Sherar Burn, which swept this area in the early 1900s.

Leaving the lake, continue south on the Kinzel Lake Trail, descending for 1.8 miles until you reach a junction with the Salmon River Trail. Turn right (west) for the final leg of this loop—but see the note for a longer loop option below if you're not ready to go home yet.

Hiking along (or more accurately, a few hundred feet above) the Salmon River, you're immersed in shady, old-growth forest with lots of campsites but sparse viewpoints. The terrain isn't quite flat, but the ups and downs are downright cushy compared to what you've hiked up to now. About a mile past the junction, you'll reach Goat Creek, a popular spot with nice camps. The trail hugs the curving ridgeline, and there are occasional views from rock outcrops, as well as several unmarked use paths toward "secret" waterfalls—but resist the temptation to try scrambling down to the river from here, even if you can hear the falls below. People regularly get injured and stuck trying to reach them.

About half a mile past Goat Creek, after a sharp switchback above Frustration Falls (audible but not visible), the trail subtly and briefly divides, with the left-hand (southern) branch looping toward an impressive Salmon River overlook. From here you can take in a long view of the thickly forested canyon, although the river itself is hard to see. This section can also be very eroded and slippery, so stick to the right-hand path if you feel unsteady or are afraid of heights. The two paths meet again after about half a mile.

Two miles past Goat Creek the trail starts to gradually descend to the river. There are good riverside camps all along this stretch, including a spacious one at Rolling Riffle, from which it's an easy 2.5 miles of mostly flat, shady, forested trail along the river back to your car.

LONGER LOOP OPTION: At the Kinzel Lake junction, you can add a lollipop tail to this trip by turning left (southeast) instead of right and following the Salmon River Trail for 5 miles. Pass a junction with the Dry Fir Trail (674A) on your left, continuing straight on the Salmon River Trail. After just over a mile, the trail turns sharply left, then in 0.75 mile, there's another junction with the Dry Fir Trail. Go left (west) at this junction (going right leads you to the east trailhead of the Salmon River Trail, 0.4 mile away) and follow Dry Fir Trail into a canyon, up a ridge, and back downhill. Note that this part of the loop trail may be faint and overgrown with rhododendrons and other shrubs, especially from the canyon onward. After 2.5 miles on the Dry Fir Trail, you rejoin the Salmon Creek Trail, completing the loop; turn right to retrace your steps to the car/trailhead.

Bridge over Mud Creek at the eastern end of the longer loop option

POSSIBLE ITINERARY

	CAMP	MILES	ELEVATION GAIN
Day 1	Kinzel Lake	7.0	3,400'
Day 2	Rolling Riffle Camp	5.8	400'
Day 3	Out	2.5	200'

8

JEFFERSON PARK TREK

RATINGS: Scenery 10 **Solitude** 3 **Difficulty** 6
MILES: 36 (40)
ELEVATION GAIN: 5,700' (6,800')
DAYS: 5–6
SHUTTLE MILEAGE: NA
MAP: USFS *Detroit Ranger District: Willamette National Forest;* National Geographic Trails Illustrated #819: *Mt. Jefferson/Mt. Washington*
USUALLY OPEN: Mid-July–October
BEST: Late July–mid-August
PERMITS: Northwest Forest Pass required at trailheads; Central Cascades Wilderness Pass required June 15–October 15 (reserve in advance, $6 reservation fee, available at recreation.gov or 877-444-6777)
RULES: No fires at Jefferson Park; no camping within 100 feet of lakes or any water source at Jefferson Park and Pamelia Lake
CONTACT: Detroit Ranger District, Willamette National Forest, 503-854-3366, fs.usda.gov/willamette

SPECIAL ATTRACTIONS

Views and mountain scenery; Jefferson Park—*wow!*

Above: Hunts Lake

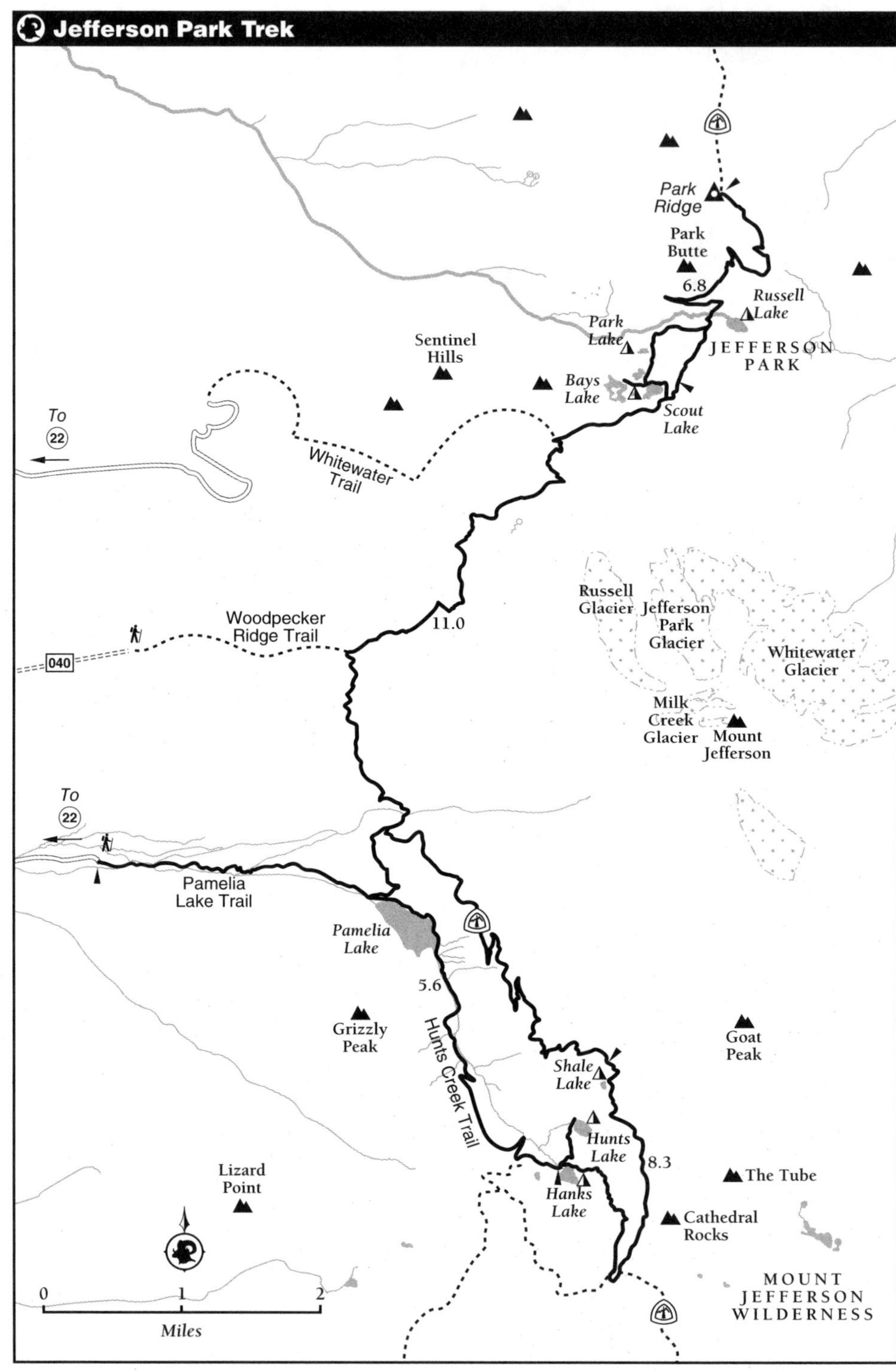
Jefferson Park Trek
Park Ridge
Park Butte
6.8
Russell Lake
Park Lake
JEFFERSON PARK
Sentinel Hills
Bays Lake
Scout Lake
To 22
Whitewater Trail
Woodpecker Ridge Trail
040
11.0
Russell Glacier
Jefferson Park Glacier
Whitewater Glacier
Milk Creek Glacier
Mount Jefferson
To 22
Pamelia Lake Trail
Pamelia Lake
5.6
Grizzly Peak
Hunts Creek Trail
Goat Peak
Shale Lake
Hunts Lake
8.3
The Tube
Lizard Point
Hanks Lake
Cathedral Rocks
MOUNT JEFFERSON WILDERNESS
0
1
2
Miles

CHALLENGES

Permits and access restrictions, burned areas, crowds, snowfields, crossing of Russell Creek, mosquitoes mid-July–mid-August

HOW TO GET THERE

To reach the Pamelia Lake Trailhead, go east on OR 22 from Detroit for 12.5 miles; turn left onto Pamelia Creek Road (Forest Service Road 2246) and go 3.7 miles to the parking lot at the end of the road.

To reach the Whitewater Trailhead, drive southeast from Detroit on OR 22 for 10 miles, then turn left onto Forest Service Road 2243 (Whitewater Road) and go 7.5 miles to the trailhead.

For the Woodpecker Trailhead, head east on OR 22 from Detroit for 12 miles to Woodpecker Ridge Road (Forest Service Road 040), then continue 5 miles to the trailhead on the left.

NOTE: The Whitewater Trail had just reopened as this book was being written, giving hikers more options for reaching Jefferson Park. You could start this hike from the Whitewater Trailhead or from Woodpecker Trailhead, located roughly between the Whitewater and Pamelia Lake Trailheads. For now, the South Breitenbush Trail is still closed due to the Lionshead Fire, and the Breitenbush Lake Trailhead, while technically open, can only be reached via increasingly terrible roads.

GPS TRAILHEAD COORDINATES:

(Pamelia Lake) N44° 39.611' W121° 53.492'
(Whitewater Trailhead) N44° 42.409' W121° 52.476'
(Woodpecker Trailhead) N44° 40.829' W121° 53.103'

INTRODUCTION

Most hikers rank the section of the Pacific Crest Trail (PCT) that goes through the Mount Jefferson Wilderness as the highlight of its route through Oregon, and it would be difficult to argue with them. There are memorable vistas at nearly every turn. But getting to this stretch of the PCT, if you're not hiking its full length, has become a bit more challenging in recent years. The Lionshead Fire swept through this area in 2020, causing destruction that in many places overlapped what had already been done by the 2017 Whitewater Fire. These events changed the landscape here, but fortunately they spared most of Jefferson Park, the justifiably beloved lake- and flower-decorated meadow at the foot of Mount Jefferson. The Whitewater Trail, the shortest and easiest path into the park, was inaccessible for several years; it's now open again but requires hiking through a shadeless forest of burned trees, as does the alternative Woodpecker Ridge Trail. A longer but more scenic way into this territory, if you can snag a permit for it, is via Pamelia Lake. This route lets you explore a pair of lakes nestled below the impressive spires of Cathedral Ridge, then ascend that ridge to skirt the west side of Mount Jefferson on your way to the idyllic Jefferson Park. The recommended route does go through the burned zone, but not for long; it also involves retracing your steps in an out-and-back hike, but you probably won't mind the opportunity to take a second look at some of these vistas.

Pamelia Lake with Mount Jefferson in the background

DESCRIPTION

The well-traveled, easy trail toward Pamelia Lake is especially soothing on a hot day. You wander gently uphill through deep forest beside lively Pamelia Creek. At 2.1 miles you reach a junction with the trail to Grizzly Peak on your right, and a potentially confusing network of use trails toward various campsites around Pamelia Lake. Skirt the lake's northwest edge, then turn right (south) onto Hunts Creek Trail and follow it around to the lake's outlet. Several camps are tucked away in the woods along this bank. Just beyond the edge of the lake is a footbridge and a beautifully mossy waterfall. The trail continues to follow Hunts Creek, at times through a thick carpet of undergrowth. There are a couple of streams to step across and one crossing of Hunts Creek on a huge fallen log.

After 3 miles, turn left at a junction onto Hunts Cove Trail. In half a mile you reach Hanks Lake. Pass another junction and some campsites amid some dangerous-looking fallen trees. Stay on Hunts Cove Trail to go north 0.3 mile to Hunts Lake, where there are also several nice camps. Forming a dramatic backdrop behind Hunts Lake, Cathedral Rocks provide shelter and maybe inspiration: You'll be up there looking down at this lake before long.

Return to Hanks Lake and go left (east) onto Old Hunts Cove Trail. Step across a pretty creek on the east side of the lake and then get ready to climb (about 800 feet in a mile—not so bad, really). At the top of the ridge, you briefly meet the Hunts Creek Trail (go left) and then the PCT.

TIP: Here you have an opportunity for an interesting side trip to Table Lake, which sits below a prominent plateau aptly named The Table. To get there, turn right onto the PCT and head east for 0.4 mile, then turn left (northeast) onto the Table Lake Cutoff trail for 1.5 miles. At a junction, go left onto Table Lake Trail to reach the lake. There are campsites here, and it's possible to scramble up to the top of The Table for epic views.

Turn left onto the PCT and go north, following it along the western side of the impressively rugged Cathedral Rocks, with several dramatic clifftop overlooks of Mount Jefferson and the diverse volcanic landscape below. This display of volcanism includes cinder cones, lava flows, and a basalt-rimmed mesa called The Table. Only the Three Sisters area showcases a more interesting and scenic variety of the volcanic forces that shaped this landscape.

Next on the list of wonders is a partially forested plateau supporting several small lakes, though only Coyote, Shale, and Mud Hole Lakes are near the trail.

TIP: These lakes are the jumping-off point for excellent cross-country explorations to Goat Peak and, for the truly ambitious hiker, up the long, steep south ridge of Mount Jefferson. Strong scramblers can get to a point a little below the summit, where a dangerously exposed traverse stops those not equipped with climbing gear.

The PCT gradually descends from the lovely high country on a series of long switchbacks to a junction with a trail you'll take later to return to Pamelia Lake. Nearby is a sweeping view up the steep canyon of Milk Creek to the top of Mount Jefferson. (There are two small tent spots tucked into the brush beside the Milk Creek overlook, which would be a great place to watch the sunrise, but it's a long way down to get water.) Make your way down to step across Milk Creek and gradually climb to a junction with the Woodpecker Ridge Trail. Stay on the PCT, which passes a small, narrow lake on the right as it makes its way across the northwest side of Mount Jefferson.

Now you confront a potential problem—the crossing of Russell Creek. As with most glacial streams, this creek's volume increases significantly on hot summer afternoons due to melting snow and glacial ice above. Try to cross in the morning, and expect a cold, possibly dangerous crossing—made worse by the brown glacial water obscuring possible footholds.

Not long after the crossing is a junction with the newly restored Whitewater Trail from the west. Keep right and follow the PCT less than a mile to Jefferson Park, a nationally famous spot that should be seen by every Oregon outdoors lover. Though wildfire crept alarmingly close to the edges of this area in 2020, it remains the perfect blend of alpine meadows, scattered trees, wildflowers, and lakes. Overlooking this scene is the snowy crown of Mount Jefferson. Camping near lakes is restricted to designated sites, and fires are prohibited.

Once you manage to drag yourself away from this paradise, the PCT climbs to the top of Park Ridge, which sustained quite a bit more damage in the fires. The burned trees might not be particularly scenic themselves, but they do open up the sightlines. Allow plenty of extra time here to gaze in amazement upon what many believe to be the best view in Oregon. The scene back down across the expanse of Jefferson Park and sweeping up to the top of Mount Jefferson is impossible to describe.

To continue your trip, retrace your steps back down the side of Park Ridge, and be sure you take time to check out several of the lakes in Jefferson Park on your way back through. Then return southward on the PCT, passing the Whitewater and then the Woodpecker Ridge Trails, until you reach the junction you passed earlier with Hunts Creek Trail down to Pamelia Lake. Turn right at the Pamelia Lake Trail, enjoy one last look at this pretty but popular lake, then make your way back down through the woods to your car.

LONGER LOOP OPTION: Hikers with plenty of time can combine this hike with the loop described in Trip 9, leaving a vehicle at the Whitewater Trailhead for a very reasonable 13-mile, 30-minute car shuttle.

POSSIBLE ITINERARY

	CAMP	MILES	ELEVATION GAIN
Day 1	Hanks Lake	5.6	2,000'
Day 2	Shale Lake (with side trip to Table Lake)	8.3	1,100'
Day 3	Jefferson Park	11.0	2,100'
Day 4	Park Ridge viewpoint, back to Jefferson Park	6.8	1,300'
Day 5	Out	8.7	300'

9

MOUNT JEFFERSON WILDERNESS LOOP

RATINGS: Scenery 9 **Solitude** 5 **Difficulty** 6
MILES: 35
ELEVATION GAIN: 6,500'
DAYS: 3–4
SHUTTLE MILEAGE: NA
MAP: USFS *Detroit Ranger District: Willamette National Forest;* National Geographic Trails Illustrated #819: *Mt. Jefferson/Mt. Washington*
USUALLY OPEN: June–October
BEST: Mid-July–September
PERMITS: Northwest Forest Pass required at trailheads; Central Cascades Wilderness Permit ($6 fee) required June 15–October 15 via recreation.gov or 877-444-6777
RULES: Wilderness restrictions apply; no fires at Marion Lake or Lake Ann, or above 5,700 feet in designated zones
CONTACT: Detroit Ranger District, Willamette National Forest, 503-854-3366, fs.usda.gov/willamette

SPECIAL ATTRACTIONS

Views and mountain scenery, alpine lakes

Above: Marion Lake

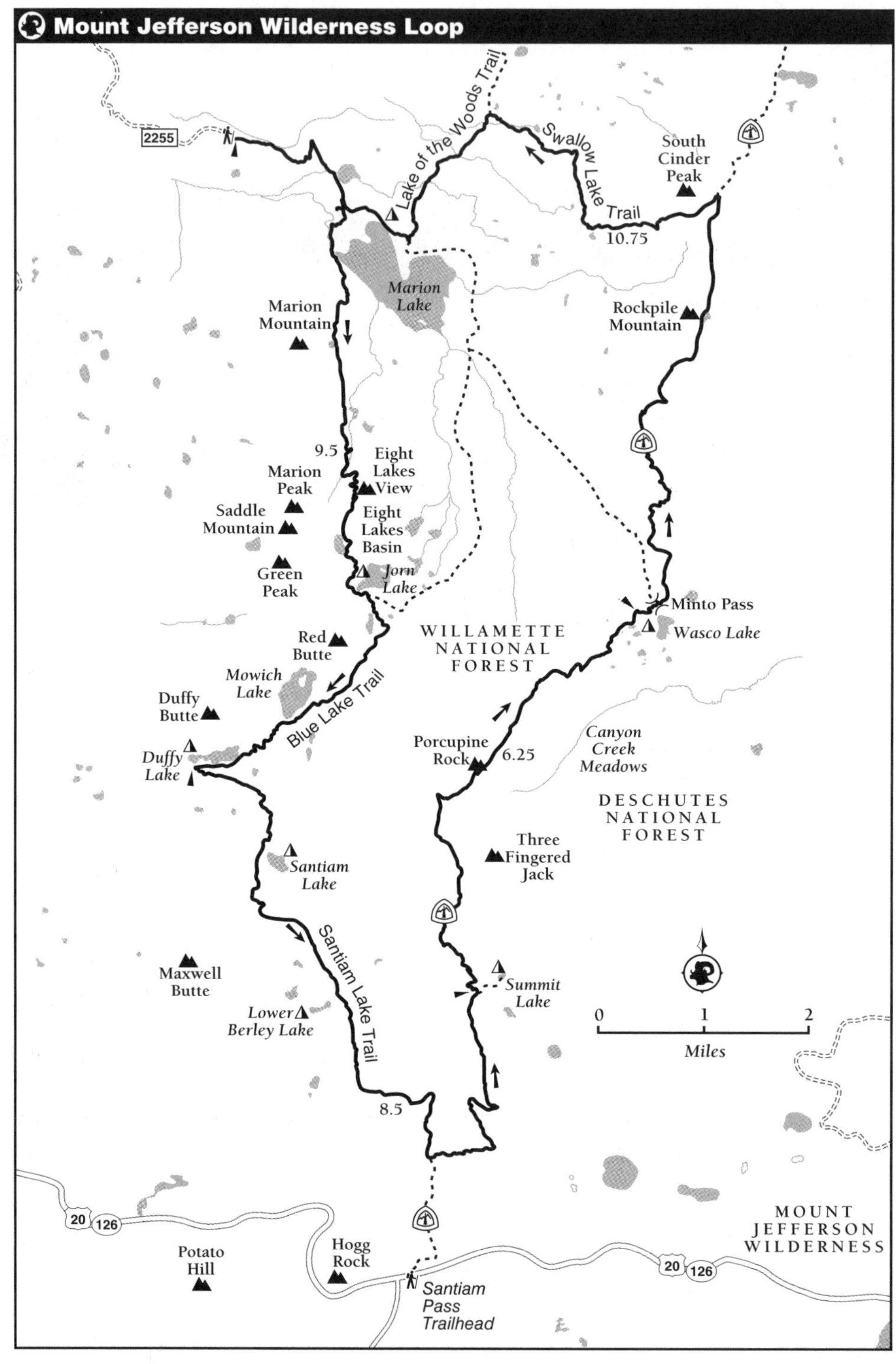
Mount Jefferson Wilderness Loop
2255
Lake of the Woods Trail
Swallow Lake Trail
South Cinder Peak
10.75
Marion Lake
Marion Mountain
Rockpile Mountain
9.5
Eight Lakes View
Marion Peak
Saddle Mountain
Eight Lakes Basin
Green Peak
Jorn Lake
Minto Pass
Wasco Lake
Red Butte
WILLAMETTE NATIONAL FOREST
Mowich Lake
Duffy Butte
Blue Lake Trail
Duffy Lake
Porcupine Rock
6.25
Canyon Creek Meadows
DESCHUTES NATIONAL FOREST
Three Fingered Jack
Santiam Lake
Santiam Lake Trail
Maxwell Butte
Summit Lake
Lower Berley Lake
0
1
2
Miles
8.5
20
126
Potato Hill
Hogg Rock
Santiam Pass Trailhead
MOUNT JEFFERSON WILDERNESS

CHALLENGES

Permits and access restrictions, crowds, burn areas, mosquitoes July–mid-August

HOW TO GET THERE

To reach the Marion Lake trailhead, go south on I-5 from Portland. Take Exit 253 for OR 22 east toward Detroit. Continue on OR 22 for 64.9 miles. Turn left on Marion Creek Road (right before the turnoff for the campground and fish hatchery). The trailhead is 4.5 miles down Marion Creek Road (FS 2255).

GPS TRAILHEAD COORDINATES:

(Marion Lake) N44° 34.593' W121° 53.626'

INTRODUCTION

Because one trip into the Mount Jefferson Wilderness just isn't enough, this loop through the southern portion of it offers more mountain scenery, more lakes, and more time along the Pacific Crest Trail (PCT) as it traces the mountainous backbone of Oregon. The loop makes use of a 14-mile stretch of the PCT and a close-up view of one of the state's most distinctive peaks, Three Fingered Jack. The route takes in a huge variety of terrain, from thick forests and wildflower meadows to otherworldly volcanic formations to some of the prettiest lakes you can reach on foot. Granted, it's not exactly a well-kept secret, so you're likely to run into day hikers anytime you're near a trailhead, but the permit system means that overnight hikers who secure a permit shouldn't have a hard time finding a place to camp.

Much of this route passes through areas that burned in the massive 2003 B&B Complex Fires, so hiking here gives you a good look at forest recovery in progress (and a sense of just how long it takes). Because it's a loop, hikers can start the trip from any of several trailheads, depending on convenience and the availability of overnight permits. If you're locked out of Marion Lake, try Santiam Pass, Duffy Lake, or the Cabot Lake Trailhead with access to Carl Lake. Marion Lake and Duffy Lake are both very popular since they provide relatively easy access to the Mount Jefferson Wilderness, so you might have to get creative. It's best to start this trip on a weekday and have a few options in mind.

DESCRIPTION

From the Marion Lake trailhead, the hike begins in a shady forest of western red cedar, Douglas fir, western hemlock, and Pacific yew. Gradually climb 1.5 miles to quiet Lake Ann, then continue a quarter mile to a junction. Take the right-hand option (Marion Lake Outlet Trail) and continue 0.1 mile to a side trail to the right. This short detour takes you to two photo-worthy waterfalls: Marion Falls and Gatch Falls.

Back on the main trail, continue toward Marion Lake until you reach a junction at its northwest corner. After admiring this large, pretty, and popular lake, continue straight (south), and after 1 mile pass a trail on the right that leads up to a viewpoint on Marion Mountain, another optional side trip. Continue heading south on the main trail, passing Jenny Lake and heading toward the Eight Lakes Basin on Blue Lake Trail.

WARNING: As you might guess by the number of lakes in this area, mosquitoes can be absolutely brutal here in summer—as early as mid-June and into mid-August.

You pass Blue Lake on the right, then larger Jorn Lake on the left, with good camps and excellent views. Keep right at a junction with the Bowerman Lake Trail. Pass tiny Alice Lake on the right, then an unofficial trail (sometimes hard to find) up to the top of Red Butte—an excellent vantage point for scoping out the territory all around you. About 0.25 mile later, go right at a junction to stay on Blue Lake Trail toward Mowich Lake, popular for swimming and camping, and Duffy Lake, which also has good camps, plus views of Three Fingered Jack and the photogenic Duffy Butte providing a scenic backdrop.

From Duffy Lake, take the Santiam Lake Trail east toward, you guessed it, Santiam Lake. The lake has nice views of Three Fingered Jack, as well as lovely wildflower fields surrounding it in spring. It's a popular destination for day hikers and is a nice lunch spot.

From Santiam Lake, continue south until the trail meets the PCT; keep left. (Turning right, or south, here leads you to the Santiam Pass Trailhead, a possible alternate start/exit point.) The PCT veers north and climbs steadily along the southern ridge of Three Fingered Jack. The woods become more open, and the scenery improves as you climb. However, the views of Three Fingered Jack remain tantalizingly limited until you round a ridge and, rather suddenly, the trees break for a full-frontal view of this craggy mountain.

TIP: Experienced scramblers can look for a steep, half-mile climber's trail up to the south ridge of the peak; all but the very last ascent can be done without specialized equipment.

The trail crosses a talus slope and probably a few lingering snowfields as it traverses the west and north faces of this peak. Keep your eyes peeled for mountain goats.

TIP: Shortly after a small pass north of the peak, look back for a final close-up view of Three Fingered Jack's northeast cliffs.

Duffy Lake

The PCT then descends through forest and recovering burn areas to a junction at Minto Pass. You'll find several designated camps at Wasco Lake, a short distance southeast of the pass.

TIP: A highly scenic alternate cross-country route to Wasco Lake drops steeply from the pass north of Three Fingered Jack to spectacular Canyon Creek Meadows. These meadows have a terrific view of Three Fingered Jack and support a riot of wildflowers in late July. Visit this popular spot on a weekday and be extra careful not to trample the flowers. To exit the meadows, hike the access trail to the northeast. Keep left when you come to a fork (now paralleling Canyon Creek) and reach a small waterfall near a trail junction. Turn left (north) for another 0.7 mile to Wasco Lake.

Continuing north from Minto Pass on the PCT, slowly climb a heavily burned ridge and cross an open slope with fine vistas south back to jagged Three Fingered Jack. Round a ridge and then reach the bowl holding Rockpile Lake. This small lake marks the beginning of an extended ridge walk, featuring more great scenery. The only significant drawback to this terrific stretch is a lack of water.

Only 1.4 miles north of Rockpile Lake is an open pass beside the reddish-colored summit of South Cinder Peak. The PCT continues its scenic route in and out of trees as it leads north toward the sharp spire of Mount Jefferson (see Trip 8). There's an option to visit Shirley and Carl Lakes for more great scenery and nice camps, 1.5 miles away on the Shirley Lake Trail—it's an excellent side trip if you have time to explore, or a possible exit point if you've left a vehicle at the Cabot Lake Trailhead. But the recommended route turns left (west) on a short cutoff toward the Swallow Lake Trail and an unmarked use trail up to South Cinder Peak.

TIP: Don't miss the easy scramble to the top of this cinder cone for an excellent viewpoint, including a look down into a cinder cone from above.

As you descend from the peak, turn right (west) to rejoin Swallow Lake Trail as it descends rather steeply past Sad Lake and then to a junction with Lake of the Woods Trail. Go left here to reach Marion Lake, where you'll pass the starting point of this loop, then briefly revisit Lake Ann and return to your car.

POSSIBLE ITINERARY

	CAMP	MILES	ELEVATION GAIN
Day 1	Duffy Lake	9.5	2,500'
Day 2	Summit Lake	8.5	1,600'
Day 3	Wasco Lake	6.25	600'
Day 4	Out	10.75	1800'

10

THREE SISTERS LOOP

RATINGS: Scenery 10 **Solitude** 2 **Difficulty** 6
MILES: 55 (75)
ELEVATION GAIN: 8,200' (10,600')
DAYS: 5–6 (6–10)
SHUTTLE MILEAGE: NA
MAP: National Geographic Trails Illustrated #818 *Bend/Three Sisters*
USUALLY OPEN: Mid-July–October
BEST: August
PERMITS: Northwest Forest Pass required at trailhead; Central Cascades Wilderness Permits required June 15–October 15 (reserve in advance, $6 reservation fee, available at recreation.gov or 877-444-6777)
RULES: No fires above 5,700' elevation; no camping within 100 feet of water; camp in designated sites only at Green, Moraine, and Matthieu Lakes
CONTACT: Sisters Ranger District, Deschutes National Forest, 541-549-7700, fs.usda.gov/deschutes; and McKenzie River Ranger District, Willamette National Forest, 541-822-3381, fs.usda.gov/willamette

SPECIAL ATTRACTIONS

Terrific mountain scenery, interesting volcanic geology

Above: South Sister over Camp Lake
photographed by Douglas Lorain

CHALLENGES

Crowds, permit and access restrictions, wildfire smoke

HOW TO GET THERE

From I-5, take Exit 194A in Eugene, and head east on OR 126. Go 6.3 miles and turn left to remain on OR 126. Go 48.4 miles and turn right onto OR 242/McKenzie Highway (closed November–mid-June). In 15.3 miles the well-marked Obsidian Trailhead will be on your right.

From the intersection of US 20 and US 97 in Bend, head northwest on US 20 toward Sisters, and go 19.2 miles. Turn left onto West Hood Avenue, and almost immediately, turn right onto OR 242/McKenzie Highway. The Obsidian Trailhead will be on your right in 21.2 miles.

GPS TRAILHEAD COORDINATES:

N44° 12.228' W121° 52.522'

WARNING: This popular trailhead leads to a heavily used area (the Sunshine Meadows), so don't expect to be lonesome. It also may be difficult to secure a permit for a particular trailhead on the dates you want, so be flexible when planning, and know that you can start this hike from any of several trailheads that provide access to the loop. (You can see which are available when making your permit reservations online at recreation.gov.)

INTRODUCTION

One of Oregon's greatest long backpacking trips, this route completely circles the Three Sisters, providing ever-changing views of these beautiful siblings. It also visits lesser-known family members (Little Brother, The Husband, and The Wife)—and craggy Broken Top, an apparent outcast without family ties. The basic loop is unsurpassed, and countless side trips visit even more lakes, high meadows, and viewpoints. A hiker could spend weeks here and never tire of the scenery or run out of places to explore. So get your permit and savor this area.

Volcanic features dominate the landscape. In addition to rugged lava flows, cinder cones, and glass-like obsidian, you'll also see pumice meadows. Formed when enormous quantities of pumice bury an area, these meadows have sparse vegetation and no surface water. Examples of this geologic oddity include Racetrack Meadow and Wickiup Plain.

DESCRIPTION

The Obsidian Trail starts by climbing gradually through thick forests, which show some evidence of the Horse Creek Complex Fire that swept through in 2017, causing several temporary closures. After 3.5 sometimes dusty miles, the trail crosses a lava flow for 0.6 mile and comes to White Branch Creek. This stream often runs dry as the water percolates into the porous volcanic soils. On the far side is a junction. To the right is the most direct route to pick up the main loop trail, but any hiker not suffering from "destinationitis" should turn left. Although this route is 0.4 mile longer, it is much more scenic.

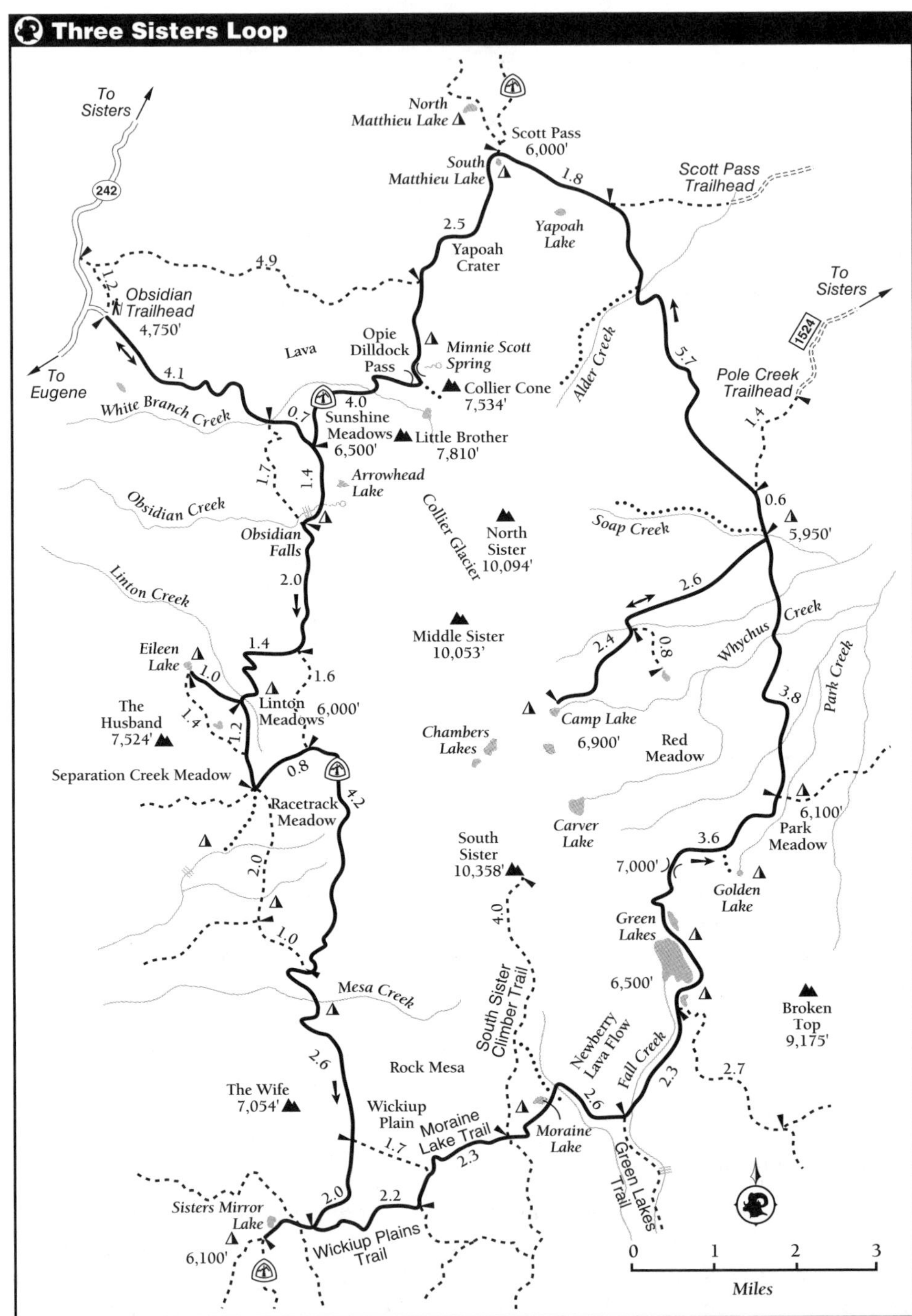
Three Sisters Loop
To Sisters
242
Obsidian Trailhead
4,750'
To Eugene
North Matthieu Lake
Scott Pass
6,000'
South Matthieu Lake
Scott Pass Trailhead
Yapoah Lake
Yapoah Crater
Lava
Opie Dilldock Pass
Minnie Scott Spring
Collier Cone
7,534'
Alder Creek
To Sisters
1524
Pole Creek Trailhead
White Branch Creek
Sunshine Meadows
6,500'
Little Brother
7,810'
Arrowhead Lake
Obsidian Creek
Obsidian Falls
Collier Glacier
North Sister
10,094'
Soap Creek
5,950'
Linton Creek
Middle Sister
10,053'
Whychus Creek
Park Creek
Eileen Lake
The Husband
7,524'
Linton Meadows
6,000'
Chambers Lakes
Camp Lake
6,900'
Red Meadow
Separation Creek Meadow
Racetrack Meadow
Carver Lake
6,100'
Park Meadow
South Sister
10,358'
7,000'
Golden Lake
Green Lakes
6,500'
Mesa Creek
South Sister Climber Trail
Broken Top
9,175'
Rock Mesa
Newberry Lava Flow
Fall Creek
The Wife
7,054'
Wickiup Plain
Moraine Lake Trail
Moraine Lake
Green Lakes Trail
Sisters Mirror Lake
6,100'
Wickiup Plains Trail
0 1 2 3
Miles

NOTE: In 2024, the Linton Creek Fire caused a temporary closure of this trail and surrounding area extending southeast from the Obsidian Trailhead. Be sure to check the latest conditions before heading out.

Choosing the left course, you climb fairly steeply through a mountain hemlock forest before arriving at the open expanse of Sunshine Meadows and a four-way junction with the Pacific Crest Trail (PCT). To the left is the return route of the loop, to the right (south) is your current route, and straight ahead is an old trail that goes through a lovely meadow topped by the summits of North and Middle Sisters. Because the mountain views from this meadow are partially obstructed, consider making a fun side trip on this old trail, past campsites and up a steep rocky slope, to a small plateau featuring tiny Arrowhead Lake and more open views.

As you head south on the PCT, a quick examination of the rocks underfoot reveals why the entry route is called the *Obsidian* Trail and why walking barefoot here is not recommended. The black glass rock chips can be razor-sharp.

You hike past a gushing spring and then drop to joyful Obsidian Falls (which makes for a *very* cold shower) and a junction. Keep left (south) on the PCT and soon leave the day hikers behind.

After 2 miles from Obsidian Falls, turn right (west) at a junction and descend sometimes steeply to the north end of beautiful Linton Meadows. This large wildflower garden is one of the trip's many highlights. A lovely clear creek cascades down from springs and then crosses this grassy expanse. Middle Sister, South Sister, and The Husband surround the basin, providing unequaled mountain scenes. The meadow is popular with backpackers, so consider hiking 1 mile northwest to tiny Eileen Lake for the night.

TIP: The best views from Eileen Lake are from the trailless northwest shore.

To continue your tour, pass the south end of Linton Meadows with its unique view of Middle Sister (a nearly perfect, unbroken cone from this angle) before reaching rather barren and burn-scarred Racetrack Meadow and a five-way junction.

TIP: A nice side trip from here goes down a gully to the south on an unmarked, unmaintained but easy-to-follow use path for 0.8 mile to large Separation Creek Meadow, with another nice creek and more views.

The main route goes sharply left through Racetrack Meadow, sometimes following posts, back to the PCT. Turn south as the PCT gradually climbs through an attractive mix of open woods and small, rolling meadows with occasional views. You pass a seasonal pond on the left, then continue on a rolling descent to Mesa Creek (with good camps).

TIP: As you switchback up the slope south of this stream, be sure to look back for a nice view of redheaded South Sister—the mountain is topped by reddish cinders.

Top out at a saddle and then pass through a barren flat nestled between Rock Mesa lava flow and the remains of a craggy mountain called The Wife. Eventually, your trail reaches the edge of Wickiup Plain, a large, flat, almost treeless expanse of volcanic pumice. As you continue south, enjoy ever-improving vistas across Wickiup Plain and Rock Mesa up to shining South Sister.

Near the south end of Wickiup Plain is a junction. Turn right and go 0.8 mile to reach the nearest camps with water at popular Sisters Mirror Lake. Although the lake is pretty, don't get your hopes up: The trees here have obviously grown since this lake was named.

TIP: Several small off-trail lakes are nearby and provide more private camping.

Returning to the Wickiup Plain junction, go east on Wickiup Plains Trail (also called Devils Lake Trail on some maps) along the meadow's south edge for 1.7 miles, and then turn left (north) and climb back into forest on the path to Moraine Lake.

NOTE: Several old trails and jeep roads cross Wickiup Plain, but unless it's foggy, it would be difficult to become lost.

At a junction, you'll cross the South Sister Climber Trail coming from the Devils Lake Trailhead 2 miles south. Energetic hikers have the option to make a difficult but highly rewarding 8-mile (round-trip) side trip to the top of South Sister, Oregon's third-highest mountain. To do so, turn left (north) at this junction and follow a well-used boot path that climbs the mountain's south side. The route requires no technical climbing equipment or experience but should be attempted only in good weather.

Continuing on the main loop, you go straight and pass Moraine Lake (which has fair camps) and then drop through woods beside a lava flow to Fall Creek and a junction. Turn left on the popular Green Lakes Trail (sometimes called Fall Creek Trail), which parallels Fall Creek across from the jumbled Newberry Lava Flow. After 2 miles, you top out at the magnificent plain containing the Green Lakes. Nestled between South Sister and Broken Top, this basin of lakes, springs, and wildflowers is one of the most beautiful places in Oregon. Judging by the number of hikers and backpackers here, a lot of people share this opinion. Try to avoid camping here. You will, however, want to linger long enough to soak in the views and make a loop of the largest Green Lake.

Continuing north, pass to the left of the final Green Lake and begin climbing out of the basin, still on Green Lakes Trail. A long switchback and well-graded trail lead to a high, windy saddle and the start of a long drop to the east.

TIP: A worthwhile but easy-to-miss side trip is the 0.6-mile unsigned path leading south to Golden Lake. This little jewel sits in a beautiful meadow basin and features a superb view of Broken Top. The route starts about 0.9 mile beyond the pass.

The descent ends at Park Meadow, yet another remarkable spot in this wilderness. A clear creek runs through this meadow, with its picturesque islands of trees, its small ponds, and its particularly photogenic view of Broken Top.

WARNING: Horse packers commonly use this meadow, so the drinking water is polluted.

TIP: The best photograph here is about 100 yards upstream from the trail crossing of Park Creek.

There are numerous camps here, although they are overused, and fires are prohibited.

To continue your loop trip, stay on Green Lakes Trail and head north from the meadow, following signs to Pole Creek.

TIP: Shortly after crossing the west fork of Park Creek, look for an unsigned side path to the left that goes to Red Meadow. Although not as scenic as Park Meadow, it is less crowded and well worth a visit.

You top a small rise and then drop through forest to a fork of Whychus Creek. Over the next low ridge is another branch of Whychus Creek—this one is dirty with glacial silt.

After another 0.7 mile of uneventful hiking, you reach the welcome banks of Soap Creek and a trail junction. Good campsites are available in the nearby trees.

Two outstanding side trips leave the main loop at this point. If the weather is good, try to make time for both of them. The first climbs the 5-mile trail to Camp Lake and the Chambers Lakes.

WARNING: Beware of a tricky crossing of Whychus Creek along the Camp Lake Trail–particularly on warm afternoons with lots of glacial ice melting above.

A night spent at popular Camp Lake is likely to be cold and windy, but it will be richly rewarded with terrific scenery. If the weather is good, we highly recommend carrying your gear up here and spending the night. From Camp Lake, you could also take an extra day to scramble up the steep, rocky south slope of Middle Sister to its summit. This climb is recommended only for confident and experienced hikers.

The second side trip from the Soap Creek crossing is less crowded, and it doesn't visit any lakes, but it is still glorious. Follow an unmarked use path going west up the north bank of Soap Creek. After about 3 miles, you'll reach a large, flat pumice meadow beneath the towering cliffs on the east face of North Sister. This is a spectacular spot, although, like Camp Lake, it's too exposed for comfortable camping in bad weather.

The sometimes-dusty main loop trail continues north from Soap Creek for 0.6 mile to a junction with the Pole Creek Trail (keep left, staying on the Green Lakes Trail), and then takes a rather monotonous course through dry, mostly viewless terrain for 5.7 miles to a junction with the Scott Trail.

TIP: A fine way to break up this segment is to follow a faint use path up splashing Alder Creek to its highly scenic headwaters beneath the northeast side of North Sister.

Turn left at the Scott Trail junction and climb 1.8 miles to Scott Pass, where there is a junction with the PCT beside tiny South Matthieu Lake. The three designated camps here are justifiably popular with both weekend backpackers and PCT thru-hikers.

TIP 1: Excellent short evening strolls lead to high points both north and south of this pool. Both are wonderful places to watch the sunset.

TIP 2: If the weather is threatening, more-sheltered camps are available at North Matthieu Lake.

Your loop trip is nearly complete now, but the remaining hike is not anticlimactic. Ahead lie still more grand scenery and the most interesting geology of the tour. Walk south on the PCT, cross a short section of lava rock, and then round the slopes of a relatively recent cinder cone called Yapoah Crater. Another 0.6 mile leads to a junction in a meadow, which is filled with blue lupine blossoms in early to mid-August. You continue straight (south) and gradually climb past tiny Minnie Scott Spring (which has fair camps) and then go back into the lava to the oddly named Opie Dilldock Pass. From here, a not-to-be-missed side trip climbs to Collier Cone and Collier Glacier viewpoint. As the name advertises, this spot provides an excellent overlook of this massive ice sheet, one of the largest in Oregon.

Back on the PCT, travel south through a lava flow to a crossing of White Branch Creek, the outflow of Collier Glacier. An up-and-down hike, mostly in forest, leads to the junction in Sunshine Meadows that you hit on day one. Turn right and follow the Obsidian Trail 4.8 miles back to your car. The hike may now be behind you, but expect the memories to last forever.

POSSIBLE ITINERARY

	CAMP	MILES	ELEVATION GAIN
Day 1	Eileen Lake	10.6	2,100'
Day 2	Sisters Mirror Lake	12.3	1,500'
Day 3	Park Meadow	12.9	1,700'
Day 4	Camp Lake	8.8	1,800'
Day 5	Soap Creek (with side trip up Soap Creek)	11.6	1,300'
Day 6	South Matthieu Lake	7.5	1,300'
Day 7	Out	11.3	900'

11

SEPARATION CREEK LOOP

RATINGS: Scenery 6 **Solitude** 7 **Difficulty** 6
MILES: 42 (44)
ELEVATION GAIN: 4,700' (5,200')
DAYS: 4–6 (4–6)
SHUTTLE MILEAGE: NA
MAP: National Geographic Trails Illustrated #818 *Bend/Three Sisters*
USUALLY OPEN: Mid-July–October
BEST: Mid-July–October
PERMIT: Central Cascades Wilderness Permit required June 15–October 15 ($6 reservation fee, available at recreation.gov or 877-444-6777)
RULES: Maximum group size of 12 people; no fires near Eileen, Husband, or Sisters Mirror Lakes; no camping within 100 feet of trails or water in Linton Meadows and around Eileen and Husband Lakes
CONTACT: McKenzie River Ranger District, Willamette National Forest, 541-822-3381, fs.usda.gov/willamette

SPECIAL ATTRACTIONS

Solitude, wildflowers, mountain meadows, lakes

CHALLENGES

Mosquitoes until about mid-August, burn areas, blowdown

Above: View of South Sister from Horse Lake

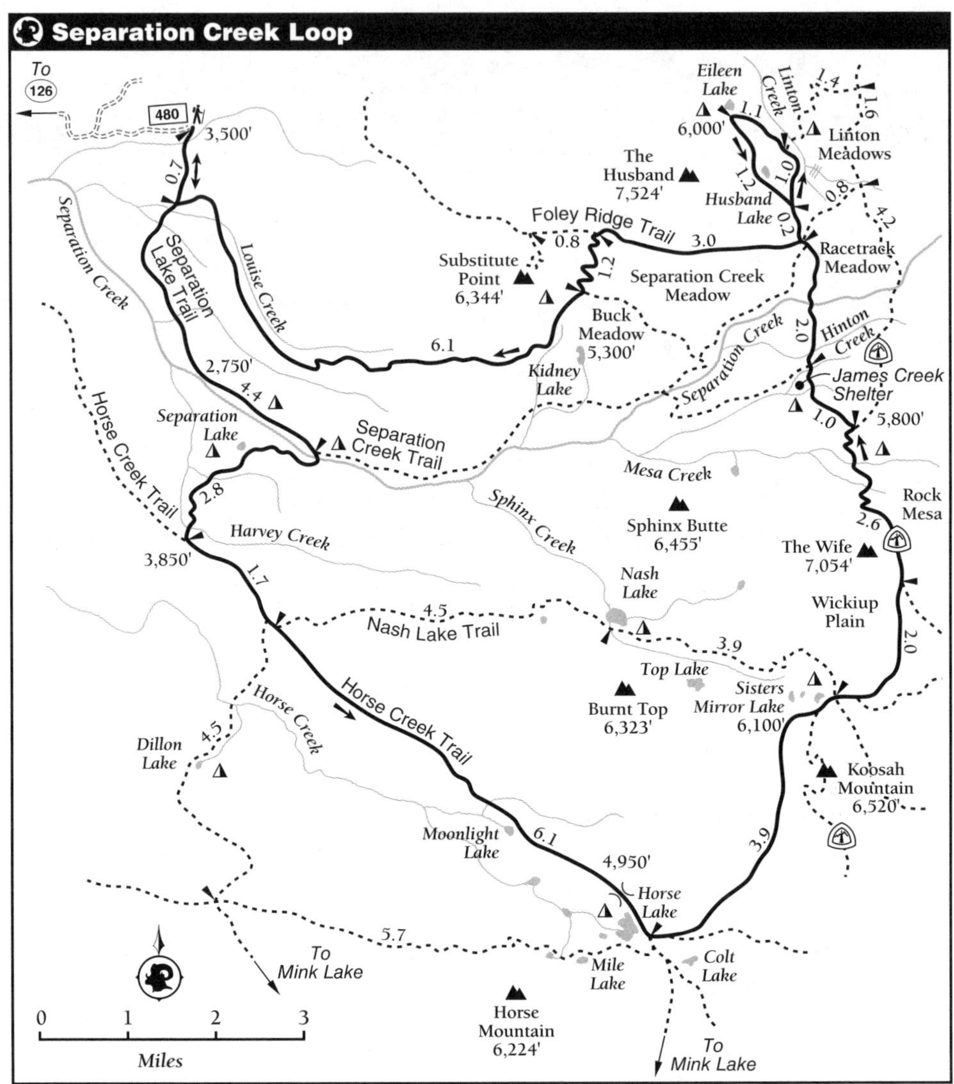

HOW TO GET THERE

From I-5, take Exit 194A in Eugene, and head east on OR 126. Go 6.3 miles and turn left to remain on OR 126. Drive 46.8 miles east on OR 126 to a junction with Forest Service Road 2643 (Foley Ridge Road), exactly 0.6 mile past the McKenzie River Ranger Station. Turn right (south) and go 7.7 miles on this one-lane paved road to a junction where the pavement ends. Veer right, drive 0.6 mile, and then bear right onto FS 480 and proceed 1.2 miles to the Separation Lake Trailhead.

GPS TRAILHEAD COORDINATES:

N44° 08.196' W121° 58.395'

INTRODUCTION

The Three Sisters Wilderness is the most visited wilderness area in Oregon, so it's not surprising that hikers sometimes have a hard time finding uncrowded trails. But solitude-loving pedestrians need not fear because such trails do exist. The key to finding them is realizing that the vast majority of visitors to this huge wilderness concentrate on a handful of very popular destinations. If you avoid these areas, there is a good chance that you will have the trail all to yourself. This loop takes you through some of the quietest parts of the preserve as it makes a long, woodsy approach to the more crowded high country. In addition to providing solitude, this warm-up period helps build anticipation for the great scenery to come, and if you start your trip on a Saturday, as most people do, it won't be until the quieter days of midweek that you reach the popular meadows and lakes around timberline.

DESCRIPTION

The trail begins in a stately old-growth forest dominated by western hemlocks and Douglas firs mixed with a few western red cedars and Pacific yews. After 0.7 mile of minor ups and downs, you reach a junction and the start of the loop.

For the recommended counterclockwise tour, go straight on the Separation Lake Trail, which over the next mile crosses two branches of Louise Creek, then larger George Creek on a convenient log. The sometimes-brushy trail then contours through viewless but attractive woods for about 1 mile before gradually descending to the bottom of the heavily forested canyon of Separation Creek. From here, the trail follows this cascading creek upstream 1.2 miles to an excellent campsite and then gradually ascends another 0.8 mile to a second campsite and a junction. To your left is Separation Creek Trail, which used to take you east via Honey Creek Falls but has been declared permanently closed due to blowdown and forest fire damage.

Turn right, cross the creek (recently there has been a footbridge), and then traverse the slope on the south side of the stream. The next 1.1 miles take you gently uphill to lily pad–filled Separation Lake, which is surrounded by skunk cabbage bogs and dense forests and has a good campsite above its southeastern shore. About 0.5 mile beyond Separation Lake, you cross an unnamed creek and then make a very steep 700-foot climb of a wooded slope. At the top of the climb, you step over tiny Harvey Creek and come to a junction. Turn left (southeast) on Horse Creek Trail and ascend this gently graded route 1.6 miles to an easily missed junction. For a really long loop, you could turn right, walk past seldom-visited Dillon Lake, and then continue about 12 miles south to the Mink Lake Basin. (This trail, #3538, goes through a 2023 burn zone, so check with rangers before you start to make sure it's passable.) From there, you would head north on the Pacific Crest Trail (PCT) and return to the main loop near Horse Lake.

Instead, the recommended trail goes straight at the faint junction and, 0.1 mile later, reaches a fork and another choice of routes. The shorter option goes left on the Nash Lake Trail, which passes its namesake lake after 4.5 miles and then climbs to a junction with the PCT near Sisters Mirror Lake. The other option is slightly longer but is recommended because it is more scenic. For this alternative, go right at the fork to stay on Horse Creek Trail and begin a mostly forested climb. After 3.5 pleasant but uneventful miles, the trail levels off near small Moonlight Lake. The trail then contours for 2 miles along a ridge on the north side of the Horse Creek valley. Shortly after it goes through an indistinct pass, the trail reaches a series of excellent campsites beside large and popular Horse Lake.

TIP: For even better campsites, take the rugged angler's path that loops around the west side of this scenic lake.

WARNING: In July, the mosquitoes are voracious around Horse Lake and often seem to rival the lake's namesake animal in size.

A peek at Horse Lake

At the east end of Horse Lake is a junction. Bear left on dusty Red Hill Trail and walk uphill 0.2 mile to a second junction. Turn left (north) and go steadily uphill through viewless forest for 3 rather monotonous miles to a group of small lakes and ponds on the meadowy Sisters Mirror Plateau. Several enchanting heather-rimmed pools here feature good campsites, though fires are prohibited. In the middle of this plateau, you merge with the PCT just before reaching Sisters Mirror Lake. Trees now mostly obstruct the view from here of South Sister, which the lake once mirrored, but this popular lake is still very beautiful.

TIP: The campsites at Sisters Mirror Lake are often crowded. For more privacy, consider going to any of several off-trail lakes to the west.

A little past Sisters Mirror Lake is a junction with the Nash Lake Trail, where you connect with the shorter loop option discussed earlier. Go straight and walk 0.3 mile to the next junction, where you bear left, staying on the PCT. From here, make a brief traverse through woods before crossing the west side of Wickiup Plain, a large and sparsely vegetated pumice-covered meadow. This plain provides excellent vistas of bulky South Sister and the large obsidian, lava, and pumice flow called Rock Mesa spread out at the mountain's base. To the northeast is Middle Sister, a sharp pyramid that rises a little to the left of her taller southern sibling. In keeping with the area's family theme, the small rocky peak on the left (northwest) side of Wickiup Plain is called The Wife.

At the north end of Wickiup Plain is a junction. Go straight, traverse a waterless depression just below the edge of Rock Mesa, and then descend two switchbacks to an excellent campsite near the second of two branches of spring-fed Mesa Creek. The trail almost immediately climbs away from Mesa Creek, gaining about 200 feet to a junction. The PCT goes straight, but for this trip turn sharply left, following signs to Linton Meadows, and wander up and down on the James Creek Trail through open forest (including lots of burned areas from fires in 2017) and past small meadows for 0.8 mile to James Creek Shelter. This well-maintained wooden structure, built by the CCC, is closed to camping to protect its historical significance, but there are wonderful places to camp nearby with water and fine views of the top third of South Sister over a lush little meadow that escaped the worst of the wildfire impact.

Immediately past the shelter, you hop over a tiny creek and reach a junction. Go straight (north, on James Creek Trail) and start a 2-mile traverse (crossing Separation Creek on a log about midway) that ends at a confusing junction at the southwestern tip of pumice-covered Racetrack Meadow. The unsigned trail that goes sharply left (south) leads in less than 1 mile to Separation Creek Meadow, a worthwhile side trip for its flowers and nice view of Middle Sister. The main trail, however, goes straight at the Separation Creek Meadow junction and, 20 yards later, reaches a signed four-way junction.

The Foley Ridge Trail, which goes left (west) here, is the return route of this loop. Before going that way, however, take the scenic side trip to Linton Meadows and Eileen Lake. So go straight, walk 0.2 mile across the west side of Racetrack Meadow, and then come to a fork. This junction is the start of a very scenic loop. Bear right (slightly downhill) and descend past great viewpoints of Middle Sister's nearly perfect pyramid to the green, flowery wonderland of Linton Meadows. The beauty of this oasis is enhanced by spring-fed Linton Creek, which tumbles down a tiered waterfall to the east before meandering across the meadow. Towering above the flower-studded grassland are Middle Sister, South

Sister, and The Husband, all vying for the title of being the most beautiful member of their extended family. It's a tough contest to judge, and one on which you can spend several happy hours trying to make up your mind. Camping is not allowed within 100 feet of water or trails in Linton Meadows.

At the north end of Linton Meadows are some possible campsites and a junction. Bear left and make a scenic 1.1-mile jaunt to spectacular Eileen Lake. This small meadow-rimmed gem has very scenic (but overused) campsites and, from the northwestern shore, views of the Three Sisters that will take your breath away. Fires are prohibited above 5,700 feet in the Eileen Lake and Husband Lake vicinity, and camping is not allowed within 100 feet of the high-water mark.

From the outlet of Eileen Lake, the trail turns south and goes gradually uphill to Husband Lake. From the east (nontrail) side of this shallow lake, there are stunning reflections of (appropriately enough) The Husband. A little beyond Husband Lake, you close the side-trip loop when you reach the junction with the trail to Linton Meadows. Go straight to return to the junction with the Foley Ridge Trail at the southwest corner of Racetrack Meadow.

Go right (west) on the Foley Ridge Trail and travel gently up and down for 3 miles through forest and past several stagnant ponds to a junction. Turn left and descend a half dozen switchbacks to a junction at the north end of long and narrow Buck Meadow. The well-used trail that goes straight dead-ends after 100 yards at a possible campsite.

WARNING: The tiny creek here usually dries up by late summer.

Your trail, which is very faint at first, veers right at the junction and travels along the west side of grassy, 0.5-mile-long Buck Meadow. From the south end of the meadow, the trail makes a brief climb to the west and then begins a long descent. The entire route is through forest, which becomes increasingly lush with a denser understory as you lose elevation. A little over 6 miles from Buck Meadow is the junction with the Separation Lake Trail and the close of the loop. Turn right and thus back to your car.

POSSIBLE ITINERARY

	CAMP	MILES	ELEVATION GAIN
Day 1	Separation Lake	6.2	200'
Day 2	Horse Lake	9.4	1,800'
Day 3	James Creek Shelter	9.6	1,700'
Day 4	Eileen Lake (with side trip to Separation Creek Meadow)	6.3	800'
Day 5	Out	12.4	700'

12

MINK LAKE AREA

RATINGS: Scenery 7 **Solitude** 4 **Difficulty** 3
MILES: 24 (38)
ELEVATION GAIN: 1,600' (3,300')
DAYS: 3 (3–5)
SHUTTLE MILEAGE: 16
MAP: National Geographic Trails Illustrated #818 *Bend/Three Sisters*
USUALLY OPEN: July–October
BEST: Late August–September
PERMITS: Central Cascades Wilderness Permit required June 15–October 15 ($6 reservation fee, available at recreation.gov or 877-444-6777); Northwest Forest Pass required at trailhead
RULES: No camping or fires within 100 feet of lakes
CONTACT: Bend–Fort Rock Ranger District, Deschutes National Forest, 541-383-5300, fs.usda.gov/deschutes; McKenzie River Ranger District, Willamette National Forest, 541-822-3381, fs.usda.gov/willamette

SPECIAL ATTRACTIONS

Fishing and swimming lakes, relatively easy hiking

Above: South Sister viewed from Elk Lake

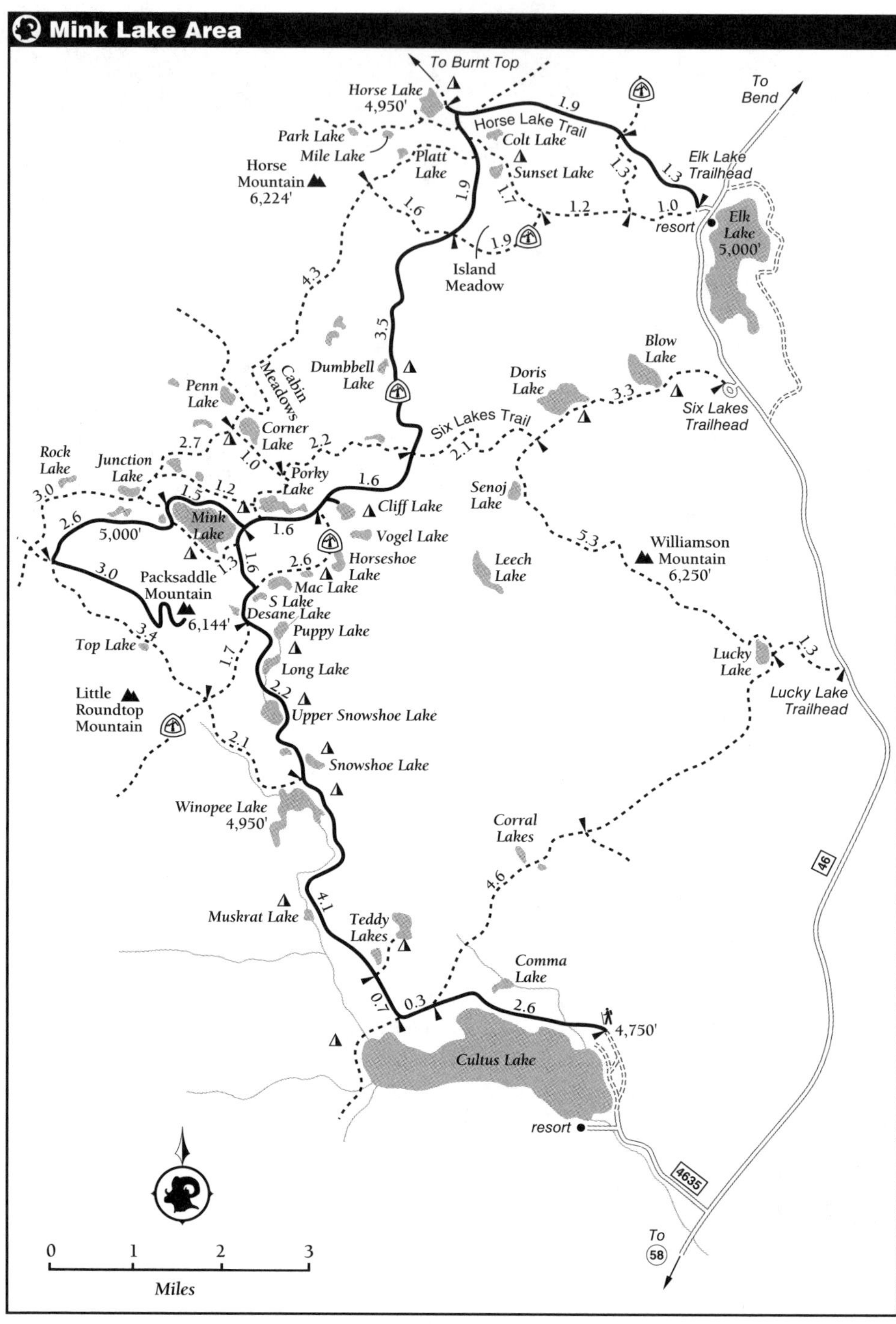

Mink Lake Area
To Burnt Top
Horse Lake
4,950'
Horse Lake Trail
Colt Lake
Park Lake
Mile Lake
Platt Lake
Sunset Lake
Horse Mountain
6,224'
To Bend
Elk Lake Trailhead
resort
Elk Lake
5,000'
Island Meadow
Dumbbell Lake
Cabin Meadows
Penn Lake
Corner Lake
Doris Lake
Blow Lake
Six Lakes Trail
Six Lakes Trailhead
Rock Lake
Junction Lake
Porky Lake
Senoj Lake
Mink Lake
5,000'
Cliff Lake
Vogel Lake
Horseshoe Lake
Leech Lake
Williamson Mountain
6,250'
Packsaddle Mountain
6,144'
Mac Lake
S Lake
Desane Lake
Puppy Lake
Top Lake
Long Lake
Lucky Lake
Lucky Lake Trailhead
Little Roundtop Mountain
Upper Snowshoe Lake
Snowshoe Lake
Winopee Lake
4,950'
Corral Lakes
46
Muskrat Lake
Teddy Lakes
Comma Lake
4,750'
Cultus Lake
resort
4635
To
58
0
1
2
3
Miles

CHALLENGES

Mosquitoes in July and early August, crowded in spots

HOW TO GET THERE

For a south-to-north tour, start from the east end of Cultus Lake. From I-5, take Exit 188A in Goshen, and head southeast on OR 58. In 72.5 miles turn left onto Cascade Lakes National Scenic Byway/Forest Service Road 61, and go 3.2 miles. Turn left to remain on Cascade Lakes National Scenic Byway/FS 46 (closed in winter; usually open by Memorial Day). Go 24.5 miles, and near the north end of Crane Prairie Reservoir, turn left (west) onto FS 4635 to Cultus Lake. At a fork in 2 miles, continue straight to stay on FS 4635, and in 0.5 mile turn left onto FS 120, then immediately turn right (staying on FS 120) to reach the trailhead.

To reach the north trailhead, from the intersection of US 20 and US 97 in Bend, head south on US 20 and take Exit 138 to Downtown/Mount Bachelor. Turn right (east) onto Colorado Avenue and go 1.6 miles. At the second traffic circle, take the third exit to head left onto Southwest Century Drive. Go 5.3 miles and continue straight onto Cascade Lakes National Scenic Byway/FS 46. Drive 25 miles, then turn right at signs for Elk Lake Resort and the trailhead, at the end of Elk Lake Resort Loop.

GPS TRAILHEAD COORDINATES:

(Cultus Lake) N43° 50.387' W121° 50.042'
(Elk Lake) N43° 59.043' W121° 48.666'

INTRODUCTION

The southern half of the Three Sisters Wilderness has a totally different character than the northern. There are no tall peaks, no glaciers, few meadows, and only limited views. What the hiker will discover, however, are miles of pleasant forest trails and enough lakes to impress even Minnesota natives. Every turn of the trail seems to reveal another lovely mountain pool, ranging from a small pond to a large lake. Each is distinct enough that lovers of fishing, swimming, rafting, or just sightseeing can stay happy for weeks. Another nice thing about this country is the easy hiking. Because almost everything is at roughly the same elevation, extended ups and downs simply don't exist—which means a lot less work for tired backpackers. This trip is perfect for hikers with knees that suffer on long downhills or as a first long backpack for beginners. Easy trails and numerous lakes allow for short hiking days and lots of time for lazy afternoons.

All that water, of course, has one big drawback—*mosquitoes!* The clouds of flying bloodsuckers here are thicker than a Dairy Queen milkshake. In July, your essential gear should include repellent, a head net, and an extra pint or two of blood to replace that stolen by the bugs. Fortunately, by mid-August or so, the number of invertebrates has dropped dramatically, and by September, you can comfortably travel without repellent or even a tent—the rain gods permitting, of course.

DESCRIPTION

From the Cultus Lake Trailhead, hike west along the lakeshore path, passing several good swimming beaches with views across this large lake. The trail veers away from the lake after 1.7 miles and leads northwest for 0.9 mile to a junction with the trail to Corral Lakes. Go straight here, and 0.3 mile farther turn right at a second junction. After 0.7 mile, you pass the side trail to Teddy Lakes (which has good camps). Another 1.4 miles of easy walking leads to a lovely meadow, which contains lily pad–filled Muskrat Lake and its quaint but disintegrating little cabin. If the ground isn't too swampy, take time to visit this cabin; it was once a nice first-come, first-served overnight shelter for backpackers, but it has deteriorated a bit too much to be tempting. Better camps are available in the woods at the lake's north end near the inlet creek.

Snowshoe Lake at dusk

Muskrat Lake is an inviting camp spot, but you probably won't be tired when you get there, since in 5 miles the elevation gain has been only 200 feet. With all that extra energy, you might prefer to continue north to other equally scenic lakes. The route gradually gains a bit of elevation as it parallels a small creek (usually nothing more than a trickle by late summer). About 2 miles from Muskrat Lake is the south shore of large, irregularly shaped Winopee Lake. The trail works around the east shore of this lake, mostly in viewless forest, to a lovely meadow at the north end. This meadow is well worth exploring, though it's rather boggy.

At the trail junction beside Winopee Lake, keep right, and in rapid succession reach Snowshoe Lake (with a good campsite or two on rocky outcrops) and two smaller, unnamed lakes as you slowly climb on this attractive route. Upper Snowshoe Lake is the next highlight, with its excellent camps and lunch spots. Here, as at all the larger lakes along this tour, hikers should look for goldeneyes (ducks), ospreys, and bald eagles—all common in the area. Continuing your hike north, the seemingly endless parade of lovely lakes continues with Long Lake and Puppy Lake. At a meadow holding Desane Lake is a junction with the Pacific Crest Trail (PCT). Turn right on the PCT to reach the shores of S Lake and another junction.

The PCT keeps right here, passing yet another string of attractive lakes. The recommended route, however, turns left, climbs a low ridge, and then drops fairly steeply into the basin containing popular Mink Lake. Dozens of excellent camps surround this scenic 360-acre lake. The best views are from the northeast shore near an old shelter. Good camps and worthwhile day hike destinations are found in almost every direction. Our favorite camps are a little to the east at Porky Lake, but other nearby lakes (some off-trail) provide more private locations.

One highly recommended day hike side trip is the path from Mink Lake to the top of Packsaddle Mountain, the area's highest viewpoint. The climb is fairly long but worthwhile, and the tired hiker can look forward to returning to a lakeside camp and a pleasant swim. The path starts near Junction Lake west of Mink Lake. Some of the less strenuous day hike options include Corner Lake, Junction Lake, and Cabin Meadows.

To continue the recommended trip, hike along the south side of Porky Lake and then climb out of the lake's basin back to the PCT. Turn north and, after about 100 yards, reach the possibly unsigned 0.1-mile side trail to Cliff Lake.

TIP: Be sure to visit this scenic lake—it features good camps, a trail shelter, and great rocks along the north shore.

The PCT continues north and east through forests and meadows. You pass several small rock formations on the way to a four-way junction with the Six Lakes Trail. Keep straight (north) on the PCT along an easy route through rolling mountain hemlock forests. The trail passes tiny Island Lake and larger Dumbbell Lake (good camps) and then drops over a gentle saddle to a four-way junction west of Island Meadow. If the weather is bad, turn right here for a quick exit back to the Elk Lake Trailhead. Otherwise, veer left to reach Horse Lake—just 2 miles away.

Horse Lake is the largest and prettiest of another cluster of lakes. Excellent campsites abound near Horse Lake, but for more privacy, try nearby Mile or Park Lake—either of which would make another good base camp for further explorations.

TIP 1: The best lunch spot at Horse Lake is on the rock peninsula on the lake's west shore—reached by an angler's path around the lake. The view from here includes a nice perspective of Mount Bachelor.

TIP 2: If you have an extra day and good route-finding skills, consider visiting Burnt Top. Take the trail going northwest from Horse Lake for about 1.8 miles and then hope to find the unmaintained 3.5-mile route to the right leading to Burnt Top's summit views.

To reach the exit point, head due east from Horse Lake on well-used Horse Lake Trail #3516. You gradually climb to a viewless pass and a junction with the PCT. Keep straight on a dusty trail, and in 1.3 miles reach civilization, in the form of the Elk Lake Trailhead.

NOTE: For loop lovers, this area provides several possible options. One alternative is to start your trip at the Lucky Lake Trailhead. Hike southwest via Corral Lakes to Cultus Lake, turn north past Winopee and Mink Lakes to the Six Lakes Trail, and then return via Senoj Lake and Williamson Mountain. Another fun approach is to set up a base camp at one of the lakes and explore via day hikes from there, returning to Elk Lake via the PCT when you're done.

POSSIBLE ITINERARY

	CAMP	MILES	ELEVATION GAIN
Day 1	Mink Lake	11.5	500'
Day 2	Day trip up Packsaddle Mountain (return to Mink Lake)	14.0	1,700'
Day 3	Horse Lake	8.8	700'
Day 4	Out	3.4	400'

13

MOUNT THIELSEN TRAVERSE

RATINGS: Scenery 7 **Solitude** 6 **Difficulty** 6
MILES: 34
ELEVATION GAIN: 5,500'
DAYS: 3–4
SHUTTLE MILEAGE: 25
MAP: USFS *Umpqua Divide Wilderness: Boulder Creek Wilderness, Rogue–Umpqua Divide Wilderness, Mount Thielsen Wilderness, Oregon Cascades Recreation Area*
USUALLY OPEN: Late June–October
BEST: July
PERMITS: Yes, free self-issued wilderness permit at trailheads; Northwest Forest Pass required at North Crater Trailhead
RULES: Maximum group size of 12 people; no camping within 100 feet of lakes
CONTACT: Diamond Lake Ranger District, Umpqua National Forest, 541-498-2531, fs.usda.gov/umpqua; Crescent Ranger District, Deschutes National Forest, 541-433-3200, fs.usda.gov/deschutes; Chemult Ranger District, Fremont-Winema National Forest, 541-365-7001, fs.usda.gov/fremont-winema

SPECIAL ATTRACTIONS

Waterfalls, mountain scenery, diverse landscapes, easy road access

Above: Mount Thielsen

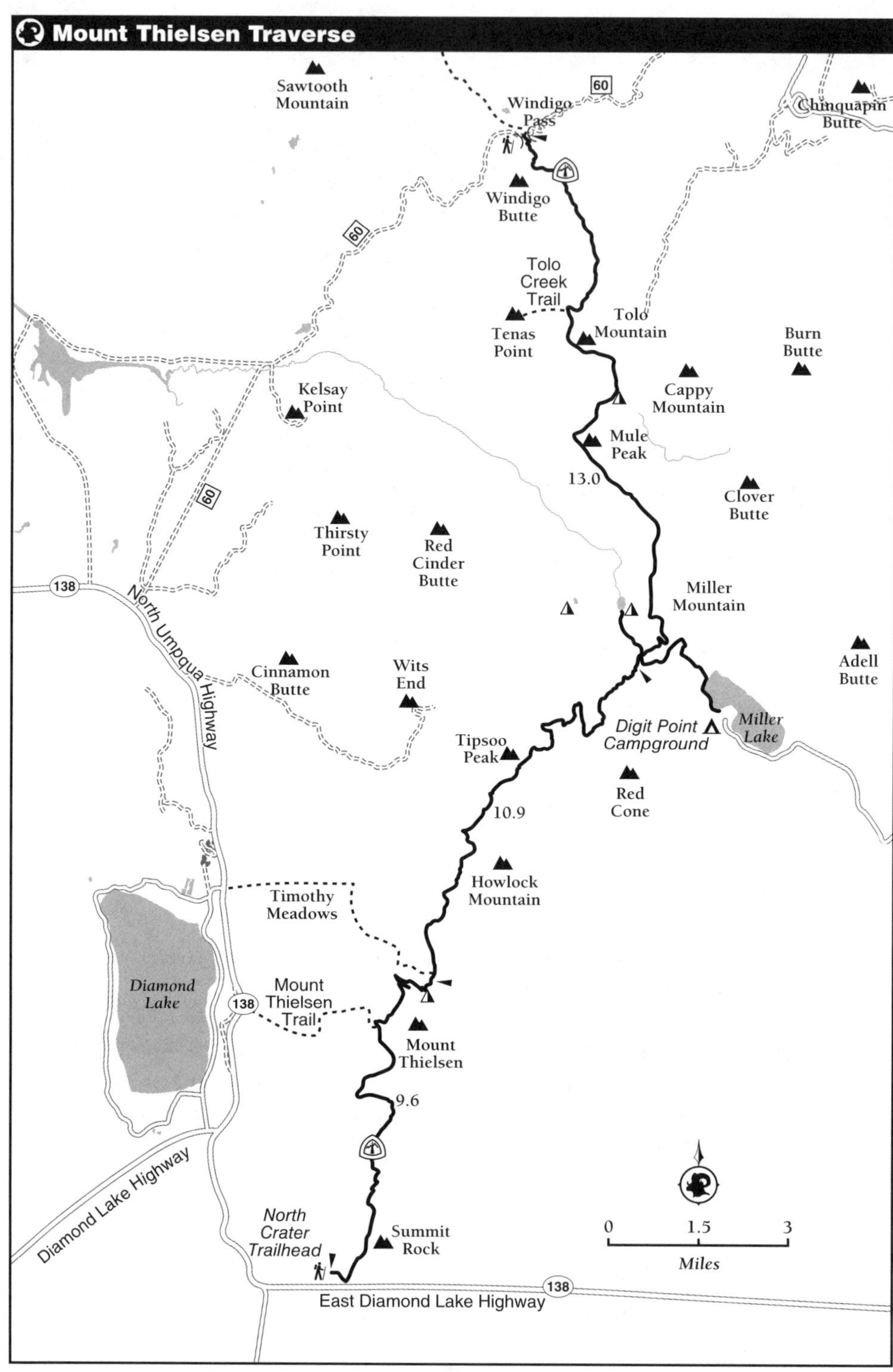
Mount Thielsen Traverse
Sawtooth Mountain
Windigo Pass
60
Chinquapin Butte
Windigo Butte
Tolo Creek Trail
Tenas Point
Tolo Mountain
Burn Butte
Cappy Mountain
Kelsay Point
Mule Peak
13.0
Clover Butte
Thirsty Point
Red Cinder Butte
138
North Umpqua Highway
Miller Mountain
Cinnamon Butte
Wits End
Adell Butte
Miller Lake
Digit Point Campground
Tipsoo Peak
Red Cone
10.9
Howlock Mountain
Timothy Meadows
Diamond Lake
Mount Thielsen Trail
Mount Thielsen
9.6
Diamond Lake Highway
North Crater Trailhead
Summit Rock
0
1.5
3
Miles
East Diamond Lake Highway

CHALLENGES

Mosquitoes at higher elevations in July, long stretches without water, crowds

HOW TO GET THERE

To reach the northern trailhead at Windigo Pass, take OR 138 east from Roseburg for 73 miles, then turn left onto Forest Service Road 60 (Windigo Pass Road). Follow FS 60 for about 4.5 miles, then keep right for 7.5 miles until the trailhead.

For the North Crater Trailhead, take OR 138 east for about 86 miles from Roseburg, then turn left (north) onto FS 4799 (a mile east of the Crater Lake National Park junction). The trailhead is at the end of the road.

GPS TRAILHEAD COORDINATES:

(Windigo Pass) N43° 22.051' W122° 01.997'
(North Crater) N43° 05.552' W122° 05.642'

INTRODUCTION

This wonderful hike takes advantage of a section of the Pacific Crest Trail (PCT) that climbs along the Cascade crest and explores the scenic meadows, crags, and views around Howlock Mountain and Mount Thielsen.

The high-country section of this route is amazingly dry. There is very little surface water and limited ground cover, and the forests consist of water-starved lodgepole pine and mountain hemlock. Porous volcanic soils around Mount Thielsen allow most of the water to percolate into the ground rather than flowing on top. This water later feeds the many springs in the lower canyon around Lemolo Lake.

DESCRIPTION

From Windigo Pass, you head south along a forested ridge, with Windigo Butte providing a looming backdrop. After 4 miles of gradual ups and downs on this ridge, you reach a junction with the Tolo Creek Trail. Turn left to stay on the PCT, unless the high point of Tenas Peak beckons to you. Once the site of a fire lookout, this peak still provides excellent views, including a preview of Mount Thielsen, where you're headed, and a glimpse of Diamond Peak through the trees.

The PCT continues south, circling around the west side of Tolo Mountain. Two miles from the junction, you reach Tolo Camp and a short trail to the left (east) leading to Six Horse Spring, a conveniently located but often measly trickling spring in a low meadow that is a favorite of mosquitoes.

Continue south along this scenic ridge for another 6 miles. At a four-way junction, turn right to visit popular Maidu Lake, surrounded by forests and excellent campsites.

TIP: Fill your water bottles here. The only trailside water for the next 11 miles is from lingering snowfields.

As always, camp well away from fragile lakeshore locations. If Maidu Lake is busy or you're not quite ready to stop yet, continue 1.3 miles northwest to forest-rimmed Lucile Lake. A pleasant trail circles this mountain pool; the best camps are on its southwest shore. There's an excellent high viewpoint between the two lakes.

WARNING: Be prepared for lots of mosquitoes at both lakes in July.

NOTE: This lake is the source of the North Umpqua River. The excellent North Umpqua River Trail parallels the river, but several sections of it have recently been closed due to landslides, blowdowns, and other dangerous conditions left in the wake of wildfires. If this stretch has reopened by the time you read this, you can follow the trail north and west from Lucile Lake for 10–12 miles to Lemolo Lake and Lemolo Falls, noting the drastic change in scenery as you descend from the high country.

To continue your tour, pass Maidu Lake and take the trail from its south end, which climbs to a forested pass and a junction with the PCT. Continue straight on the Maidu Lake Trail for 2 miles to reach comparatively enormous Miller Lake, where there are restrooms, drinking water, a campground, and road access.

Back at the PCT junction, turn left (south) and begin a long, viewless climb through mountain hemlock forests. After 2.2 miles, the trail reaches a marvelous viewpoint atop a rocky promontory. Rest and enjoy the scenery and then reshoulder your pack and resume climbing. The trail circles the remains of a flattened volcanic butte, passes another viewpoint, and comes to a saddle on the northeast side of Tipsoo Peak. Ice age glaciers ripped deeply into this reddish-colored peak's north side, though no ice remains today. Continue climbing beside a gully and then come to a meadow leading to another broad pass, where posts mark the way across a pumice-covered flat. Tired hikers rejoice—this 7,560-foot pass is the highest point on the PCT in Oregon!

TIP: Don't miss the relatively easy scramble to the excellent overlook atop Tipsoo Peak.

From the pass, your trail returns to the trees and begins a gradual descent. Now you round a ridge and begin to enjoy occasional views of craggy Howlock Mountain. Shortly after you pass a junction, the PCT skirts around the left side of a large pumice flat called Howlock Meadows.

TIP: For an exceptionally scenic vista of Howlock Mountain, take the time to visit the middle of this meadow. From here, it's easy to see how this section of the Cascade crest got the name Sawtooth Ridge.

Although camping here seems inviting, lingering snowfields provide the only water. Forced, therefore, to continue south, you can look for intermittent views of Diamond Lake and Mount Bailey to the west as you make a long, irregular descent. About 3 miles from Howlock Meadows is Thielsen Meadow and the welcome waters of Thielsen Creek. Please camp back in the trees, well away from the fragile meadows.

Thielsen Meadow is a popular place for several reasons. Water from the spring-fed stream attracts PCT hikers. Abundant wildflowers provide delicate beauty and draw their share of admirers. Most outstanding of all, however, is the jaw-dropping view of the north face of Mount Thielsen. The towering cliffs rise almost 2,300 feet above the meadow to the mountain's famous pointed summit. The incredible scenery has earned this spot a place on our list of Oregon's most spectacular locations.

TIP: Photographers will need a wide-angle lens to capture this scene.

You could easily spend an extra day here just gazing up in amazement. For more exercise, venture out on any of several highly rewarding day hikes. Nearby are the boulder field and springs at the head of Thielsen Creek and the small glacier at the base of the cliffs on the north face of Mount Thielsen. More ambitious hikers can scramble up an unnamed high point northeast of Mount Thielsen, where an outstanding overlook of the peak and surrounding country awaits. Another option is to scramble over a bouldery pass to the east and then drop steeply to the huge pumice flat at the head of Cottonwood Creek, directly beneath the steep east face of Mount Thielsen.

The PCT continues south from Thielsen Creek, making a long, gradual climb to a ridge, where you are treated to a frontal view of the colorful scree slopes on Mount Thielsen's northwestern face. The mountain's impressive summit spire is prominently displayed. This pinnacle is a favorite target of Mother Nature's wrath, earning Mount Thielsen the nickname Lightning Rod of the Cascades. The trail cuts across a scree slope to a second ridge, where there is a junction with the Mount Thielsen Trail from Diamond Lake.

If the weather is good, strong hikers who aren't afraid of heights should take the time to climb Mount Thielsen. The unofficial trail is easy to follow as it winds through twisted mountain hemlocks and whitebark pines and passes numerous delicate rock gardens. Views of distant peaks and lakes improve with every heart-pounding step. Above the treeline, the "trail" charges up a super-steep slope of scree and loose rocks, eventually topping out on a small ledge at the base of the summit pinnacle. The world-class landscape from here includes most of the state of Oregon, as well as parts of California. A sharp eye will even be able to see over the rim of Crater Lake, not far to the south. The final 100 feet or so to the top of the mountain is definitely not for everyone. While not technically difficult, it requires using handholds and footholds to crawl carefully up the rock face. To the north and east, sheer cliffs drop 2,000–3,000 feet, so vertigo is a real concern.

WARNING: Given this mountain's nickname, hikers should avoid this climb when there is any threat of a thunderstorm.

After returning to the PCT, continue south and make a long, gradual, and rather uneventful descent around forested ridges to a dirt road. Cross the road and shortly thereafter turn right at a junction with the 0.2-mile trail that drops down a forested gully to the official Pacific Crest Trailhead and your car.

POSSIBLE ITINERARY

	CAMP	MILES	ELEVATION GAIN
Day 1	Maidu Lake	13.0	900'
Day 2	Thielsen Creek	10.9	2,100'
Day 3	Out (with side trip up Mount Thielsen)	9.6	2,500'

14

SKY LAKES LOOP

RATINGS: Scenery 7 **Solitude** 5 **Difficulty** 6
MILES: 59
ELEVATION GAIN: 6,000'
DAYS: 5–7
SHUTTLE MILEAGE: NA
MAP: USFS *Sky Lakes Wilderness; Siskiyou Mountain Club Sky Lakes Wilderness North & South*
USUALLY OPEN: July–October
BEST: Mid-August–early September
PERMITS: None
RULES: Maximum group size of 8 people/12 stock; near lakes, camping is allowed only at designated sites
CONTACT: Klamath Ranger District, Fremont–Winema National Forest, 541-883-6714, fs.usda.gov/fremont-winema

SPECIAL ATTRACTIONS

Huckleberries, swimming and fishing lakes

CHALLENGES

Mosquitoes (through mid-August), crowded in spots, a few burn areas

Above: The fire-scarred but beautiful Sky Lakes Wilderness

HOW TO GET THERE

Multiple trailheads provide access to this loop, but Cold Springs combines relatively easy car access and a short approach to the most scenic part of the wilderness. To get there from Medford, take I-5 to Exit 30. Head northeast on OR 62 and go 5.6 miles to OR 140. Turn right (east) on OR 140 toward Klamath Falls, drive 40 miles, then turn left onto Forest Service Road 3651, following signs for the Cold Springs Trailhead. Go 10 miles to the trailhead at road's end.

TIP: There are a few established car-camping spots and a pit toilet at the trailhead, handy for those who want to get an early start through the unshaded burn zone at the beginning of the hike.

GPS TRAILHEAD COORDINATES:
N42° 32.574' W122° 10.855'

INTRODUCTION

The Sky Lakes Wilderness is perfectly designed for a series of choose-your-own-adventure side trips. We've described a wobbly figure-eight loop route here, but it's only a suggestion; hike the whole route or use it as a starting point to design the tour you want. This area is rich in lake basins that are ideal for setting up base camps and exploring from there. And there's certainly plenty to explore: This narrow, mountainous strip of the Cascade Range south of Crater Lake is a beautiful land of open forests, deep canyons, craggy mountains, and countless lakes. This highly attractive hike samples most of the charms of this wilderness and, although the suggested loop involves briefly retracing your steps a couple of times, it avoids the hassle of car shuttles and trailhead fees. The terrain is equally scenic in any direction, but is described here looping first north and then south, so you can enjoy a gradual approach to Mount McLoughlin, the area's principal landmark. You'll also notice plenty of options for shortcuts and early exits; this is an area you'll want to come back to, and there's no shame in breaking this hike into multiple excursions.

WARNING: The numerous lakes and ponds of the Sky Lakes Wilderness are a nursery for a tremendous population of invertebrate vampires (mosquitoes). If you come in July, when the crags are streaked with snow and pictures are at their prettiest, be prepared with repellent, a head net, and a well-enclosed tent. Otherwise, consider visiting mid-August–early September, when the bugs are mostly gone and the huckleberries are ripe.

DESCRIPTION

From the Cold Springs Trailhead, walk past a shelter and freshwater spring into an eerily beautiful forest of fire-scarred tree snags and recovering undergrowth. There's not much protection from the sun for the first mile or so of the trip, so it's best to get it done early in the day. The trail meanders gently uphill and quickly enters the Sky Lakes Wilderness. In half a mile, you reach a junction with the South Rock Creek Trail, which, like your route, ends up at the Heavenly Twin Lakes. This might look like a shortcut, but it goes through the heart of the area burned in the 2017 North Pelican Fire and is therefore not

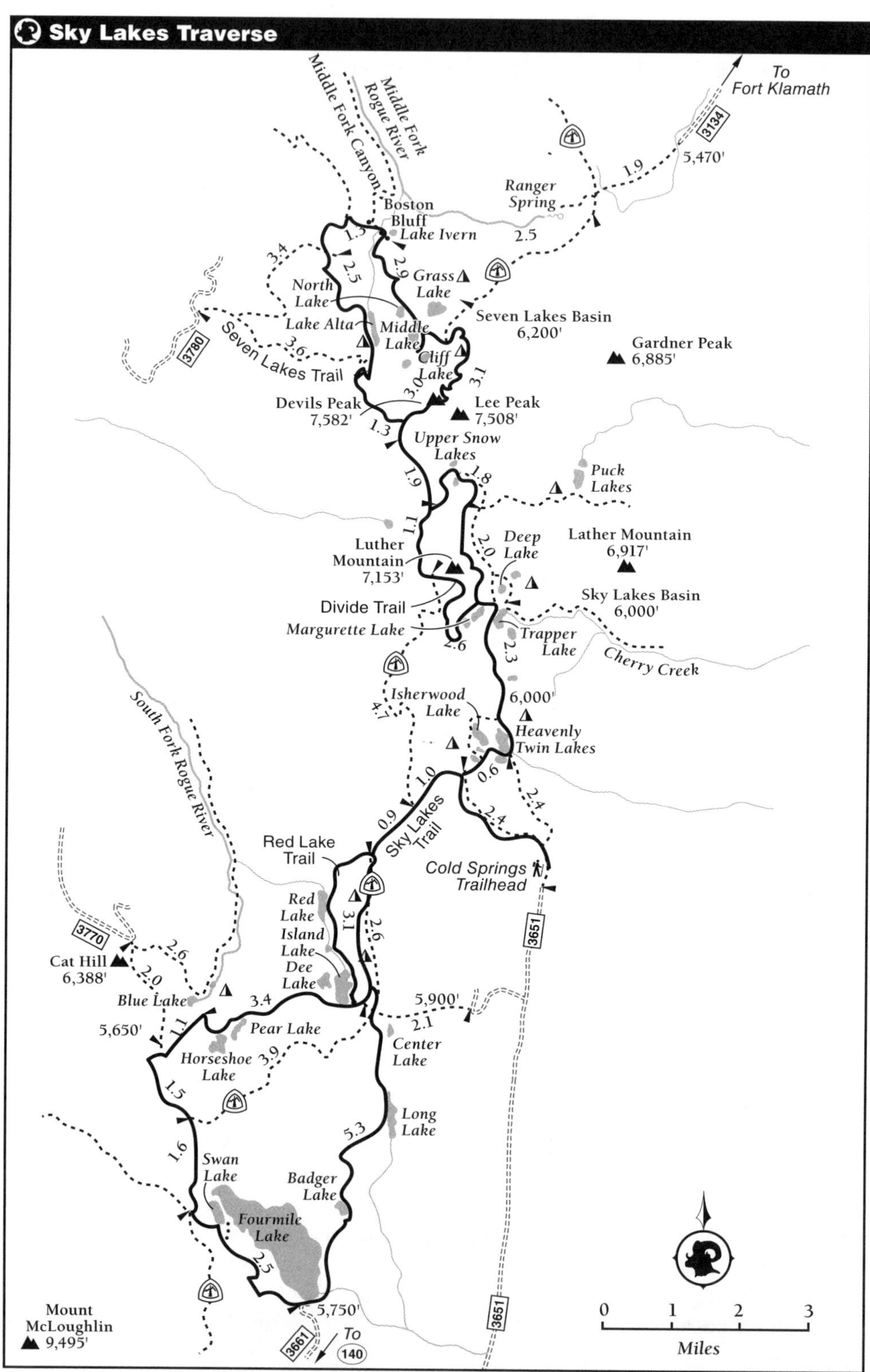
Sky Lakes Traverse
To
Fort Klamath
3134
5,470'
Middle Fork Canyon
Middle Fork
Rogue River
Ranger
Spring
Boston
Bluff
Lake Ivern
2.5
1.9
Grass
Lake
North
Lake
Lake Alta
Middle
Lake
Cliff
Lake
Seven Lakes Basin
6,200'
Gardner Peak
6,885'
3780
Seven Lakes Trail
Devils Peak
7,582'
Lee Peak
7,508'
Upper Snow
Lakes
Puck
Lakes
Luther
Mountain
7,153'
Deep
Lake
Lather Mountain
6,917'
Divide Trail
Sky Lakes Basin
6,000'
Margurette Lake
Trapper
Lake
Cherry Creek
Isherwood
Lake
6,000'
Heavenly
Twin Lakes
South Fork Rogue River
Sky Lakes
Trail
Red Lake
Trail
Cold Springs
Trailhead
Red
Lake
Island
Lake
Dee
Lake
3651
3770
Cat Hill
6,388'
Blue Lake
5,650'
Pear Lake
5,900'
Horseshoe
Lake
Center
Lake
Long
Lake
Swan
Lake
Badger
Lake
Fourmile
Lake
5,750'
Mount
McLoughlin
9,495'
3661
To
140
0
1
2
3
Miles

as pleasant (and not as well cleared of blowdown) as the Cold Springs Trail, so keep left at the junction. You crest a hill and exit the burn zone into thick forest.

Two miles past the Rock Creek junction, your trail meets the Sky Lakes Trail. You can turn either way here, but the recommended route goes right (north) toward the aptly named Heavenly Twin Lakes, with nice camps. You pass a junction with the Isherwood Trail on your left (it forms an easy loop around Isherwood Lake before rejoining the main trail) and the other end of the South Rock Creek Trail on your right. Here, the Sky Lakes Trail becomes the Snow Lakes Trail and skirts the east side of the larger of the two Heavenly Lakes, heading north.

TIP: As you can already tell by the number of trail junctions, it is crucial to have a good, up-to-date trail map on hand for this trip.

Go past the other end of the Isherwood loop trail and then, 0.8 mile later, a junction with the Sky Lakes Cutoff Trail heading west. Continue north, passing several smaller lakes, and then reach Trapper Lake, one of the largest and clearest in the area. At its north end, you pass a junction with the Cherry Creek Trail (leading east to a trailhead with road access) and then the short Donna Lake Trail—keep left at both to visit lovely Margurette Lake, which offers excellent camps.

Between Trapper and Margurette Lakes, you'll reach a junction with the Divide Trail; turn left (south) and climb on this spectacular trail past multiple ponds and viewpoints. The trail skirts the south side of Luther Mountain and meets the Pacific Crest Trail (PCT), where you turn right (north). You'll briefly pass through a burned area from wildfires in 2014. At a junction with the Snow Lakes Trail, stay left on the PCT for now.

Follow the PCT across Shale Butte and beside Lucifer Peak to a junction; turn right, staying on the PCT, for 3 miles as you descend into the Seven Lakes Basin.

TIP: It is easy and highly rewarding to climb the ridge from here to the summit of Devils Peak.

Turn left at a junction with Cliff Lake Trail. The dramatic Cliff Lake sits directly beneath the towering north face of Devils Peak, so you should allow time to admire this spectacular spot.

Leaving Cliff Lake, take Seven Lakes Trail north toward Middle Lake. All the nearby lakes, including Middle Lake, have good to excellent camps. Northeast of Middle Lake, at aptly named Grass Lake, a short side trail leads to a camping area on the lake's northeast shore and another good view of craggy Devils Peak.

TIP: An interesting side trip from here goes north and then west to the gushing Ranger Spring—the source of the Middle Fork Rogue River.

One of the best ways to enjoy this basin is to pick your favorite scenic lake, set up a base camp, and explore via day hikes in all directions. The recommended loop, however, continues north from Middle Lake along a path that goes past North Lake on its way to tiny Lake Ivern.

TIP: A few hundred feet north of this pool is Boston Bluff, as well as an outstanding viewpoint of the impressive glacial canyon of the Middle Fork Rogue River.

Notasha Lake pops into view just before you reach the Heavenly Twin Lakes.

From Lake Ivern, set a northwest course and walk cross-country 0.4 mile to reach a trail coming up from the Middle Fork Canyon. Turn left and follow this trail to a junction, where you turn left again and climb a ridge to narrow and remarkably straight Lake Alta, a nice place for a swim.

Continue south to a junction with the western access trail for the Seven Lakes Basin and turn right (turning left will close the loop and return you to your possible base camp at Middle Lake). Almost immediately, go left onto the Devil's Peak Trail heading south and back to the PCT the way you came in, exiting the basin.

You retrace your steps along the PCT and into the 2014 burn zone, but this time, at the Snow Lakes Trail junction, turn sharply left to descend past several unnamed ponds and into the Cherry Creek valley. The trail makes a 3-mile loop and passes Lower Snow Lakes, directly below the cliffs of Luther Mountain, then curves south to end up back at Margurette Lake.

Turn left, staying on the Snow Lakes Trail east of Trapper Lake. Continue retracing your steps past Heavenly Twin Lakes (where the trail becomes Sky Lakes Trail) and the junction with the Cold Springs Trail you came in on. You could, of course, go back to your car from here, but there are more lakes to see!

So ignore Cold Springs for now and turn right to stay on Sky Lakes Trail, continuing southwest to a junction with the PCT, which has made a mostly forested descent from Luther Mountain. You now follow the PCT 0.9 mile to another junction and once again turn off the main path, this time to the right on the Red Lake Trail.

You pass the shores of the trail's namesake before reaching appropriately named Island Lake. In addition to a forested island, this lake features a nice vista of Mount McLoughlin from a camp on its northeast shore. The path then works southeast away from the lake to a junction. Turn right and pass near the southern shore of Island Lake and an interesting historical landmark. In 1888, Judge John B. Waldo, for whom Waldo Lake in Willamette National Forest was named, carved his name in a tree here during his epic exploration of the Cascade Range.

Leaving Island Lake and the Waldo Tree behind, go west on Blue Canyon Trail and make a forested descent into yet another lake basin. This one features Pear and Horseshoe Lakes, both barely touched by the trail, and several off-trail pools. The prettiest, and most popular, of the lakes here is Blue Lake, backed by a 300-foot cliff. You reach this lake via a short side trip to the north at a junction west of Horseshoe Lake. There are plenty of options for campsites throughout this basin.

Turn southwest from Blue Lake and climb 1.1 miles to a ridgetop junction. Turn left here and travel over Cat Hill, where an opening in the trees provides a nice, if partly obstructed, view of Mount McLoughlin.

When you yet again reach the PCT, turn right (south). (There's also an option here to skip the sometimes-busy Fourmile Lake by turning left instead and returning to Island Lake via the PCT.) Gradually go up and down, mostly in forest, to a saddle with a four-way junction. Turn left and soon reach shallow Swan Lake.

TIP: Don't miss taking a short side trip up the trailless east shore of Swan Lake. Photographers will especially like the excellent reflection of Mount McLoughlin in the tranquil early morning waters.

From here you have an almost level forest walk to the south end of Fourmile Lake (actually a human-made reservoir), where you can take advantage of the developed campground, or exit the hike if you've left a car at this trailhead; otherwise, continue around the lake and go north on Badger Lake Trail, passing Long Lake on the right. After 4 miles you pass Center Lake on the right and then a junction with the PCT, where you turn right (north) to get on the PCT.

Continuing north along the PCT, you'll pass the junction with Red Lakes Trail, but stay on the PCT until the next junction, where you turn right (northeast) onto Sky Lakes Trail. In 1 mile you meet the Cold Springs Trail and turn right (south) to return to the start of this long, lake-filled adventure.

POSSIBLE ITINERARY

	CAMP	MILES	ELEVATION GAIN
Day 1	Margurette Lake	5.6	500'
Day 2	Cliff Lake	8.5	1000'
Day 3	Deep Lake	13.0	1,400'
Day 4	Horseshoe Lake	12.0	1,600'
Day 4	Fourmile Lake	7.5	1000'
Day 5	Out	12.0	500'

15

STRAWBERRY MOUNTAINS TRAVERSE

RATINGS: Scenery 9 **Solitude** 6 **Difficulty** 7
MILES: 35 (52)
ELEVATION GAIN: 7,600' (11,700')
DAYS: 4 (5–6)
SHUTTLE MILEAGE: 31
MAP: USFS *Strawberry Mountain and Monument Rock Wilderness*
USUALLY OPEN: Late June–early November
BEST: Early to mid-July and mid-October
PERMITS: None
RULES: No camping within 100 feet of lakes or streams; maximum group size of 12 people/18 stock
CONTACT: Prairie City Ranger District, Malheur National Forest, 541-820-3800, fs.usda.gov/malheur

SPECIAL ATTRACTIONS

Mountain scenery, views, fall colors, solitude (for most of the trip), wildlife

CHALLENGES

Long stretches without water, several burn areas

Above: Strawberry Mountain from a ridge near Indian Creek Butte
photographed by Douglas Lorain

HOW TO GET THERE

To find the west trailhead, from the intersection of US 26 and US 395 in John Day, head south on US 395. In 10 miles, turn left (east) onto paved Canyon Creek Road/Forest Service Road 15, and go 3 miles. Turn left onto gravel FS 1510, which becomes FS 6510, and follow it 4.9 miles to its end at the Joaquin Miller Trailhead.

To reach the east trailhead, follow the directions above to Canyon Creek Road/FS 15. Turn left (east) onto FS 15 and go 13.7 miles to FS 16. Turn left (northeast) onto FS 16, and drive 13.8 miles through Logan Valley to Summit Prairie. Turn left (north) onto Summit Prairie Road/FS 14/County Road 62 and go 3.2 miles; then turn left (west) onto rough gravel FS 101. Drive 1.4 miles to the Skyline Trailhead.

GPS TRAILHEAD COORDINATES:

(Joaquin Miller) N44° 17.367' W118° 53.400'

(Skyline) N44° 14.385' W118° 32.280'

NOTE: In 1996, the Wildcat Fire swept through a large section of the Strawberry Mountain Wilderness. On this hike, the still-noticeable affected area extends from Indian Creek Butte in the west to Twin Springs Basin on the east side of Strawberry Mountain. You'll also see damage from the 2015 Canyon Creek Complex Fire, especially around Indian Creek Butte. At this stage, the main thing you'll notice about the burn zones is expanded views. In places, however, blowdown from the fire has made the trail faint, so be sure to carry a good map and compass. While flowers and grasses tend to benefit from wildfires, the larger trees have yet to fill in, and many views still include snags and blackened timber. Shade is at a premium on this section of the trail.

INTRODUCTION

The narrow spine of the Strawberry Mountains packs a lot of scenic punch in a small package. Its snowy line of peaks provides a lovely backdrop, seen both from the north over the upper John Day River Valley near Prairie City and from the south over Logan Valley. Happily, the backcountry trails deliver scenery at least as good as that seen from a distance. Views are spectacular throughout, flowers are abundant, and wildlife is unusually common. The range is crowded only near the few lakes in it, so there are miles of rarely traveled trails. For those who do make the scenic traverse of the Strawberries, most begin at the Canyon Mountain Trailhead near Iron King Mine. The route described here is shorter, involves less climbing, and has better road access. It also passes through some of the range's best wildlife habitat, so your chances of seeing elk, bighorn sheep, and other animals are significantly improved.

DESCRIPTION

This trip starts with a short climb along Rattlesnake Ridge, followed by three long downhill switchbacks to a saddle. Now you contour around two hills and then drop a bit to another saddle and a junction with the Tamarack Creek Trail, where you go left.

TIP: This is one of the best areas in Oregon to spot bighorn sheep. Keep your binoculars handy for the next few miles. If you're really lucky, you may also see black bears

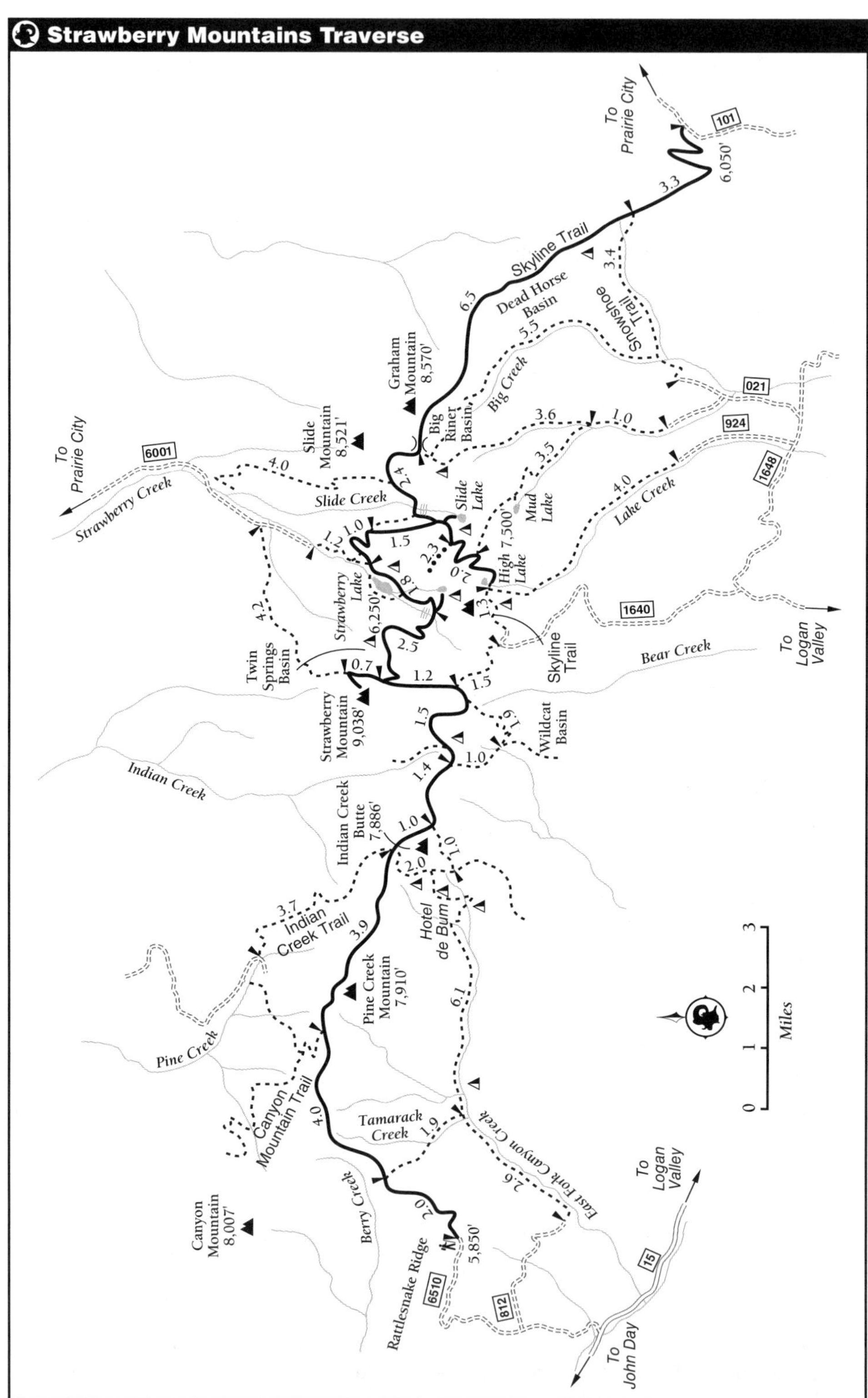
Strawberry Mountains Traverse
To Prairie City
101
6,050'
3.3
Skyline Trail
3.4
Snowshoe Trail
6.5
Dead Horse Basin
5.5
Graham Mountain 8,570'
Big Creek
Big Riner Basin
021
3.6
1.0
924
Slide Mountain 8,521'
To Prairie City
6001
4.0
Strawberry Creek
Slide Creek
2.4
Slide Lake
3.5
Mud Lake
4.0
Lake Creek
1648
7,500'
High Lake
1640
To Logan Valley
Strawberry Lake
6,250'
4.2
Twin Springs Basin
2.5
Skyline Trail
Bear Creek
0.7
1.2
1.5
Strawberry Mountain 9,038'
Wildcat Basin
Indian Creek
1.4
1.0
Indian Creek Butte 7,886'
2.0
3.7
Indian Creek Trail
3.9
Hotel de Bum
Pine Creek Mountain 7,910'
6.1
Pine Creek
Canyon Mountain Trail
4.0
Tamarack Creek
1.9
East Fork Canyon Creek
2.6
To Logan Valley
Berry Creek
Canyon Mountain 8,007'
2.0
5,850'
Rattlesnake Ridge
6510
812
15
To John Day
0
1
2
3
Miles

or the elusive mountain lion. Watch for movement on the steep canyon walls of Berry and Tamarack Creeks.

From the junction, your trail climbs steeply along a ridge and then contours around the head of Tamarack Creek.

TIP: At a saddle on the side of this ridge, be sure to visit a small rise south of the trail to check out the view and look for animals.

The climb eases somewhat as you approach a pass along the high ridge of the Strawberry Mountains. For the next several miles, the route follows this view-packed ridge. Water is scarce except for a few snow patches into July.

Keep right at a junction with the Canyon Mountain Trail and then cut across the steep north face of Pine Creek Mountain. Snow lingers here for much of the season. Your route climbs to a pass on the east slopes of Pine Creek Mountain and then makes a long traverse along the south side of the ridge. The trail remains on the south side as it makes a gradual descent to a four-way junction, immediately north of prominent Indian Creek Butte.

TIP: Camps in this area are best made near the previous crossings of two small creeks, or turn right and drop 500 feet in 1.5 miles to a spring with a good campsite. The as-fancy-as-it-sounds Hotel de Bum, a small camp at the headwaters of the East Fork of Canyon Creek, offers good views of Indian Creek Butte.

The main trail stays straight at the four-way junction and cuts across the east face of Indian Creek Butte. To the east, across the deep canyon of Indian Creek, rises Strawberry Mountain, the highest point in this range. The trail contours through a low saddle to a junction. Turn left and travel east along the ridge to a large meadow, which supports scattered wildflowers in July and has an exceptionally picturesque view of Strawberry Mountain. From here the trail drops to a junction where there is a choice of trails. To the right, the main trail drops to the wildflowers of Wildcat Basin (decent camps) before climbing through an interesting eroded "badlands" back up to the ridge. A shorter but equally scenic route, described here, from the junction goes left, passes a junction with the Indian Creek Trail, and soon reaches a beautiful little meadow at the head of Indian Creek. This marshy basin holds lots of wildflowers, provides a fine vista of the cliffs to the south, and has good camps.

WARNING: This boggy area supports a healthy mosquito population through July.

From Indian Creek, you make several switchbacks up to a ridge and then reunite with the main trail climbing from Wildcat Basin. Hike east and climb to the end of a closed jeep road that now serves as a trail. You turn left here and follow this exposed and rocky path north, passing several exceptional vistas to the west.

At a ridgetop junction, drop your heavy pack, pick up a camera, and then head north for an excellent side trip to the summit of Strawberry Mountain. The route first cuts across the rocky east face of the peak, where you'll enjoy terrific scenes to the east. A short side trail climbs the northeast ridge to the top. On a clear day there seems to be no end to the views from this overlook. The John Day River Valley lies to the north. To the west is the crumpled spine of the Strawberry Range, with the Aldrich and Ochoco

Mountains in the distance. On very clear days even the snowy peaks of the Cascades can be seen. To the south are the forested Blue Mountains and distant Steens Mountain. Turning east you will see the scenic peaks, cliffs, and lake basins that will occupy your attention for the next couple of days. A sharp eye will even be able to spot the Elkhorn Range and part of the Wallowa Mountains to the northeast.

After absorbing the views, return to your pack and begin the long descent east toward Strawberry Lake. The highly scenic trail goes through Twin Springs Basin (good camps) and then rounds a ridge with excellent vistas of Strawberry Lake and the cliffs surrounding this basin. About 1,000 feet farther down, you reach a crossing of Strawberry Creek and a junction. To the right is a highly recommended 0.6-mile side trip to beautiful Little Strawberry Lake. The lake sits at the base of 1,500-foot cliffs, so bring an extra-wide-angle lens for photographs. There are good camps at both Little Strawberry Lake and Strawberry Creek.

TIP: These camps are generally less crowded than those farther down the trail at popular Strawberry Lake.

To continue your trip, return to the main trail and switchback down the forested slope to the north, stopping along the way to enjoy Strawberry Falls. At the south end of 31-acre Strawberry Lake is a junction. The trail along the west shore is more scenic, but the shorter route along the east side is the usual choice.

TIP: At the north end, be sure to take a short detour along the lake's northwest shore to enjoy a classic scene across the lake of the jagged snowy ridge above. Afternoons provide the best lighting for photographs. Because the lake's water level fluctuates considerably, early summer is best.

Camps (and people) are abundant near Strawberry Lake, so if you camp here, expect plenty of company and heed all U.S. Forest Service restrictions on where to set up your tent.

Keep right at two junctions not far below the lake's outlet, following signs to Slide Lake. The trail climbs steadily to a junction at a flat spot on the ridge. The quickest exit goes left, but taking it would bypass too much great scenery, so keep right and make a long up-and-down traverse across an open slope. The distinctive peak to the east is Slide Mountain. Reenter woods and keep right at a junction before climbing to a second junction. To the left a short side trail leads to pretty Slide Lake, which has excellent camps.

Slide Lake makes an outstanding base camp for day hikes. Possible hikes range from the short stroll to Little Slide Lake, a small pool about 0.2 mile south of Slide Lake, to the long scramble up Slide Mountain. The two spectacular destinations could be combined in one rugged day. Begin by climbing the trail heading southwest from the Slide Lake junction. Leave the trail near the base of a steep talus slope and scramble up the ridge to the northwest. The climb ends at the top of the high cliffs above Little Strawberry Lake.

To continue your day hike excursion, return to the trail, turn right, and climb across a steep, rocky slope to a pass.

WARNING: This slope is usually covered with steep snowfields until about mid-July.

Keep right at a junction and travel along the top of an open ridge, where windswept trees and small alpine wildflowers enhance the wonderful scenery. The path now makes a long descent to High Lake—a spectacular pool backed by high cliffs and ridges. Once you've had your fill, return to Slide Lake the way you came.

At the junction north of Slide Lake, turn right. As the trail drops to a junction, look for fine views up to Slide Mountain. Turn right and continue downhill to a creek crossing.

TIP: Impressive Slide Falls is a short bushwhack upstream.

The trail now makes a long 1,200-foot climb out of Slide Basin. Along the way you turn right at a junction with the Slide Basin Shortcut Trail and then complete your climb to a pass with another trail junction. South of the pass is Big Riner Basin (good campsites), and to the left is Graham Mountain.

Turn left at the junction, staying on the Skyline Trail as it makes a long traverse across the southwest slopes of Graham Mountain. You reach a saddle and begin following a scenic up-and-down ridge. To the east, across the forested upper John Day River Valley, are Lookout and Glacier Mountains. As the route loops south around Dead Horse Basin, it stays on the west side of the ridge and passes two welcome springs. Views to the west are superb.

The trail returns to the increasingly forested ridgecrest and eventually meets the Snowshoe Trail coming up from a fire-scarred area to the west. The Skyline Trail continues straight, staying along the ridge for another mile before dropping in very long switchbacks to the eastern trailhead on FS 101.

POSSIBLE ITINERARY

	CAMP	MILES	ELEVATION GAIN
Day 1	Spring below Indian Creek Butte	11.4	3,000'
Day 2	Twin Springs Basin (with side trip up Strawberry Mountain)	9.6	3,100'
Day 3	Slide Lake (with side trip to Little Strawberry Lake)	7.3	1,300'
Day 4	Day hike to High Lake and Strawberry Ridge (return to Slide Lake)	11.0	2,400'
Day 5	Out	12.5	1,900'

ELKHORN CREST TRAIL

RATINGS: Scenery 9 **Solitude** 6 **Difficulty** 6
MILES: 27 (34)
ELEVATION GAIN: 3,000' (5,700')
DAYS: 3 (3–4)
SHUTTLE MILEAGE: 35
MAP: USGS *Elkhorn Peak, Bourne,* and *Anthony Lakes*
USUALLY OPEN: July–October
BEST: Mid-July
PERMITS: Northwest Forest Pass required at Anthony Lake and Marble Pass Trailhead
RULES: Maximum group size of 12 people/18 stock; no camping within 100 feet of lakes and streams.
CONTACT: Whitman Ranger District, Wallowa-Whitman National Forest, 541-523-6391 or 541-742-7511, fs.usda.gov/wallowa-whitman

SPECIAL ATTRACTIONS

Views; granite peaks, cirque lakes, and generally excellent mountain scenery; relative solitude; mountain goats

CHALLENGES

Poor road access to southern trailhead, motorbikes

Above: Anthony Lake

HOW TO GET THERE

To reach the north trailhead at Anthony Lake, take I-84 to Exit 285 for North Powder. Head west on River Lane, and go 4 miles. Turn left (south) onto Ellis Road, and go 0.7 mile. Turn right (west) onto Anthony Lakes Highway, and go 8.2 miles. Anthony Lakes Highway becomes Forest Service Road 73. Follow signs to Anthony Lake as you climb paved FS 73 for 7 miles to the Anthony Lake Campground.

TIP: The best place to park is a bit east of the campground at the well-marked Elkhorn Crest Trailhead.

The traditional southern entry point to this hike, Marble Pass Trailhead, is extremely difficult to reach without a high-clearance, four-wheel drive vehicle. (That said, if you have the vehicle for the job, starting at Marble Pass saves you significant initial climbing.) From I-84, take Exit 302 in Baker City. Head west on OR 86, and go 0.8 mile. Turn right (west) onto Hughes Lane, and drive 1.2 miles. Continue straight onto Pocahontas Road, and go 7.2 miles (making a right turn and then a left turn to stay on Pocahontas). Turn left (west) onto Marble Creek Road, and in 0.3 mile, turn left (south) to stay on Marble Creek. Go 3.7 miles, and continue straight on FS 6510, which enters national forest land and passes the Marble Creek Picnic Area. In 3.7 miles from the beginning of FS 6510, you top out at a pass and the (signposted) Marble Pass Trailhead.

For an easier drive and the recommended starting point, use the Twin Lakes Trailhead at the end of FS 030. From I-84, take Exit 304 in Baker City. Head west on Campbell Street. In 0.9 mile turn left (south) onto Main Street, and go 0.5 mile. Continue straight on OR 7 S for 22.5 miles. Make a right turn (north) onto Deer Creek Road/FS 6550, continue 3.3 miles, and then veer right (northwest) onto FS 6540. In 0.6 mile keep straight on FS 030. In 2.5 miles the road becomes a hikable track at a trailhead entrance sign, and another parking area is 0.5 mile farther.

TIP: For around $100/person, local shuttle services (Range Tour & Shuttle, Fridays only, 541-523-1668, thetrailheadbakercity.com) will pick you up at the Elkhorn Crest Trailhead, where you leave your car, and drop you at the Marble Pass Trailhead.

GPS TRAILHEAD COORDINATES:

(Anthony Lake/Elkhorn Crest) N44° 57.797' W118° 13.505'

(Marble Pass) N44° 46.402' W118° 02.631'

(Twin Lakes) N44° 46.780' W118° 05.518'

INTRODUCTION

The jagged spine of the Elkhorn Range rises dramatically above Baker City and the Powder River Valley. Strangely, although countless people drive past these impressive peaks on I-84, relatively few stop to explore. This narrow range hides many of the same treasures that make the nearby Wallowa Mountains so popular (granite peaks, glacial lakes, and clear streams), but for some reason it receives only a tiny fraction of the publicity. Lovers of solitude would prefer it if it stayed that way. Unfortunately, most of this range is unprotected and therefore open to mining (once an important business in these mountains), logging, and motorbikes. A trip along the view-packed Elkhorn Crest Trail

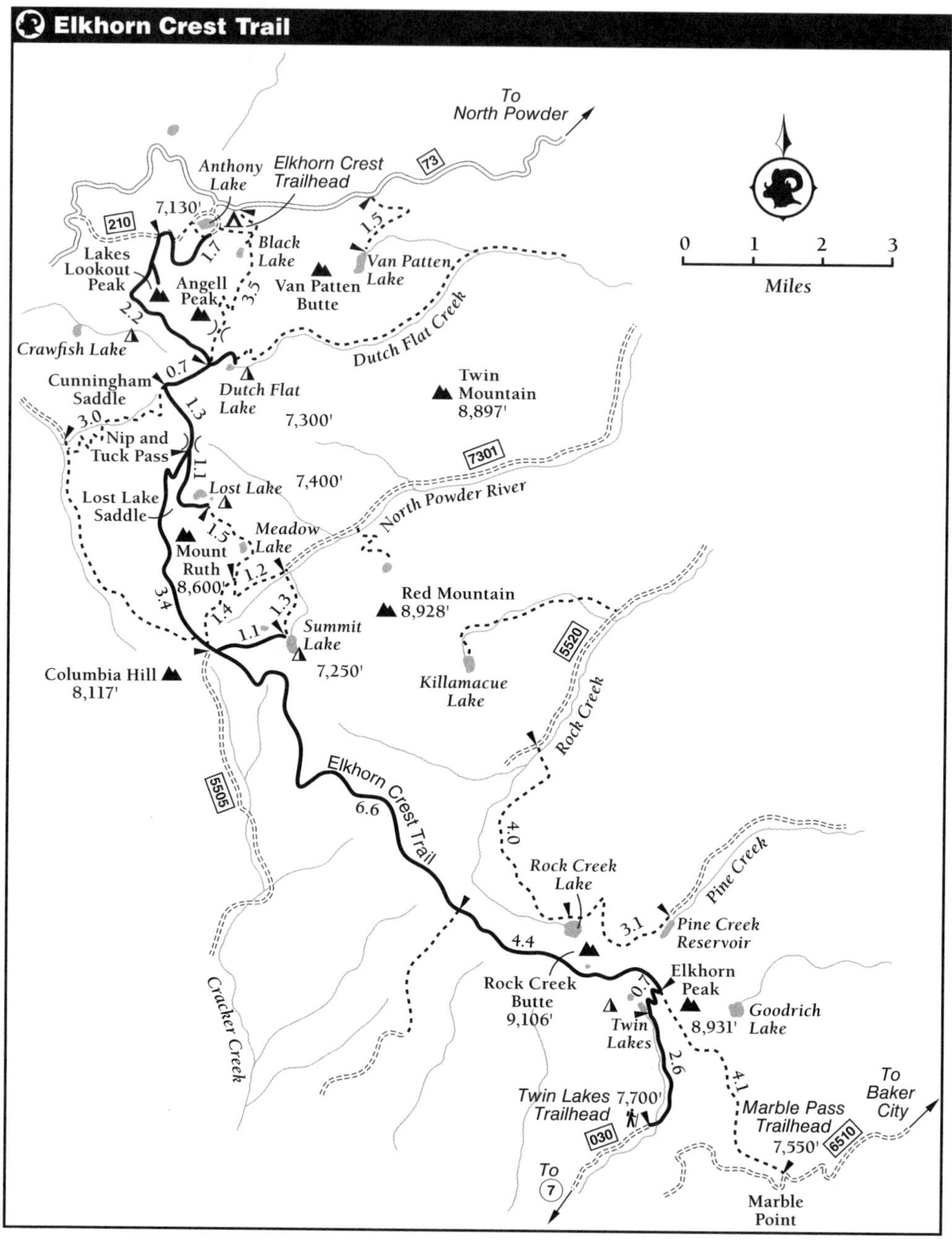

is the ideal way for backpackers to enjoy this lovely range and learn what is at stake. This relatively easy trail closely follows a high ridge for its entire length. Side trails drop to numerous lakes and meadows with scenic campsites. The trip is beautiful in either direction, but south to north is marginally easier because the start is some 400 feet higher.

WARNING: The southern half of this trail is open to motorbikes. Be prepared to have the quiet disrupted on occasion.

DESCRIPTION

Your route climbs gradually (if you start from Marble Pass) or steeply (if you start from the Twin Lakes Trailhead) along a mostly open ridge to the northwest. Views here, as well as along most of this route, are superb, as they alternate between the forested Blue Mountains and Sumpter Valley to the southwest, and the Powder River Valley and the distant Wallowa Mountains to the northeast. For most of the trip, the trail stays on the west side of the Elkhorn Crest, so vistas west dominate.

The outstanding scenery, particularly of the picturesque basin holding the Twin Lakes, with brown and reddish peaks all around, continues along the next stretch of trail. The high point on the east side of this basin is Elkhorn Peak, an inviting mountain with reasonably easy access up its south ridge. The crest trail continues its scenic course—sometimes on the ridge's west side, sometimes at or near the crest—another 3 miles to a trail junction in a saddle. If you started the hike at the Twin Lakes Trailhead, you'll have come up this way; if not, don't miss this excellent side trip, which turns left and drops 0.7 mile in a series of long switchbacks to Lower Twin Lake, backed by rugged cliffs. Smaller Upper Twin Lake is also worth exploring, though there is no official trail. The lower lake is prettier and has better camps.

Fill your water bottles (there is precious little of the stuff along the ridge), climb back to the crest trail, turn left, and round the head of the Twin Lakes Basin.

TIP: An outstanding cross-country side trip climbs moderately steep slopes to the summit of Rock Creek Butte. At 9,106 feet, this is the highest point in the range, and it commands a breathtaking view in all directions. Most impressive of all is the look down to sparkling Rock Creek Lake, which sits in a stark basin beneath sheer cliffs. Bring binoculars to check for what appear to be small moving snowfields but are actually mountain goats.

After another 0.7 mile on the crest trail, scramble up to a second cliff-edge viewpoint, this time of tiny Bucket Lake. Mountain goats are common here as well.

The delightful and gently graded trail passes a junction with a rarely used path from the west and then continues another 6.6 joyous miles of open ridges and views. Notice how the rock changes from reddish volcanic rocks to predominantly white granite. The soils also become more suitable for forests, and the trees grow thicker and healthier than in the sparsely vegetated Twin Lakes Basin. The only blemish on the landscape is the remains of mining activity along Cracker Creek. In a saddle about 0.5 mile northeast of prominent Columbia Hill is a trail junction. From here, a worthwhile side trip goes east to popular Summit Lake. This is a large, beautiful lake with good fishing, several excellent campsites, and photogenic granite cliffs above its southwest shore.

From the Summit Lake junction, go west and quickly reach a four-way junction with a jeep track (still in use), where you go straight and soon reach a pass beside Columbia Hill. Your route goes north, sticking to the Elkhorn Crest Trail (#1611). The trail gradually climbs toward Mount Ruth and soon enters the North Fork John Day Wilderness, so the motorbikes are finally left behind.

TIP: The summit view from Mount Ruth amply rewards the scrambler.

The path skirts the west side of this peak before dropping first to Lost Lake Saddle and then Nip and Tuck Pass and a junction. A highly recommended side trip drops southeast from this junction across a rocky slope and then loops around the basin holding Lost Lake (one of at least 14 lakes in Oregon holding this unimaginative name). An easy walk through open woods and meadows leads to the lake's southeast shore with views back up to Mount Ruth. Several good camps are located around this lake.

Back at Nip and Tuck Pass, the crest trail continues to Cunningham Saddle and a junction with a path coming up from the west. To the north are terrific vistas of spacious Crawfish Meadows backed by a jagged ridge. Now you cross a slope, with intermittent views of this spectacular basin, to a pass and a junction. To the right a recommended side trail drops 600 feet to small but pretty Dutch Flat Lake, with good views and nice camps. From the pass, the official Elkhorn Crest Trail climbs north to a saddle beside Angell Peak, then drops past Black Lake on its way to the trailhead on FS 73. This scenic route is the quickest way out for those in a hurry.

There is another alternative, however, that allows you to savor still more of this country. Turn left and drop about 400 feet before contouring across the slope on the north side of Crawfish Basin. You round another ridge and then climb to a junction with the 0.7-mile trail to the top of Lakes Lookout Peak. This peak provides a particularly good perspective of the Anthony Lakes area, so the side trip is well worthwhile. A short distance north is the end of FS 210 coming up from the west, as well as the top of several ski lifts for the Anthony Lakes ski area.

Keep right and descend on a road/trail that makes a long switchback. At the second switchback, keep straight on a trail leading to the small but very scenic Hoffer Lakes. Finally, drop steeply to busy Anthony Lake with its mountain views, campground, and, of course, your waiting vehicle.

POSSIBLE ITINERARY

	CAMP	MILES	ELEVATION GAIN
Day 1	Lower Twin Lake	4.8	800'
Day 2	Summit Lake	12.8	1,300'
Day 3	Dutch Flat Lake (with side trip to Lost Lake)	9.8	1,800'
Day 4	Out (with side trip to Lakes Lookout Peak)	6.1	1,800'

17

WENAHA RIVER TRAVERSE

RATINGS: Scenery 6 **Solitude** 7 **Difficulty** 5
MILES: 25
ELEVATION GAIN: 2,100'
DAYS: 3–4
SHUTTLE MILEAGE: 21
MAP: USFS *Wenaha-Tucannon Wilderness*
USUALLY OPEN: April–November
BEST: May and October
PERMIT: Northwest Forest Pass required at Elk Flats Trailhead
RULES: Camp at least 75 feet from water
CONTACT: Pomeroy Ranger District, Umatilla National Forest, 509-843-1891, fs.usda.gov/umatilla

SPECIAL ATTRACTIONS

Canyon scenery, early-season access, solitude, wildflowers, wildlife

CHALLENGES

Wildfire damage, heat, rattlesnakes, poison ivy, ticks

Above: The town of Flora, en route to the trailhead

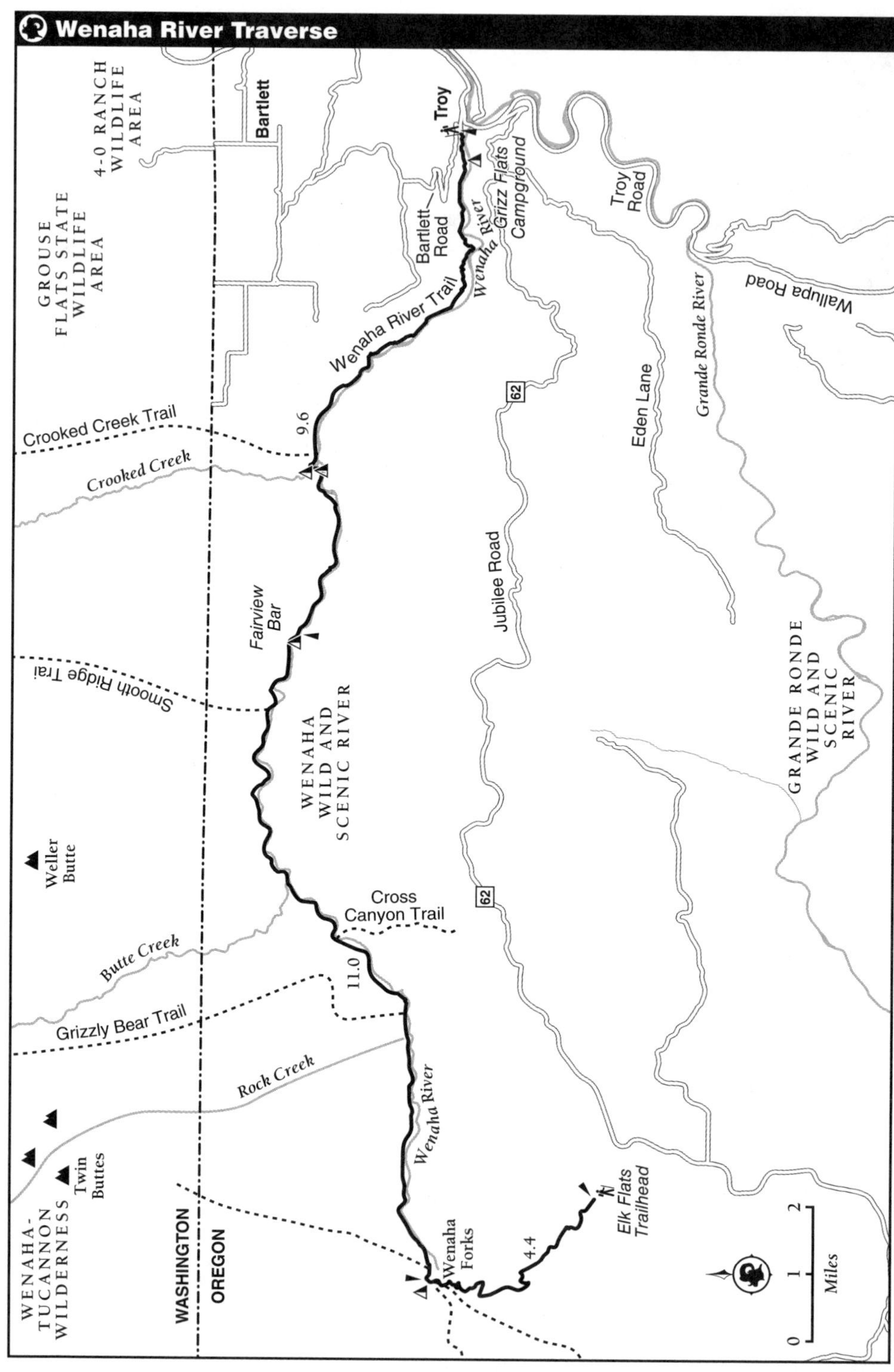
Wenaha River Traverse
4-0 RANCH WILDLIFE AREA
GROUSE FLATS STATE WILDLIFE AREA
Bartlett
Troy
Bartlett Road
Wenaha River Trail
Wenaha River
Grizz Flats Campground
Troy Road
Wallupa Road
Grande Ronde River
Eden Lane
62
Crooked Creek Trail
9.6
Crooked Creek
Jubilee Road
Fairview Bar
Smooth Ridge Trail
WENAHA WILD AND SCENIC RIVER
GRANDE RONDE WILD AND SCENIC RIVER
Weller Butte
Cross Canyon Trail
Butte Creek
11.0
Grizzly Bear Trail
Rock Creek
Twin Buttes
WENAHA-TUCANNON WILDERNESS
WASHINGTON
OREGON
Wenaha Forks
4.4
Elk Flats Trailhead
0
1
2
Miles

HOW TO GET THERE

To reach the tiny community of Troy, drive north from Enterprise on OR 3 for 33.7 miles. Turn left on the signed road to Flora and Troy. The road goes through farmland and the dilapidated buildings in Flora and then turns left onto Redmond Grade Lane after 6 miles. Continue 7.6 miles on Redmond Grade Lane as it winds steeply down into the Grande Ronde River Canyon toward Troy. Cross the bridge and turn left onto Troy River Road. After 1.6 miles turn right onto Bartlett Road. You will reach the marked trailhead at a switchback in the road just 0.3 mile from town.

If it's not snowed in, you can reach the upstream trailhead at Elk Flats by driving west on Forest Service Road 62. Drive south on Grande Ronde River Road and turn right onto FS 62 in 0.5 mile. After 20 miles turn right on FS 290 and go 0.7 mile to the signed trailhead.

GPS TRAILHEAD COORDINATES:

(Troy) N45° 56.851' W117° 27.267'
(Elk Flats) N45° 54.970' W117° 46.165'

INTRODUCTION

For countless thousands of years, the Wenaha River has been carving a canyon into the lava tablelands of Oregon's Blue Mountains. The result of these relentless efforts is a spectacular 2,000-foot-deep chasm. The scenic mix includes a clear rushing stream, open ponderosa-pine forests, steep grasslands covered with wildflowers, and rugged rock outcrops. The best way to appreciate the river's handiwork is to hike the full length of the Wenaha River Trail—one of Oregon's classic wild-river and canyon tours. But that has been virtually impossible to do in recent years because of the devastation caused by the Grizzly Complex Fire in 2015. Among other things, it knocked out the bridge over Crooked Creek and obliterated trails in much of the area it swept through.

Happily, the Crooked Creek bridge was restored in 2023 as part of continuing trail repair work. Dedicated trail-keepers have made a lot of progress on clearing and restoring the trail at either end, enough that determined bushwhackers are thru-hiking the Wenaha River Trail once again. Maintenance efforts continue, and we're optimistic that the hike will be increasingly enjoyable as time goes on. In the meantime, it's well worth doing an out-and-back hike at least to Crooked Creek, or as far along the trail as you feel comfortable, in order to experience this unique landscape. Although it's only a short distance from much better-known Hells Canyon, the Wenaha River Canyon has a character all its own. True, that character has changed since the fire—most of the once-stately shade trees are gone, but the wildflowers are thicker than ever, and down-canyon views have opened up. Just remember to stay hydrated, bring sun protection, and save this hike for the cooler seasons.

DESCRIPTION

With the cooperation of Mother Nature, this would be an easy, point-to-point, downhill hike. Unfortunately, in the spring (when the lower canyon is at its best), the upper trailhead at Elk Flats is typically snowed in. One solution is to do this trip in October, when the sumac bushes and maples turn color and temperatures have cooled. The other alternative is an out-and-back hike in the spring from the lower trailhead at Troy, which also lets you hike just as far along the trail as you feel like going before turning around.

TIP: If the upper trailhead is open, reverse the route described here to hike downstream from Elk Flats to Troy—a trip that involves almost no elevation gain and ends near a well-loved swimming beach where the Wenaha meets the Grande Ronde River.

For an upstream trip from Troy, begin by gradually dropping to the first of several grassy, river-level flats. This one features a row of pungent lilac bushes and a riot of other wildflowers in spring. The trail alternates between river-level flats and grassy slopes and benches; you walk right into the wildfire burn zone, so there are a lot of snags where there once was a forest of ponderosa pines, but there are also inspiring signs of recovery, as well as breathtaking views down the canyon. The steep slopes and rocky ledges above and beside you continue to put on a display of colorful spring flowers. As the trail goes up the canyon, the canyon walls get steeper and rockier.

TIP: Keep a sharp eye on the ledges above the trail for bighorn sheep—common in this area.

You enter the Wenaha-Tucannon Wilderness at 6 miles. About a quarter mile later is a trail junction and the crossing of Crooked Creek, with its new footbridge as of 2023. It's worth a detour up the Crooked Creek Trail a ways, both to find good camps and to explore the terrain. Be alert for white-tailed deer (found in only a few parts of Oregon), as well as

The Wenaha River

coyotes, porcupines, rattlesnakes, and a wide variety of birds. There have also been bear and cougar sightings here and elsewhere along the trail.

Another 2 miles west is a junction with the steep, switchbacking Hoodoo Trail, popular with anglers seeking river access. There's no bridge at this crossing. The ford is easy in the fall but too dangerous for most hikers in the spring. If you can cross, you'll be rewarded with some excellent views from the trail that climbs the opposite canyon wall.

The main Wenaha River Trail continues its tour upriver to aptly named Fairview Bar—a large, grassy flat with good camps. From Fairview Bar, you can take a recommended side trip north along Smooth Ridge Trail, which climbs the hillside before leveling out and continuing north for 15 miles toward Oregon Butte (a tempting longer-trek opportunity, although the trail is rough in places). About 1.5 miles up this sometimes-steep trail, you reach a huge, dry, grassy slope. Flowers here include phlox, lupine, balsamroot, and clarkia, and the views up the canyon are outstanding.

Back on the Wenaha River Trail, 5 miles upstream from Fairview Bar is the junction with the Cross Canyon Trail, which has dropped to the river from a trailhead on the south rim. Energetic hikers might want to take a side trip up this steep, view-packed trail, although the forest service warns that it may not be maintained. The main river trail continues to fair camps near Rock Creek and a junction.

A potentially outstanding side trip turns right at Rock Creek onto Grizzly Bear Trail, but call ahead to make sure the trail is passable; at last check it hadn't been recently maintained all the way down to the river. The route closely follows the stream for about 0.7 mile and then turns away from the brushy creek and climbs to a switchback on Grizzly Bear Ridge, from where there are some especially photogenic views downstream. This is a great place to spend some time enjoying the river's handiwork and admiring nature's resilience.

Continue upriver on the Wenaha River Trail for 4.7 miles, finally leaving the worst of the burned area behind and reaching Wenaha Forks, where several canyons and their braided streams converge. In this area, Slick Ear Creek, Beaver Creek, and the north and south forks of the Wenaha River all come together to form the main stream. Beavers work these waters, and other wildlife is abundant. Good camps can be found in several places, and a half dozen paths radiate up the various creeks and ridges here, allowing for a variety of interesting side trips.

Wenaha Forks is a good place to leave the main trail, as the next 10 miles follow the much smaller South Fork with increasingly restricted views until reaching Timothy Springs Trailhead, the official end of the Wenaha River Trail. Our recommended exit point is the Elk Flats Trailhead, so cross the South Fork Wenaha River and head south on Elk Flats Trail, climbing a moderately graded trail for 3 miles to a large flat area, then more steeply for 1.5 miles to the trailhead and your waiting vehicle.

POSSIBLE ITINERARY

	CAMP	MILES	ELEVATION GAIN
Day 1	Fairview Bar	9.6	500
Day 2	Wenaha Forks	11.0	1,500
Day 3	Out	4.4	100

18

MINAM RIVER LOOP

RATINGS: Scenery 7 **Solitude** 6 **Difficulty** 7
MILES: 35 (41)
ELEVATION GAIN: 5,300' (5,900')
DAYS: 3–6 (4–6)
SHUTTLE MILEAGE: NA
MAP: Green Trails *Wallowa Mountains*
USUALLY OPEN: June–October
BEST: July
PERMIT: Yes (free self-issued wilderness permit at the trailhead); Northwest Forest Pass required at trailhead
RULES: Maximum group size of 12 people
CONTACT: Wallowa Mountains Office, Wallowa-Whitman National Forest, 541-426-4978, fs.usda.gov/wallowa-whitman

SPECIAL ATTRACTIONS

Diverse scenery, including deep canyons, high ridges, and fine viewpoints; solitude

CHALLENGES

Confusing junctions with unmapped trails, faint trails, heavy horse use

Above: Overlooking Little Minam River

HOW TO GET THERE

From I-84 take Exit 261 in La Grande, and turn right (northeast) onto OR 82. Drive 1.5 miles to a major junction. Go straight (east) on OR 237 and proceed 13.5 miles to Cove. One block after the road makes a 90-degree turn to the right (west), turn left (south) onto French Street, which soon becomes Mill Creek Lane. Remain on this road, which turns to gravel after 3.1 miles and becomes Forest Service Road 6220, and drive another 4.3 miles to the trailhead at the east end of horse-oriented Moss Springs Campground.

GPS TRAILHEAD COORDINATES:

N45° 16.480' W117° 40.754'

INTRODUCTION

Although this western third of the Eagle Cap Wilderness is easier to reach for most Oregonians, who drive from the populous Willamette Valley, it receives far fewer visitors than the central portion of the preserve. The reason for this seeming incongruity is that this part of the wilderness has none of the fish-filled lakes or high granite peaks that draw crowds to other parts of the Wallowa Mountains. Nonetheless, there is still plenty of great scenery, most notably high alpine ridges that boast terrific views, plenty of wildflowers, and the remarkably clear Minam River, which flows through an impressive 3,500-foot-deep forested canyon. In addition, while you probably won't have the trails all to yourself, you also won't have to fight off other backpackers for a good campsite, which is sometimes a problem in the more popular areas to the east.

DESCRIPTION

Start by walking east from the trailhead and soon pick up a dusty, horse-pounded trail that goes through a pleasant forest of western larches, mountain hemlocks, Engelmann spruces, lodgepole pines, and subalpine firs. After only 70 yards, the trail splits at the start of the loop.

A counterclockwise tour is preferable because it avoids a long climb out of the Minam River Canyon, so bear right, following signs to Upper Little Minam River (Lackeys Hole Trail on some maps/signs). For 1.5 miles you gradually lose elevation in four lazy switchbacks to the bottom of the canyon of the Little Minam River. Here you hop over a tiny creek and then walk 0.5 mile through an open lodgepole pine forest to a junction with the Art Garrett Trail. Go straight and, 100 yards later, make a log crossing of clear Dobbin Creek. Just 50 yards later is a nice campsite and another junction, this time with Crib Point Trail. Veer left and immediately cross the gravel-strewn Little Minam River on a log.

The route now goes upstream, gradually gaining elevation through a mix of forest and small meadows. In early July these meadows are filled with tall wildflowers, including false hellebores, mariposa lilies, horsemint, sunflowers, pink geraniums, and bluebells. About 0.8 mile from the crossing of the Little Minam River, go straight at a confusing and unmapped junction with an unofficial horse trail that goes uphill to the left. Just 0.5 mile farther, go straight again at a junction with another unmapped equestrian trail, this one an unofficial shortcut to Jim White Ridge.

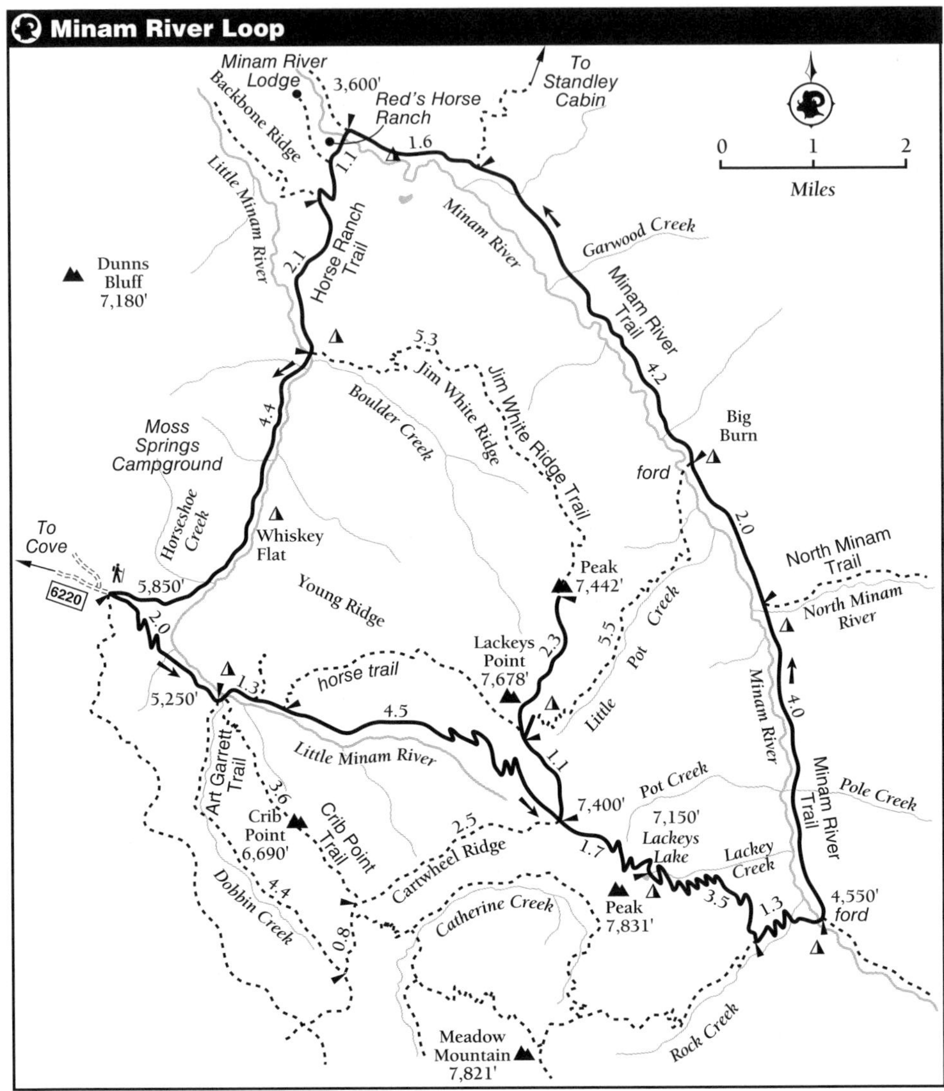

WARNING: These are only the first of many unofficial horse trails that you will encounter on this trip. Confusingly, many of these paths appear to get more use than the official U.S. Forest Service trails. Keep your map and GPS handy and consult them often to ensure that you are headed in the proper direction.

After these junctions, the trail gradually pulls away from the river (now just a creek), ascending at a steady but moderate grade on a partly forested hillside. Several tiny side creeks provide water on this long 2,200-foot climb. About one-third of the way up, you enter the Little Minam Burn, a decades-old blaze that left many snags but opened up fine views of the high ridges flanking this canyon. The most interesting of these ridges lies straight ahead to the southeast, tempting hikers with its open, rounded slopes that promise fine views. This enticing ridge is your goal, but it is still a long way up, so settle in for a lengthy trudge. Six switchbacks add variety along the way, but the increasingly excellent scenery is what really keeps you going. Vistas of the nearby ridges and the distant Grande Ronde Valley and Elkhorn and Blue Mountains are more impressive with each upward step. In July wildflowers compete with the views for your attention. Expect colorful displays of Sitka valerian, Indian paintbrush, buckwheat, lupine, and scarlet gilia. The large sloping meadows here seem even more expansive because many of the trees were burned in the Little Minam Fire. At 7.8 miles from the trailhead, you reach a four-way junction marked by a prominent post just below the top of Cartwheel Ridge.

Here you have a choice. The recommended longer trail goes straight, heading for Lackeys Lake and the Minam River. If you prefer a shorter, 21-mile loop that skips the Minam River, you can take the Jim White Ridge Trail to the left. Even if you choose the longer loop, however, take a day to explore the first few miles of Jim White Ridge, because this area features terrific wildflower displays and outstanding views. So turn left (north) and ramble up and down through rolling alpine meadows that feature the usual assortment of high-elevation flora and fauna. Of the latter, look for elk lounging in the meadows, coyotes trotting by in search of ground squirrels, and mountain bluebirds and Clark's nutcrackers flying overhead. Plant life here includes pink heather, whitebark pines, and numerous grasses and small wildflowers. At 1.1 miles from the four-way junction, there is a signed junction with the Little Pot Creek Trail.

TIP: Just 0.1 mile down the Little Pot Creek Trail is an excellent campsite on a scenic little bench beside a small spring. This makes a good base camp for exploring Jim White Ridge.

WARNING: If you look at the map, the Little Pot Creek Trail appears to be a good shortcut to the Minam River. This route, however, is often sketchy and involves a tricky ford of the river at the end. The longer trail via Lackeys Lake, described below, is a much better option.

About 100 yards past the Little Pot Creek junction, the Jim White Ridge Trail comes to a fork at a cairn. The unofficial horse trail to the left is the route mentioned earlier that drops to the Little Minam River Trail at the unsigned junction 1.3 miles from the crossing of that stream. The less obvious and lesser-used official trail goes right (uphill) from the cairn. This sketchy but wildly scenic path along Jim White Ridge soon climbs to nearly the top of 7,678-foot Lackeys Point and then drops briefly but steeply on a rocky trail (not recommended for livestock) before going up and down along the ridge to the north. There are acres of flowers here in July and terrific views in all directions. You can hike for several miles, but a logical turnaround point is a high viewpoint about 2 miles past Lackeys Point.

Returning to the four-way junction on Cartwheel Ridge, those taking the recommended loop should go southeast and, 0.1 mile later, top the rounded ridge at a point featuring fine vistas southwest down to the forests and meadows beside Catherine Creek, nearly 2,000 feet below. The often narrow but mostly level trail then cuts across the steep slopes on the southwest side of a ridge for 0.7 mile before crossing over to the northeastern side of this ridge. Here views shift to the high snowy peaks of the central Wallowa Mountains towering above the deep chasm of Minam River Canyon. From here four downhill switchbacks and a gently descending traverse of a mostly wooded slope take you down to a small saddle over a spur ridge. You then drop briefly in one switchback to a crossing of Lackey

Creek just below marshy and hard-to-see Lackeys Lake. Nice camps can be found above the east side of this pretty little lake, but the water is too shallow for fish.

From the lake the path goes steadily downhill, losing 2,600 feet on its way to the bottom of the Minam River Canyon. Fortunately, the route is well graded, but anyone taking this loop in the opposite direction will find the climb very tiring. Initially, the descent is through a sloping meadow immediately below the lake. Then the trail crosses Lackey Creek a couple of times and enters forest. A dozen switchbacks over the next 3.5 miles take you to an unsigned junction with the lightly used trail to Meadow Mountain and North Catherine Creek. Go left (downhill) and make 19 short switchbacks in 1.1 miles to an aging wooden bridge over Rock Creek. Another 0.2 mile of downhill leads to a small meadow with an inviting campsite just before a ford of the crystal-clear Minam River. The water here is usually over knee-deep and quite cold, but the ford is not dangerous. Just 75 yards after the ford is a junction with the Minam River Trail.

Turn left and walk downstream on a trail that includes some minor uphill sections but that is generally a long, gradual descent that never strays far from the winding Minam River. The forest and shrubbery near the water are surprisingly lush and include ponderosa pines, Pacific yews, and thimbleberries, all species that prefer these lower elevations to the high ridges. The trail also skirts the edge of the 2022 Sturgill Fire, of which there are some signs on your right. After crossing Pole Creek on a log, you continue descending, mostly in forest, but with many lovely views of the river with high ridges rising in the background. At 4 miles from where you started on the Minam River Trail is a good camp below the trail, just before a crossing of the North Minam River. (There was a bridge, but it's been declared unsafe and scheduled for removal—go 15 feet upstream to ford.) About 100 yards later is a junction with the North Minam Trail, where you go straight.

About 2 miles past the North Minam junction, you come to a lovely meadow named, for no obvious reason, Big Burn, with nice camps and a cairn marking the junction with the Little Pot Creek Trail. The tread of this side trail is so faint that it is hard to locate. Go straight and, for the next 4.2 miles, spend most of your time well away from the river and, illogically, seeming to go uphill. The forest scenery is rather mundane, though it is more varied as large cottonwoods now grow in the bottomlands near the river. At the end of this section, go straight at a junction with a faint trail to Standley Cabin and then return to the banks of the now quite large Minam River.

TIP: A couple of very nice, secluded camps are along the river here, which you can reach via unsigned use paths that drop down to the left.

About 1.6 miles from the Standley Cabin junction is an intersection with the Horse Ranch Trail. Turn left, immediately cross an elaborately large wooden bridge over the river, and then climb briefly to the huge meadow holding the buildings, fences, and corrals of historic Red's Horse Ranch (now run by the U.S. Forest Service). The trail goes through a gate (cleverly latched in place with horseshoes) and then across a large pasture, part of which is mowed and used as a wilderness airstrip.

NOTE: Be sure to close all gates behind you to keep the horses from straying.

At the west end of the meadow, or pasture, you go through another gate and immediately come to a junction with a spur trail to the privately owned Minam River Lodge.

This rustic but very comfortable facility offers cabin accommodations, hearty homemade meals, and a variety of outdoor-oriented activities. If you are interested in staying here as part of your trip, contact the lodge at minam-lodge.com (booking ahead is essential).

After the Minam River Lodge junction, you return to the forest, some of which has been partially burned, and begin a 700-foot climb to the top of narrow Backbone Ridge. Most of this climb is a long traverse, though there are two switchbacks as you approach the top. Just 0.1 mile past the top of the ridge is a junction with the Little Minam River Trail, which goes downhill and sharply to the right. You go straight and continue uphill, now on the west side of the ridge, before finally leveling off and then contouring until you meet up with the Little Minam River. About 2.1 miles from the last junction is a spacious but horsey campsite at the junction with the Jim White Ridge Trail. This is where you rejoin the main route if you took the shorter, 21-mile loop mentioned earlier.

Go right at the junction, crossing the Little Minam on a wooden bridge, and then follow that sparkling river upstream. This clear, rushing stream is a haven for dippers, chunky little gray birds that live along mountain streams and sing all year long. Depending on the time of year, you might also see an astounding variety of fungi along the trail. About 2.2 miles after the bridge is an excellent campsite on your left at a place called Whiskey Flat. From here, you follow the river another 0.7 mile before crossing Horseshoe Creek on a bridge and then climbing away from the water across open, sunny slopes with blooming snowberry bushes in July and nice views up the Little Minam River's canyon. After 1.5 miles of climbing, you return to the Moss Springs Trailhead and your car.

POSSIBLE ITINERARY

	CAMP	MILES	ELEVATION GAIN
Day 1	Little Pot Creek Camp	8.9	2,400'
Day 2	Minam River (after day hike out Jim White Ridge)	12.3	900'
Day 3	Minam River before Red's Horse Ranch	11.2	200'
Day 4	Out	8.2	2,400'

19

BEAR CREEK LOOP

RATINGS: Scenery 8 **Solitude** 8 **Difficulty** 8
MILES: 39 (40)
ELEVATION GAIN: 6,300' (6,800')
DAYS: 3–6 (4–6)
SHUTTLE MILEAGE: NA
MAP: Green Trails *Wallowa Mountains*
USUALLY OPEN: July–October
BEST: Mid-July
PERMIT: Yes (free at the trailhead); Northwest Forest Pass required at trailhead
RULES: Maximum group size of 12 people; no camping within 50 yards of spring by Standley Cabin
CONTACT: Wallowa Mountains Office, Wallowa-Whitman National Forest, 541-426-4978, fs.usda.gov/wallowa-whitman

SPECIAL ATTRACTIONS

Spectacular alpine ridge, wildlife, solitude

CHALLENGES

Faint trail that often disappears, rugged hiking

Above: Minam River above Red's Horse Ranch
photographed by Douglas Lorain

HOW TO GET THERE

From I-84 take Exit 261 in La Grande, and turn right (east) onto OR 82. In 1.4 miles turn left (north) to remain on OR 82. Go 17.7 miles and turn right (east) to again remain on OR 82. Drive 25.8 miles to the town of Wallowa. Turn right (west) onto West Fifth Street, following signs for Boundary Campground, and drive 0.3 mile. Turn left (south) onto Bear Creek Road. Follow Bear Creek Road for 7.5 miles, after which it becomes Forest Service Road 8250 and transitions from paved to well graveled. Then turn right (south) onto FS 040 and follow it 0.8 mile to the trailhead at the south end of Boundary Campground.

GPS TRAILHEAD COORDINATES:

N45° 28.378' W117° 33.495'

INTRODUCTION

Tucked away in a lesser-used corner of the Wallowa Mountains, this loop provides an excellent opportunity for experienced hikers to explore some outstanding country, see plenty of wildlife, and enjoy lonesome trails. Though there is only one lake along the way, anglers have ample opportunity to try their luck in catching Bear Creek's many brook and rainbow trout. (Artificial flies or lures are required, and any bull trout must be released unharmed.) The hike also features two historical log cabins, both of which are worth exploring. This trip's main attraction, however, at least from a scenery standpoint, is the spectacular hike along Washboard Ridge, one of the most outstanding ridge walks in Oregon. Although the vistas are awe-inspiring, the hike is quite rugged, so only fit hikers should consider this trip.

DESCRIPTION

The well-used Bear Creek Trail travels south, paralleling the cascading waters of boulder-strewn Bear Creek through an open forest of western larches, Engelmann spruces, grand firs, ponderosa pines, and Douglas firs. A few stately black cottonwoods—along with several shrubs, including wild rose, thimbleberry, snowberry, alder, birch, and vine maple—grow near the stream. After 0.2 mile cross the creek on a bridge beneath moss-draped cliffs. The trail then closely follows the stream for almost 1 mile through dense riparian vegetation. The path next climbs a bit to a cliff-edged bluff overlooking the stream before dropping to a pleasant creekside campsite at 1.8 miles.

At 2.1 miles you hop over the trickle of water in Baker Gulch, after which you gradually ascend in open forest with occasional glimpses of the wooded ridges to the south and west. By 3.3 miles you drop back down to Bear Creek and pass two good campsites. Then it's another mile to a large meadow with a cluster of landmarks: first a junction with the Goat Creek Trail (go straight), then a bridge over that trail's namesake creek, and finally a spacious and inviting camping area in the trees at the meadow's south end. Just 0.4 mile past this camp is an unsigned but obvious spur trail that goes right 150 yards to the beautifully built log structure of the old Bear Creek Guard Station. This historical cabin is now locked, but good camps are nearby, and use trails lead to Bear Creek for water.

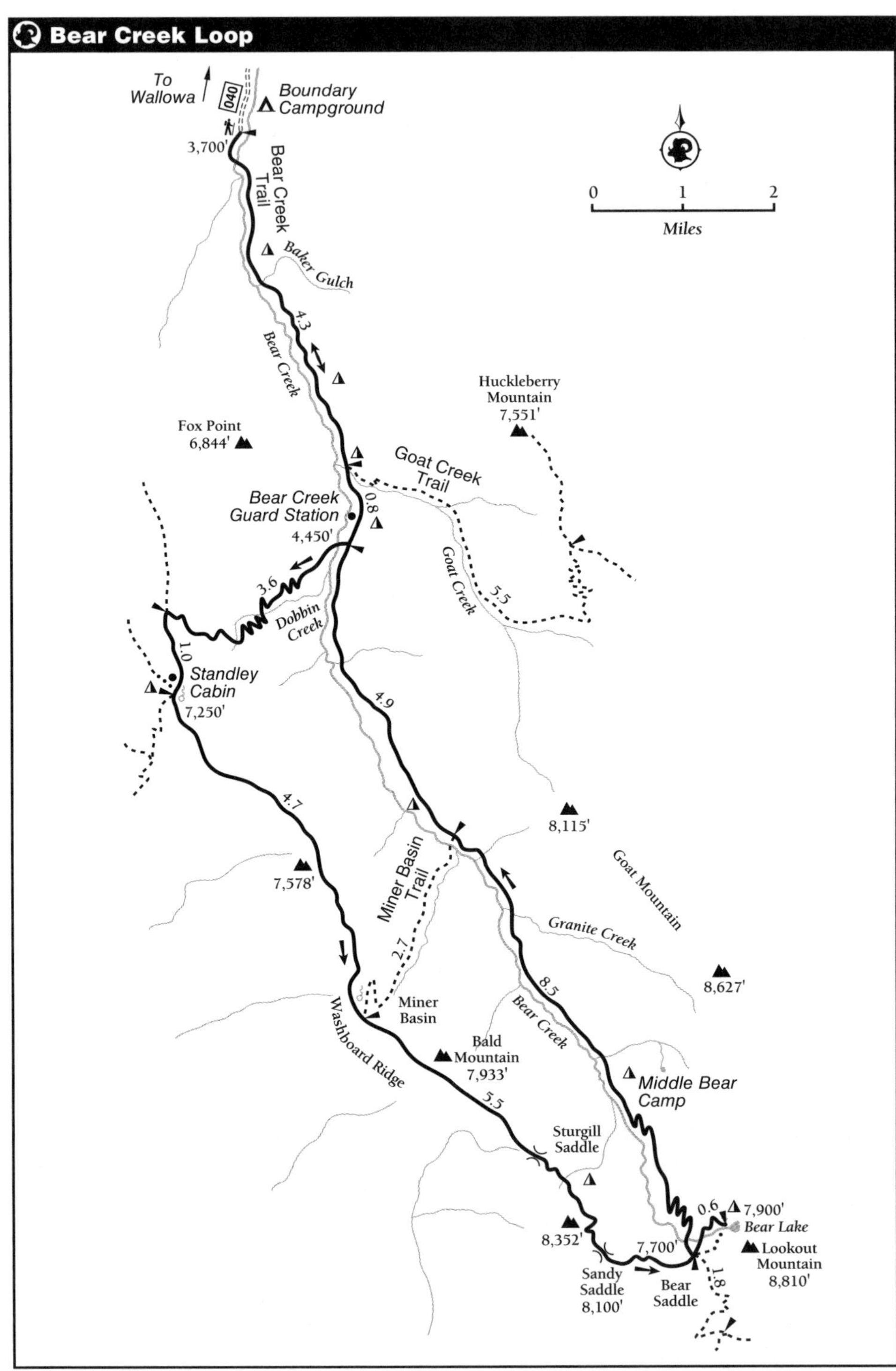
Bear Creek Loop
To Wallowa
040
Boundary Campground
3,700'
Bear Creek Trail
Baker Gulch
4.3
Bear Creek
Huckleberry Mountain 7,551'
Fox Point 6,844'
Goat Creek Trail
Bear Creek Guard Station
4,450'
0.8
Goat Creek
5.5
3.6
Dobbin Creek
1.0
Standley Cabin
7,250'
4.9
4.7
8,115'
Goat Mountain
Miner Basin Trail
7,578'
Granite Creek
2.7
8,627'
Miner Basin
Washboard Ridge
8.5
Bear Creek
Bald Mountain 7,933'
Middle Bear Camp
5.5
Sturgill Saddle
0.6
7,900'
Bear Lake
8,352'
7,700'
Lookout Mountain 8,810'
Sandy Saddle 8,100'
Bear Saddle
1.8
0
1
2
Miles

Back on the Bear Creek Trail, it's another 0.4 mile before you come to a junction at the start of the loop. Turn right and, 120 yards later, encounter an easy ford of Bear Creek, which after mid-July probably won't even get your ankles wet.

To this point the hike has been very easy, but the gentle creekside ramble is now over, as you rapidly ascend the western side of Bear Creek Canyon. The mostly open slopes here are surprisingly dry, hosting both western juniper and mountain mahogany, species that are normally found in the desert mountains of southeastern Oregon, not in the relatively wet Wallowa Mountains. In addition to botanical interest, these slopes provide nice views of the Bear Creek drainage and the high peaks at the stream's headwaters.

The first mile of steady uphill includes six switchbacks to ease the steepness somewhat, but the ascent is still a challenge for both thighs and calves. At 1.4 miles from the Bear Creek ford, you cross Dobbin Creek, whose cool, rapidly falling waters are a welcome relief from the heat of the climb. The next mile uses numerous short switchbacks to climb through a shady forest, where the trail is often overgrown with a mix of thimbleberry, gooseberry, currant, bracken fern, tall larkspur, coneflower, cow parsnip, bluebell, false Solomon's seal, and (beware) stinging nettle. The uphill is unrelenting, but the shade makes things more comfortable. That shady comfort comes to an abrupt halt at 2.4 miles from Bear Creek when you enter an area still scarred by the old Fox Point Fire.

Look for abundant July blossoms of false hellebore, aster, Lewis's monkeyflower, penstemon, pearly everlasting, and Indian paintbrush, among other wildflowers taking advantage of the sunshine here. After a little less than 1 mile of uphill walking through the burn, you pass a marshy pond backed by a red-tinged ridge. You then climb a bit more before finally returning to unburned forest shortly before a junction.

Turn left on a well-used trail and go gradually uphill 1 mile through forest and rolling ridgetop meadows to Standley Cabin. This quaint log cabin, which formerly served as a U.S. Forest Service guard station, is now locked, but it is fun to poke around the outside and take pictures. A tiny but reliable spring nearby feeds a creek that flows through a lush green meadow. Camping is prohibited within 50 yards of the spring, but plenty of legal sites are nearby.

About 0.1 mile south of Standley Cabin the trail forks. Bear left, following signs to Upper Bear Creek, and begin what is perhaps the most magnificent ridge walk in Oregon. Following Washboard Ridge for its entire length, the route starts high and remains so, never dipping below 7,300 feet and topping out at more than 8,000. The views are tremendous, especially west across the great depths of the Minam River Canyon to the distant Elkhorn Mountains, and southeast to the highest peaks of the Wallowa Mountains. Trees rarely block the vista, with only a few scattered whitebark pines, subalpine firs, and mountain hemlocks. Gentle breezes (and occasionally strong winds) help to keep you comfortable in the hot sun and create waves in the acres of grasses and wildflowers. And there are plenty of wildflowers to blow around, with fine displays of lupine, Cusick's speedwell, buckwheat, penstemon, campion, yarrow, orange mountain dandelion, and other blossoms that usually peak in mid-July. All in all, it is great fun. But that fun is reserved for hardy and experienced backpackers because the trail is often very faint, frequently disappearing in the meadows, and Washboard Ridge is true to its name, with lots of ups and downs. The trail is also steep and narrow in places, making it dangerous for stock, though horses sometimes use it.

The first mile is all uphill on the west side of the ridge, as the trail ascends a huge meadow where the tread soon disappears. A few large cairns guide you, but they are surprisingly hard to find. The best plan is to angle uphill to the southeast until you meet the tread again just below the ridgecrest. Now on clearer trail, descend a steep section with impressive views of the knife-edge ridge ahead and the Minam River Canyon below. Wildlife frequent this area. Two common species to look for include Rocky Mountain elk and calliope hummingbirds—the first is one of Oregon's largest wild mammals, and the latter its smallest bird. You can also expect families of blue grouse to suddenly flush up from your feet, often in a startling flurry of activity.

The next 2 miles stay almost exclusively on the west side of the ridge, with easterly views only at the few places where you hit saddles. The most notable feature of this section, however, is that it can be rather scary for hikers who are afraid of heights. In several places, the rocky and dangerously sloping trail cuts across dizzying ledges that are frequently no more than a foot across. So even though the views are distracting, keep a close eye on your footing. After negotiating this section, an easier (but no less scenic) segment follows as the path goes through long grassy saddles and rolling ridgetop meadows.

At 4.8 miles from Standley Cabin, you pass 50 feet above a tiny spring (the first potential water along the ridge) and, 30 yards later, come to a junction with the Miner Basin Trail. Go straight and then cut across the steep slopes of Bald Mountain before traversing a large sloping meadow, where, once again, the tread fades away. The proper route goes downhill and then traverses a long basin on the west side of Washboard Ridge. If you lose the tread, simply head toward Sturgill Saddle, an obvious low point in the ridge a little more than 1 mile to the southeast. Once you are there, the tread becomes obvious again as it drops into an exceptionally scenic alpine basin beneath an unnamed 8,352-foot peak. Alpine buttercup, Cusick's speedwell, pink heather, and other alpine wildflowers seem to be everywhere, and small creeks provide much-needed water. There are several places to camp here, and you will probably have the basin all to yourself.

From the south end of this basin, the trail climbs 500 feet to 8,100-foot Sandy Saddle and then turns left (east) and follows a ridge. The route initially contours but soon begins descending, steeply at times, to a meadow-filled saddle. This place has no official name, but it is locally referred to as Bear Saddle. Though the trail disappears here, it is easy to make your way east across the meadow to an obvious cairn marking the junction with Bear Creek Trail.

Several trails converge at this remote location. To the right (south), hikers with extra time could spend several days exploring such worthwhile destinations as Wilson Basin and North Minam Meadows. Another option is to go straight (east) on an initially promising use path that heads uphill toward Bear Lake. Unfortunately, this trail soon disappears, forcing hikers to make a rather rugged scramble to that lake. Two trails go to the left at Bear Saddle, neither of which is initially easy to see. The one angling slightly left is the official trail to Bear Lake. The tread of this path becomes obvious about 100 feet from the junction as it contours and then climbs sharply for 0.6 mile to the shores of clear, 20-foot-deep Bear Lake. This lovely 10-acre pool is ideal for fishing (it's filled with hungry brook trout), swimming (if you don't mind chilly water), and camping (with a good site above the north side of the outlet creek).

The return route of the recommended loop goes sharply left at the Bear Saddle junction. The tread is initially hidden in meadow but becomes obvious after about 50 yards. After 0.2 mile the trail crosses the outlet of Bear Lake and then descends 15 well-graded switchbacks through an area covered with white granite boulders to the bottom of Bear Creek Canyon. For the next 1.5 miles the trail stays on the forested hillside above the stream, though from time to time you can see meadows below you beside the creek.

TIP: Look for herds of elk in these meadows, especially early in the morning.

After this traverse, four lazy switchbacks take you down to the creek and, at 4.5 miles from Bear Saddle, to Middle Bear Camp, a nice spot in the trees at the south end of a small but particularly inviting meadow.

Below Middle Bear Camp the hiking is easy and enjoyable, though views are infrequent through the forest. Occasional meadows provide westward vistas to Washboard Ridge, the rugged high points of which you will recognize from earlier in the trip. A little more than 2 miles below Middle Bear Camp is a rock-hop crossing of Granite Creek, after which you continue mostly downhill, often in large sloping meadows. Deer frequently browse in these meadows, and ground squirrels squeak loud alarms at your passing. In the forested sections between the meadows, look for snowshoe hares bounding away with their summer-brown bodies and flashing white back feet.

At 8.5 miles from Bear Saddle, you pass two small cairns on your left that mark the junction with Miner Basin Trail. Go straight on the main trail, and a little less than 1 mile later, pass two unsigned trails that drop to pleasant campsites near Bear Creek. At 13.4 miles from Bear Saddle, though the distance seems less than that with all the easy downhill, you return to the junction with the trail to Standley Cabin and the close of your loop. Go straight and retrace your steps back to your car.

POSSIBLE ITINERARY

	CAMP	MILES	ELEVATION GAIN
Day 1	Standley Cabin	9.6	3,700'
Day 2	Basin below Sturgill Saddle	8.0	1,800'
Day 3	Middle Bear Camp (with side trip to Bear Lake)	8.0	1,000'
Day 4	Out	14.0	300'

20

LOSTINE–MINAM LOOP

RATINGS: Scenery 9 **Solitude** 4 **Difficulty** 6
MILES: 43 (51)
ELEVATION GAIN: 8,700' (11,000')
DAYS: 4–6 (5–8)
SHUTTLE MILEAGE: NA
MAP: Green Trails *Wallowa Mountains*
USUALLY OPEN: July–October
BEST: Late July–September
PERMITS: Yes (free, self-issued at trailhead); Northwest Forest Pass required at Two Pan Trailhead
RULES: No fires within 0.25 mile of Chimney, Laverty, Mirror, Moccasin, Steamboat, or Swamp Lakes; maximum group size of 6 people/9 stock in Lakes Basin and at Minam and Blue Lakes
CONTACT: Wallowa Mountains Office, Wallowa-Whitman National Forest, 541-426-4978, fs.usda.gov/wallowa-whitman

SPECIAL ATTRACTIONS

Great mountain scenery

CHALLENGES

Crowded in spots, short road walk, unbridged stream crossings, thunderstorms

Above: Lostine River Trail at Two Pan Trailhead

HOW TO GET THERE

From I-84 take Exit 261 in La Grande, and turn right (east) onto OR 82. In 1.4 miles turn left (north) to remain on OR 82. Go 17.7 miles and turn right (east) to again remain on OR 82. Drive 34.2 miles to the town of Lostine. Continue straight (south) on Lostine River Road, signed LOSTINE RIVER CAMPGROUNDS. The road turns to gravel after 7 miles and becomes Forest Service Road 8210/Upper Lostine Road. The route gets rougher and bumpier as it goes up the canyon but remains passable for passenger cars. Reach the Bowman Trailhead 7.7 miles after the road turns to gravel. If you have two cars, leave one here and the other 3.3 miles farther south at the spacious Two Pan Trailhead.

GPS TRAILHEAD COORDINATES:

(Two Pan) N45° 15.018' W117° 22.571'

(Bowman) N45° 17.639' W117° 23.681'

INTRODUCTION

This is one of several classic loop hikes in the Wallowa Mountains. Like the others, this one includes all the major attractions of this wonderful range. There are mountain lakes, alpine passes, wildflower-filled meadows, clear streams, and granite peaks. These features make this hike fairly popular, but it's not as crowded as the Wallowa River Loop (Trip 21). For those with less time or ambition, this route lends itself nicely to a shorter version. In fact, the most common way this trip is done skips East Lostine Canyon and Minam Lake and heads directly up the West Lostine River to the Copper Creek Trail. Without side trips, this alternate loop is only about 32 miles long. Don't forget your fishing gear (lots of lake and stream fishing is available); binoculars (to search for elk, bighorn sheep, and mountain goats); swimsuit; and, most of all, your camera (the scenery is terrific).

DESCRIPTION

From Two Pan Trailhead, hike up the trail 0.1 mile to a junction. The short version of this loop goes to the right. For a longer, more satisfying trip, keep left on the popular East Fork Lostine River Trail. The wide path makes a moderately steep climb through forests for the first 2.5 miles as it ascends toward the stream's high glacial valley. Views become more impressive near the top of the climb, especially of imposing Hurricane Divide to the east. All that climbing is rewarded when you enter the impressive glacier-carved upper East Lostine River Valley. Jagged ridges rise steeply on either side, while the crystalline river flows lazily through wildflower meadows on the valley floor. At the 3.2-mile point, a large, swampy, wide spot in the stream goes by the name of Lost "Lake."

For the next several miles, the path remains nearly level as it wanders up this beautiful valley.

TIP: Look for elk, deer, and mountain goats in this area, especially in the early morning and evening.

You are walking through a classic U-shaped glacial canyon, which adds geologic interest to the fine scenery. The trail travels through a delightful mix of open forests, meadows, and boulder fields. At the head of the valley looms the distinctive shape of Eagle Cap.

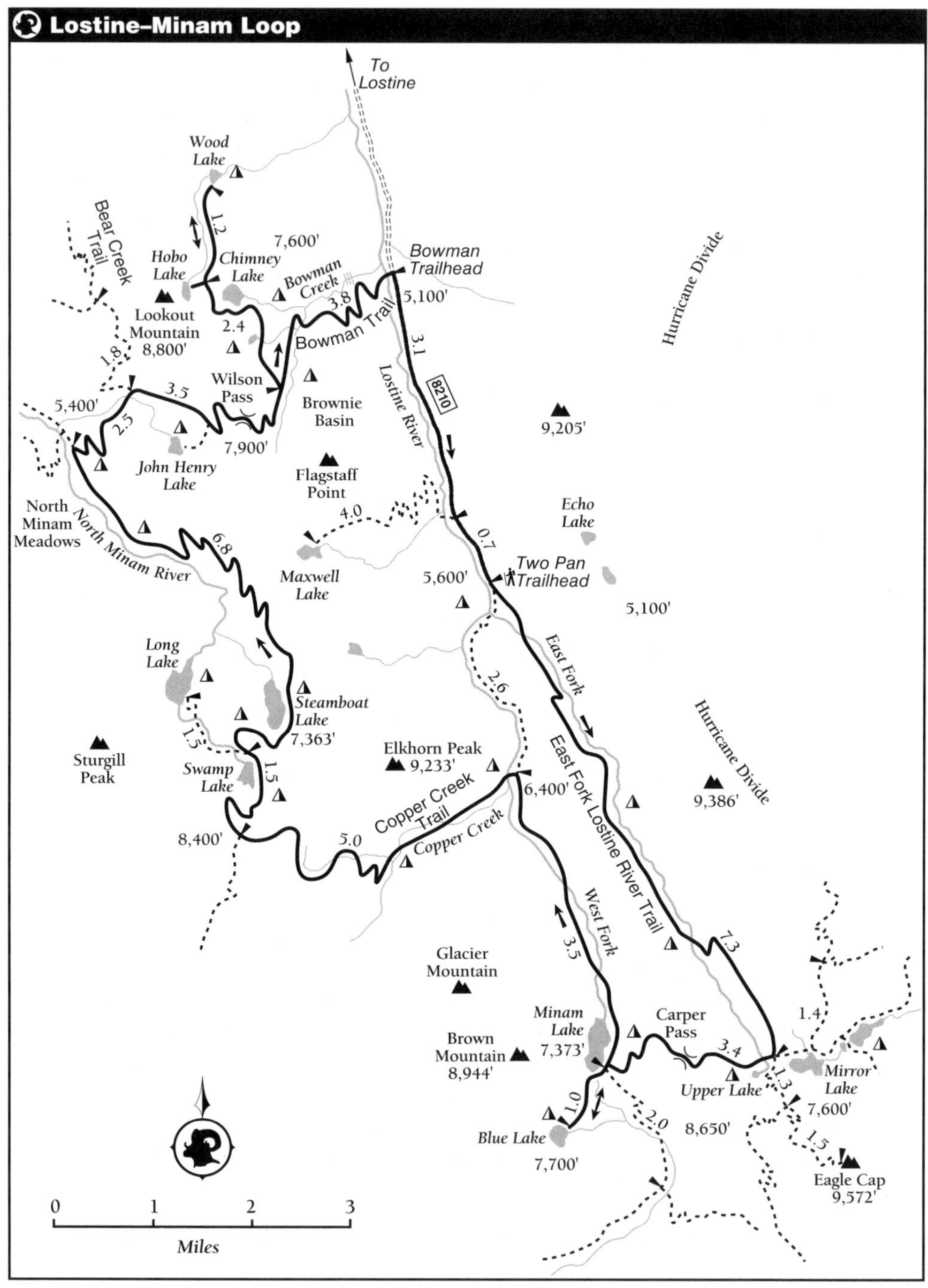

Cross the stream near the head of the valley and increase the rate of your climb as you switchback through open forests to a four-way junction. Most visitors turn left here to visit lovely Mirror Lake—well worth a side trip. Your route, however, turns right, passing below Upper Lake and providing excellent views down the East Lostine Canyon. If you choose to camp in this popular but fragile basin, be even more careful than usual to leave no trace. The trail now begins a moderately steep climb toward Carper Pass. Frequent views of Eagle Cap, resembling Yosemite's Half Dome from this angle, make the climb more of a joy than a strain. As expected, the views from the pass are exceptional. From the high point, the trail makes a rolling descent before dropping more consistently to the south end of large Minam Lake.

An earthen dam blocks this lake's former outlet to the south, so it now drains principally north into the West Lostine River. Aptly named Brown Mountain dominates the skyline to the west.

TIP: To visit lovely Blue Lake, cross the dam and follow a trail 1 mile to this round jewel below a serrated ridge of granite peaks. The lake's outlet is the source of the Minam River.

To continue your tour, turn north as the trail loops around the east shore of Minam Lake and then gradually descends to the valley of the West Lostine River. If the scenery in the East Lostine Valley rates a 10, then the West Lostine has to be a 9.9. You cross the stream twice as you wind down through the meadows and forests of this lovely valley. Not all the crossings have bridges, so be prepared to wade (chilly but not dangerous).

About 3.5 miles from Minam Lake is a poorly marked junction at a talus slope. Turn left on the Copper Creek Trail to a ford of the West Lostine River. Good camps are in the meadows nearby. The trail then begins to climb through the valley of Copper Creek, crossing the stream four times along the way.

WARNING: Through July these crossings will be wet and sometimes treacherous.

Though the climb is moderate in grade, it seems to go on forever. However, the excellent scenery is ample compensation. Camps are abundant in this section of bouldery areas and meadows, with a terrific variety of wildflowers throughout the summer.

Eventually the trail veers away from the creek and climbs to a high, sandy plateau. Swamp Lake lies in the basin to the right. More distant views extend to the Matterhorn, Eagle Cap, and the other distinctive peaks of this range. Now the trail gradually loses a bit of elevation to a junction, where you turn right. This route makes a long, switchbacking descent into the meadowy basin holding Swamp Lake, which has good camps near the north end. The south end of this irregularly shaped pool is an intricate mix of meadows, creeks, and small ponds that looks like a Japanese garden.

TIP: A side trail drops from here to large Long Lake, which features secluded camps and good fishing but has only limited views.

To continue your tour, top a low saddle near two small ponds (good camps) and enjoy a nice view down to Steamboat Lake. The route makes a series of switchbacks down a mostly open slope to the south end of this lake, where the best camps are along the east shore. A large rock island apparently looked like a steamboat to imaginative early travelers. The trail veers away from Steamboat Lake over a low rise before descending through a meadow to an overlook of the North Minam River Canyon. For the next few miles, the trail leads down into this canyon in a series of irregular switchbacks over semi-open terrain. Numerous side creeks provide ample water. Several good campsites highlight the last couple of miles of the descent as the trail follows an attractive stream to spacious North Minam Meadows.

TIP: Though the trail skirts this large meadow, it is worthwhile to walk over for a visit.

Near the north end of the meadow, you turn right at a junction with the Bowman Trail. Climb in a series of moderately steep switchbacks, enjoying several nice views down to North Minam Meadows along the way. You pass an unseen waterfall and then reach a junction with the Bear Creek Trail. Keep right, and 1.2 miles later look for the unsigned and unmaintained path to John Henry Lake. The lake, 0.5 mile away, features nice camps.

The main trail climbs to Wilson Pass, which offers an excellent view to the east of Twin Peaks and the Hurricane Divide. Your route then switchbacks down to the trees above Brownie Basin, a long, scenic meadow with a lovely setting that is well worth a visit. The trail goes north along the slope above the meadow to a junction. Here you have the option of either heading directly out to your car or investing a bit more time and energy in the worthwhile side trip to Chimney and Hobo Lakes.

To do the side trip, keep left at the junction, traverse a view-packed slope to Laverty Lake, and then round a ridge to large and beautiful Chimney Lake. Granite peaks rise to the west, and two small islands add to the scene. To reach the more alpine setting of Hobo Lake, climb above Chimney Lake to a saddle. From here turn left at a junction and climb over rocky meadows to the high basin holding Hobo Lake.

TIP: Ambitious hikers can also make the cross-country scramble to overlooks atop Lookout Mountain and take the trail down to the lovely meadow basin holding Wood Lake.

Back at Brownie Basin, the well-graded trail crosses Bowman Creek and then drops in long gentle switchbacks to FS 8210/Upper Lostine Road. Near the bottom, a nice sloping waterfall on the creek adds scenic interest. From the Bowman Trailhead, it's an easy 3.8-mile walk up the road to Two Pan Trailhead and your car. (So easy, in fact, that you may be able to talk your companion into doing the extra walk while you volunteer for the difficult task of guarding the packs and daydreaming about this wonderful trip.)

POSSIBLE ITINERARY

	CAMP	MILES	ELEVATION GAIN
Day 1	Mirror Lake	7.3	2,100'
Day 2	Minam Lake (with side trip to Blue Lake)	5.4	1,500'
Day 3	Swamp Lake	10.0	2,200'
Day 4	John Henry Lake	11.1	2,000'
Day 5	Brownie Basin (with side trip to Chimney, Hobo, and Wood Lakes)	9.7	2,600'
Day 6	Out (with road walk to Two Pan Trailhead)	7.6	600'

21 WALLOWA RIVER LOOP

RATINGS: Scenery 10 **Solitude** 2 **Difficulty** 7
MILES: 36 (54)
ELEVATION GAIN: 7,100' (11,700')
DAYS: 4–5 (5–10)
SHUTTLE MILEAGE: NA
MAP: Green Trails *Wallowa Mountains*
USUALLY OPEN: July–October
BEST: Late July and September
PERMITS: Yes (free and self-issued)
RULES: No fires within 0.25 mile of Glacier, Mirror, Moccasin, or Upper Lakes; maximum group size of 6 people/9 stock in Lakes Basin and at Ice Lake
CONTACT: Wallowa Mountains Office, Wallowa-Whitman National Forest, 541-426-4978, fs.usda.gov/wallowa-whitman

SPECIAL ATTRACTIONS

Stunning mountain scenery

CHALLENGES

Crowded, thunderstorms, horse-pounded trails

Above: Overlooking Wallowa Lake from the trail

Wallowa River Loop

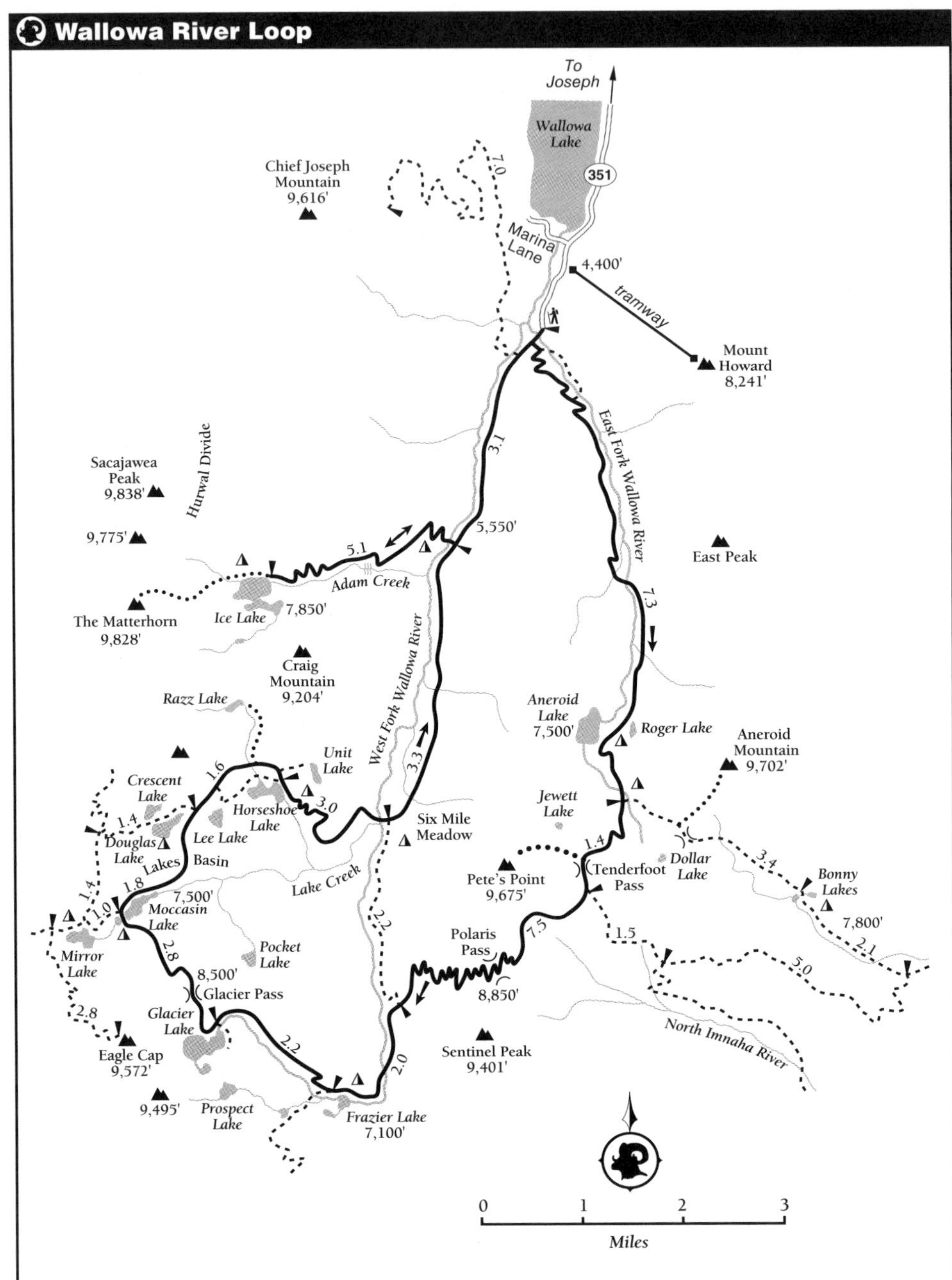

HOW TO GET THERE

From I-84 take Exit 261 in La Grande, and turn right (east) onto OR 82. In 1.4 miles turn left (north) to remain on OR 82. Go 17.7 miles and turn right (east) to again remain on OR 82. Drive 44.2 miles to the town of Enterprise. Turn right (south) onto OR 82, and go 6.3 miles to Joseph. OR 82 becomes OR 351; continue 6.9 miles past the south end of Wallowa Lake to the end of the road. Parking is available on the side of the road.

GPS TRAILHEAD COORDINATES:

N45° 16.034' W117° 12.765'

INTRODUCTION

This trip features the best scenery in the most beautiful mountains in Oregon. Crystal-clear lakes and streams, meadows filled with wildflowers, glacier-polished white granite peaks . . . the list of joys excites the imagination, and the reality lives up to those high expectations. Unfortunately, the trails here are also the most popular in the Eagle Cap Wilderness, traveled by thousands of hikers and horses. However, the beauty more than compensates for the lack of solitude. If you can plan your hike for after Labor Day, you'll encounter fewer crowds (though temperatures drop radically up here), and even if not, you can usually find more secluded campsites by venturing away from the main lakes.

DESCRIPTION

Go left on the East Fork Wallowa River Trail, following signs to Aneroid Lake. You switchback up the mostly forested hillside, and after 1.6 miles you pass a small waterfall and a diversion dam, part of the Wallowa Falls Hydroelectric Project. The trail enters the official wilderness just beyond this point. Continue climbing at a gentler pace, keeping your eyes peeled for thimbleberries to snack on, and enter the stream's more level upper valley. As the path leads upstream, views of meadows and the surrounding peaks become more frequent and enticing. Cross the stream (on a recent visit, the footbridge was broken, but crossing was easy) 3.9 miles from the trailhead and continue up its east bank, eventually reaching the shores of large and very scenic Aneroid Lake. Good though sometimes crowded camps abound in the woods around the lake, and if they're full, you can backtrack slightly to the camps at smaller Roger Lake.

Aneroid Lake makes an excellent base camp for exploring the highly scenic terrain nearby. Don't miss the easy stroll around the lake itself, including a stop at the privately owned cabins at the lake's south end. A much more strenuous option is the scramble to the top of Aneroid Mountain (a long, tiring, trailless climb, but *what a view!*). Another worthwhile trip is Dollar Lake and the easy climb along the ridge behind it. Jewett Lake, on a bench southwest of Aneroid Lake, is also worth a visit. Finally, the climb to the summit of Pete's Point is extremely rewarding. This peak is most easily reached by a sketchy boot path that climbs steeply on the exposed ridge on the peak's northeast side.

Once you've sampled the day hike possibilities from Aneroid Lake, pack up your gear and continue south. The trail climbs through a typically glorious Wallowa Mountains meadow on the way to exposed Tenderfoot Pass. The trail then traverses a slope and climbs to the fine view from Polaris Pass.

WARNING: The trail to Polaris Pass is steep and exposed; it's been in good shape recently, but allow more time than you think you'll need to get up and over.

The landscape west of this overlook is stunning, as most of the rugged Wallowa Mountains spread out in front of you. From the pass the trail drops almost 2,000 feet in a seemingly endless series of very gradual switchbacks all the way to the bottom of the valley. There is no water on the long descent, which explains why this loop is less attractive in the opposite direction.

Once you reach the bottom, turn left (upstream) at the junction with the West Fork Wallowa River Trail and soon enter the highly scenic upper valley of this stream. Cross the creek—there is no bridge, so expect a chilly wade—and continue another mile to the good camps at pretty Frazier Lake.

TIP: A nice side trip from Frazier Lake leads south past beautiful Little Frazier Lake to the view from Hawkins Pass–2.3 miles from Frazier Lake.

The trail now climbs a series of meadowy benches beside the waterfalls and cascades of the West Fork Wallowa River to Glacier Lake—one of the classic beauty spots in the state of Oregon. Camping here is *not* recommended due to the fragile alpine terrain and the exposed nature of camps, but you'll want to make sure you've saved some camera battery life.

WARNING: The water of this aptly named lake is bone-chillingly cold even on the hottest days of summer.

TIP: While views across any part of Glacier Lake are terrific, perhaps the best is from the east shore looking toward Eagle Cap and Glacier Peak. Reach this viewpoint by crossing the outlet creek and following a use path beside the lake for a few hundred yards.

Once you manage to pull yourself away from the beauty of Glacier Lake, climb in a series of short switchbacks to the tremendous vista from windswept Glacier Pass. Spread out to the north are the forested Lakes Basin and myriad distant peaks. Spend some time here to rest and pick out the many landmarks.

Dollar Lake and Pete's Point are two worthwhile side trips.

The path now drops 1,200 feet into the Lakes Basin, a heavily used area that consists of a series of large, beautiful lakes that seem to pop up at every turn in the trail. Every lake features a different scene of the surrounding peaks. The first one you'll reach is Moccasin Lake, perhaps the prettiest of all, where numerous excellent camps can be found (as is the case at all of the lakes). Side trips abound, but the easy stroll to Mirror Lake and tiny Upper Lake should be included in any itinerary. More ambitious hikers can follow exposed but view-packed routes to Carper Pass or even the top of Eagle Cap.

TIP: A superior side trail, though unmarked and hard to find, leads from the east end of Moccasin Lake to the austere setting of Pocket Lake.

To continue the loop trip, turn right at Moccasin Lake and take Moccasin Trail #1810A. Pass Douglas Lake, with an unnamed but spectacular granite ridge for a backdrop, and then Lee and Horseshoe Lakes as you slowly descend through the Lakes Basin. Side trips from Horseshoe Lake lead to forest-rimmed Unit Lake or lovely Razz Lake (the trail to the latter is not marked or maintained). Reluctantly, you must now leave the Lakes Basin and descend through forest to the West Fork Wallowa River. Several moderate switchbacks eventually lead down to a stream crossing just before you enter Six Mile Meadow (good camps). Turn left at the trail junction here and follow the river downstream as you gradually leave the high country behind. There are several nice cross-canyon views, and small side creeks provide water.

If time and energy allow, a highly recommended side trip switchbacks up to Ice Lake, located in a high basin on the Hurwal Divide to the west. This large, scenic lake provides a good base camp for scrambles up the Matterhorn and Sacajawea Peak, the highest summits in the Wallowa Mountains. Other rewarding pursuits there include angling, scanning for the area's mountain goats, and simply sitting and enjoying the landscape. To reach Ice Lake, leave the main trail 3.3 miles north of Six Mile Meadow and turn left on a path that climbs a seemingly endless series of switchbacks to the lake. The tedium of this climb is broken by ever-improving views and a terrific look at a long waterfall on Adam Creek.

Once you convince yourself to leave this paradise, make your way back down all those switchbacks to the West Fork Wallowa River Trail. Turn north and follow this woodsy path back down to your car.

POSSIBLE ITINERARY

	CAMP	MILES	ELEVATION GAIN
Day 1	Aneroid Lake	6.3	3,200'
Day 2	Day hike up Pete's Point (return to Aneroid Lake)	8.0	2,300'
Day 3	Frazier Lake	11.8	2,200'
Day 4	Horseshoe Lake	8.5	1,500'
Day 5	Ice Lake	11.1	2,400'
Day 6	Out	8.2	100'

22

SOUTHERN WALLOWAS TRAVERSE

RATINGS: Scenery 9 **Solitude** 6 **Difficulty** 8
MILES: 40 (55)
ELEVATION GAIN: 9,400' (13,400')
DAYS: 4–5 (6–8)
SHUTTLE MILEAGE: 42
MAP: Green Trails *Wallowa Mountains*
USUALLY OPEN: July–October
BEST: Mid-July–September
PERMITS: Yes (free, self-issued at trailheads); Northwest Forest Pass required at both trailheads
RULES: No fires within 0.25 mile of Eagle Lake; maximum group size of 12 people/18 stock
CONTACT: Wallowa Mountains Office, Wallowa-Whitman National Forest, 541-426-4978, fs.usda.gov/wallowa-whitman

SPECIAL ATTRACTIONS

Mountain landscapes, relative solitude

CHALLENGES

Fairly remote trailheads, thunderstorms

Above: View of China Cap from the trail

HOW TO GET THERE

The east trailhead is at Boulder Park, a former horse-outfitting ranch on Eagle Creek. From I-84 take Exit 298, north of Baker City, and head east on OR 203 N. Go 18.2 miles to the village of Medical Springs, and turn right (south) onto Big Creek Road, following signs for Tamarack Campground. After 1.7 miles keep left on Forest Service Road 67. In 13.9 miles, just before a bridge over Eagle Creek, turn left onto FS 77/Eagle Creek Road. After another 0.7 mile keep right at a fork and travel on FS 7755 for 3.5 miles to the road-end Main Eagle trailhead.

The west trailhead is reached by taking I-84 to Exit 265 near La Grande. Turn right to head southeast on OR 203 S. In 10.8 miles turn left (east) onto East Beakman Street/OR 203. Go 11.3 miles, and turn left (east) onto FS 7785/Catherine Creek Lane. This gravel road follows the North Fork of Catherine Creek 4.1 miles to a fork. Turn right (southeast) onto FS 7787 and go 3.7 miles. Turn left (east) and go 0.3 mile to the Buck Creek Trailhead.

TIP: Both the Buck Creek Forest Camp and (especially) Two Color Campground, 3 miles up the road from the Main Eagle trailhead, are nice places to camp before or after your hike.

GPS TRAILHEAD COORDINATES:

(Main Eagle) N45° 03.936' W117° 24.614'
(Buck Creek) N45° 08.899' W117° 34.356'

INTRODUCTION

The southern Wallowa Mountains are both very similar to and quite different from the northern part of the range. As in the areas to the north, the scenery is spectacular, with the same enchanting combination of granite peaks, alpine lakes, and wildflowers. The southern part, however, has a very different character. First of all, the trail population is smaller. While you won't be lonesome, longer road access and more rugged trails mean that far fewer people choose to hike in this region. The terrain also differs from the northern Wallowas. Granite peaks are still found in abundance, but the geology here is more varied, with many prominent peaks being more reddish than white. Finally, the forests are more open and the meadows more expansive, so vistas are wider and more common. This attractive but difficult hike traces a rugged up-and-down route as it alternates between the high passes and deep canyons that characterize the southern Wallowas. For the fit hiker who longs for the beauty of the Wallowas without the crowds, this is a wonderful choice. The hike is described here from east to west (although endless variations are possible).

DESCRIPTION

Begin by hiking northeast up an abandoned jeep road across the remains of a landslide to a bridged crossing of Eagle Creek. Now a pleasant footpath, the route climbs through forests as it closely parallels the stream. You recross Eagle Creek on a narrow log bridge and soon reach the ford of Copper Creek—sometimes on a handy log, but otherwise expect to get your feet wet until late summer—just downstream from impressive Copper Creek Falls.

Southern Wallowas Traverse

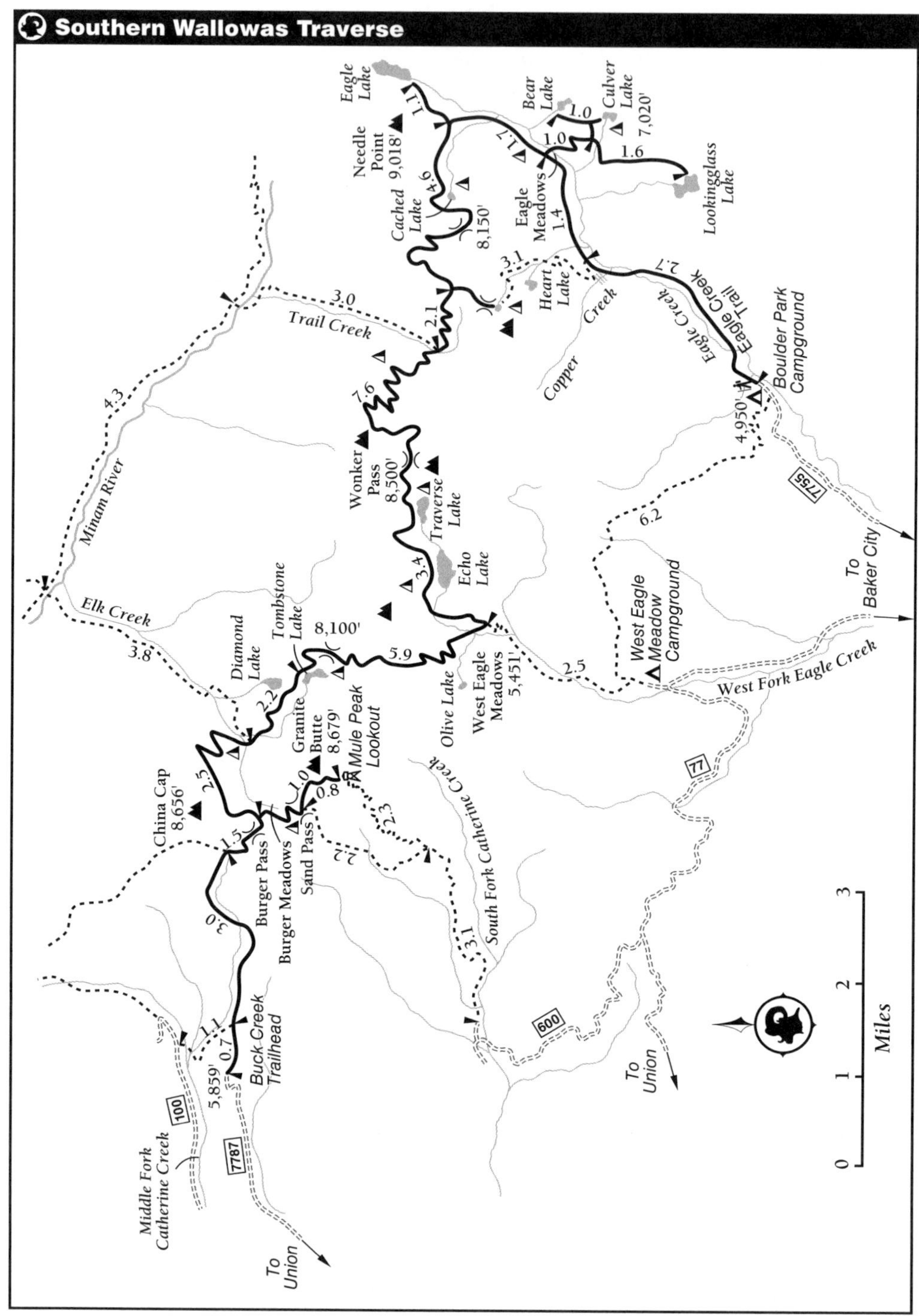

TIP: For the best photo opportunity of this falls, take a short spur trail north of the creek.

Keep straight at a trail junction a little past Copper Creek, sticking with the Eagle Creek Trail. The trail gets rougher, but the terrain is more open, with meadows and views of the surrounding peaks. At 4.1 miles is large Eagle Meadows, with good camps. There is also a junction here with the route to Lookingglass Lake.

To visit the lovely lakes in the high cirques to the south and east, ford Eagle Creek and climb a fairly steep trail along the canyon wall. Views to the north of Needle Point and the basin of Eagle Lake improve as you ascend to a trail junction near the base of a meadow. To the right, a 1.6-mile path climbs over a mostly open ridge before dropping a bit to large Lookingglass Lake. This deep lake has good fishing but is artificially dammed, so when the water is lower, it resembles a bathtub. The rocky terrain around the lake makes for generally poor camping, but the views are excellent. Back at the last junction, the left fork quickly enters the basin holding very scenic Culver Lake. Towering cliffs behind the east shore of this lake present a challenge for even the widest-angle camera lens. The trail continues north another mile to Bear Lake. This pool is attractive but less spectacular than Culver or Lookingglass Lake.

TIP: The best plan is to camp down at Eagle Meadows and day-hike up to these lakes.

Continuing north on the Eagle Creek Trail, wildflowers brighten the canyon ascent as the landscape changes from meadows and open slopes back into forest. Not long after the trail begins to make a switchbacking climb is a rock cairn (and possibly a sign) marking the junction with the trail to Eagle Lake. Though Eagle Lake is artificially dammed and has generally poor campsites (great views but very exposed), it's still well worth the side trip. The last 0.3 mile of the trail to this lake goes up a steeply tilted granite ridge with a few stunted whitebark pines, framing excellent if dizzying views back down the canyon. The lake itself sits in a spectacular alpine basin rimmed by 9,000-foot granite peaks. There are few trees in this high bowl, but the scenery is impressive.

For better camps, return to the main trail and climb to the meadow holding tiny Cached Lake. Nice, sheltered camps are in the trees on this pool's north side.

TIP: Be sure to walk around to the lake's southwest shore for some excellent views across Cached Lake to Needle Point—dominating the local skyline.

As is true in many parts of the Wallowas, friendly deer are likely to visit your camp in the evening.

TIP: Peak baggers will want to make the steep, but not technically difficult, scramble to the top of Needle Point. The vistas from the summit are truly outstanding, especially of the deep, curving Minam River Canyon to the north.

From Cached Lake your trail makes a long looping climb to a windswept pass and then descends back into forest to a meadow with a trail junction. An excellent side trip turns left here, climbs steeply over a rocky pass, and drops to the alpine cirque holding tiny Arrow Lake. With a high granite peak, small islands, and a rocky wildflower meadow, Arrow Lake is a magical place.

Returning to the main trail, you switchback steadily downhill to Trail Creek. You'll have to get used to this pattern of alternating between high passes and deep canyons because that pretty much describes the rest of this trip. There are precious few stretches of level trail. Fortunately, frequent lakes and views provide ample compensation. A break in the trees partway down this particular descent offers an excellent glimpse of the peaks to the west.

At the bottom of the canyon, you go left at a junction and then cross Trail Creek. Rest awhile and refill your water bottle before tackling the long 2,300-foot climb to Wonker Pass. The well-graded trail climbs gradually for 1 mile to a nice meadow with a good campsite. From here you ascend through forest and then up a series of airy switchbacks on an exposed talus slope with increasingly good views to the pass.

From Wonker Pass it's only a short descent to the alpine basin holding beautiful Traverse Lake, with excellent camps. The lake has an idyllic setting in a large meadow surrounded by scattered islands of trees. The most impressive view is from the northwest shore looking back toward a prominent granite monolith beside Wonker Pass—outstanding!

To continue your tour, head away from the waters of Traverse Lake and soon reach a grand overlook of Echo Lake and the canyon below. (Yes, you're going *all the way down there.*) Walk past a nice spring and then drop to Echo Lake, which can be reached by any of several short side trails. A serrated ridge south of this lake makes a nice backdrop.

WARNING: Later in the summer, the water level drops in this artificially controlled lake, making it much less attractive.

You continue downhill, making a few switchbacks, and then cross a marshy area near a small pond. Switchbacks resume as the trail crosses semi-open slopes with high peaks on either side.

In a brushy area, long before the switchbacks end, is a junction. Turn right, cross the West Fork Eagle Creek, and brace yourself for the next big climb, as the trail regains all the previously lost elevation on a long and rather uneventful ascent toward the pass above Tombstone Lake. There are nice views as you climb, but only intermittent shade. It's all worthwhile once you top out at a high pass because the vistas, as usual, are superb. From the pass the trail contours along a ridge for a bit then drops to the shores of Tombstone Lake, which has several choice camps for the weary hiker. The lake's name comes from a large pinnacle rising from the southwestern shore. With some imagination, it might be said to resemble a tombstone.

The path continues to the northwest, traveling above the basin holding woodsy Diamond Lake, which can be reached by steep side trails, and then continues to lose elevation to a trail junction beside Elk Creek. Turn left and cross the stream to an excellent campsite where two creeks meet. The meadow here is a lovely foreground for craggy Granite Butte to the south, and trees provide welcome shade.

WARNING: Bugs can be an annoyance here because the meadow is rather boggy.

Leaving this meadow basin, you'll notice an older trail that climbs steeply along a slope to the left, but the well-graded newer trail climbs gradually to the right in two very long switchbacks with several good views along the way. Near the top of this climb, the trail

Views of surrounding peaks open up along Burger Pass.

contours around sloping Burger Meadows and then climbs another hillside to a junction in the trees. For a quick exit, turn right, but keep straight for a terrific side trip.

The side trip first visits a beautiful meadow with a fine campsite, wildflowers, and small ponds. The view across this meadow toward prominent China Cap is particularly fetching. Leaving this meadow, you travel up very steep, sandy switchbacks to aptly named Sand Pass, often snowbound until late summer. Turn left at Sand Pass and follow a more gently graded trail that climbs through semi-open forest on a ridge east of Sand Pass. The route traverses an open slope a few hundred feet below the summit of Granite Butte and then crosses a saddle and goes up the spine of a narrow ridge to Mule Peak Lookout. This is one of Oregon's least-visited fire lookouts, but the lack of visitors is due only to its isolation because outstanding panoramas extend in all directions. Fire-scarred forests below the peak testify to the need for this facility; the 2016 Mule Peak Fire even caused the lookout to be evacuated.

Back at the junction above Burger Meadows, turn west and climb to Burger Pass. The peaks on either side are not the typical white granite of the Wallowas but are reddish summits instead.

TIP: For those with energy to burn, the scramble up China Cap to the north is particularly rewarding.

The trail drops a few hundred feet to a junction below the pass. To the right (northwest) is a long, view-packed ridge walk, but keep left to reach your car.

The final part of the hike is a pleasant downhill stretch, mostly in forest, along Middle Fork Catherine Creek. Keep straight at a trail junction near the bottom and soon reach the Buck Creek Trailhead—the end of an exhausting but glorious hike.

POSSIBLE ITINERARY

	CAMP	MILES	ELEVATION GAIN
Day 1	Eagle Meadows (with side trip to Lookingglass and Bear Lakes)	11.3	2,700'
Day 2	Arrow Lake (with side trip to Eagle Lake)	9.6	3,000'
Day 3	Traverse Lake	10.8	2,400'
Day 4	Tombstone Lake	9.3	2,200'
Day 5	Meadow below Sand Pass (with side trip to Mule Peak Lookout)	7.8	2,500'
Day 6	Out	5.7	600'

23

EAST EAGLE–IMNAHA LOOP

RATINGS: Scenery 10 **Solitude** 4 **Difficulty** 6
MILES: 39 (46)
ELEVATION GAIN: 7,900' (10,400')
DAYS: 5–6 (5–7)
SHUTTLE MILEAGE: NA
MAP: Green Trails *Wallowa Mountains*
USUALLY OPEN: Mid-July–October
BEST: Mid-July–August
PERMITS: Yes (free, self-issued at trailhead)
RULES: No fires within 0.25 mile of Glacier, Mirror, Moccasin, or Sunshine Lakes; maximum group size of 6 people/9 stock in Lakes Basin and at Frazier and Glacier Lakes
CONTACT: Wallowa Mountains Office, Wallowa-Whitman National Forest, 541-426-4978, fs.usda.gov/wallowa-whitman

SPECIAL ATTRACTIONS

Great mountain scenery, alpine lakes, wildlife

CHALLENGES

Crowded in spots, thunderstorms

Above: Eagle Cap over upper Moccasin Lake
photographed by Douglas Lorain

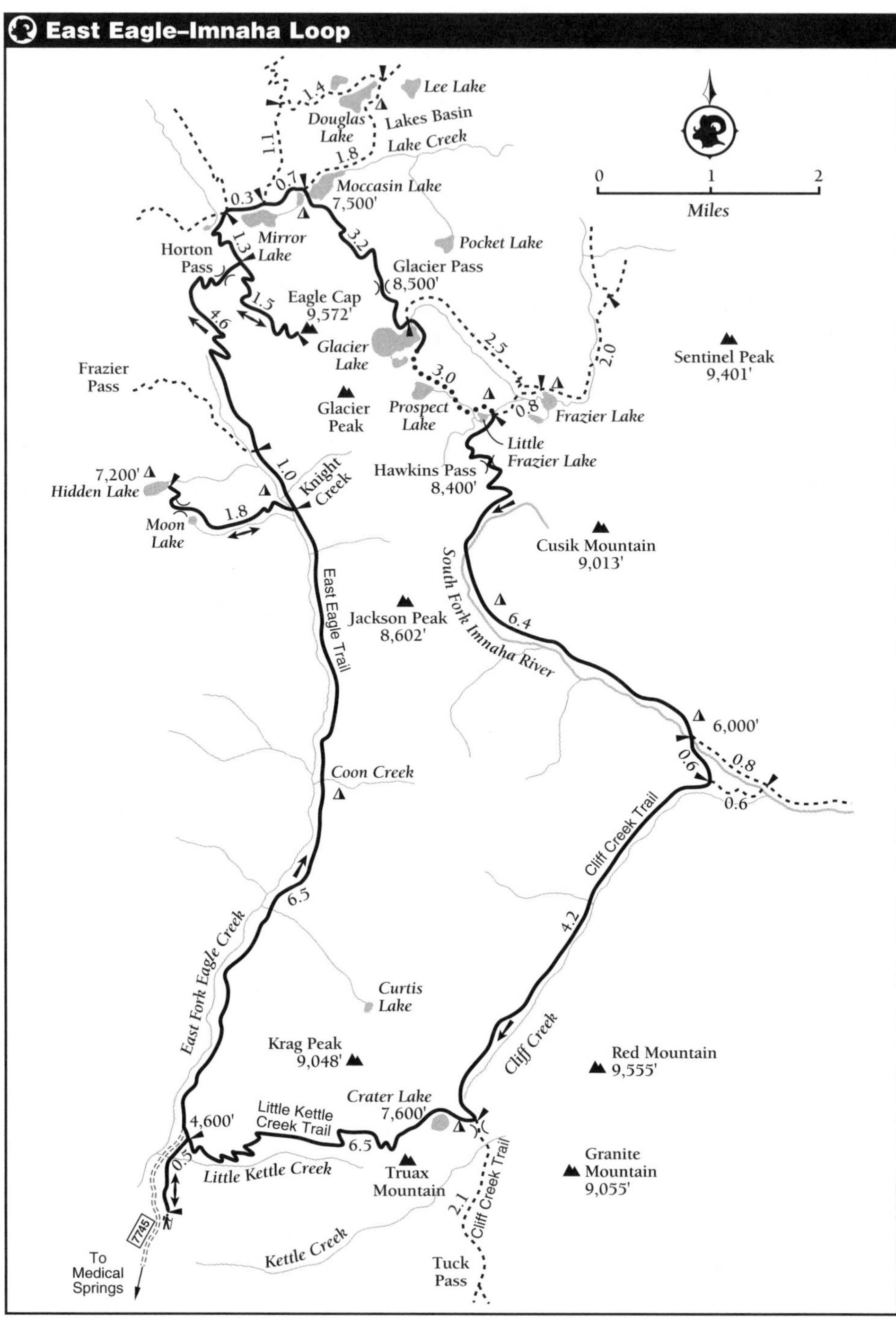

East Eagle–Imnaha Loop
Lee Lake
Douglas Lake
Lakes Basin
Lake Creek
Moccasin Lake
7,500'
Miles
Mirror Lake
Horton Pass
Pocket Lake
Glacier Pass
8,500'
Eagle Cap
9,572'
Glacier Lake
Sentinel Peak
9,401'
Frazier Pass
Glacier Peak
Prospect Lake
Frazier Lake
Little Frazier Lake
Hawkins Pass
8,400'
7,200'
Hidden Lake
Knight Creek
Moon Lake
Cusik Mountain
9,013'
East Eagle Trail
South Fork Imnaha River
Jackson Peak
8,602'
6,000'
Coon Creek
Cliff Creek Trail
East Fork Eagle Creek
Curtis Lake
Krag Peak
9,048'
Cliff Creek
Red Mountain
9,555'
Crater Lake
7,600'
4,600'
Little Kettle Creek Trail
Little Kettle Creek
Truax Mountain
Granite Mountain
9,055'
Kettle Creek
Tuck Pass
7745
To Medical Springs

HOW TO GET THERE

To reach the start of this adventure, from I-84 take Exit 298, north of Baker City, and head east on OR 203 N. Go 18.2 miles to the village of Medical Springs, and turn right (south) onto Big Creek Road, following signs for Tamarack Campground. After 1.7 miles keep left on Forest Service Road 67. Drive 14 miles, cross a bridge over Eagle Creek, and then go another 0.6 mile to Tamarack Campground. The road turns right and becomes FS 77. After another 5.8 miles, turn left onto FS 7745, following signs to the East Eagle Trailhead. Drive this gravel route 6.2 miles to the hiker trailhead at the end of the road (passing a larger stock-trailer parking area and equestrian trailhead on the right).

GPS TRAILHEAD COORDINATES:

N45° 03.461' W117° 19.404'

INTRODUCTION

Here is yet another remarkably beautiful loop hike through the spectacular Wallowa Mountains. The focus here is on the southeast part of the range. As is true everywhere in these mountains, this trip features a wealth of breathtaking mountain scenery, largely through peak-framed open meadows. The hike takes you right past Eagle Cap itself, with the opportunity to summit this impressive landmark.

DESCRIPTION

From the trailhead at the end of the road, you go north through an attractive forest of beautiful old-growth ponderosa pine, grand fir, and western larch. Off to your right is the Little Kettle Creek Trail, the return leg of your loop. You go straight as the trail drops to creek level near the old trailhead. From here the route makes a gradual up-and-down climb with frequent views extending up 4,000-foot canyon walls. Your path alternates among forests, brushy slopes, and meadows. Look for views of Krag Peak and several waterfalls across the canyon. Water from tributary creeks is abundant. The lower canyon offers limited camping opportunities, though comfortable camps are possible a little south of Coon Creek and near Eagle Creek a bit farther along.

At 7 miles, a little before the waterfall on Knight Creek, is a possibly unsigned junction with the trail to Hidden Lake. To make this excellent side trip, turn left and drop to a fairly easy ford of East Eagle Creek. A good campsite is a bit farther up the far bank. The trail climbs fairly steeply about 1 mile before leveling off below Moon Lake. You climb over a low ridge and then drop down the other side to large and beautiful Hidden Lake. There are numerous excellent camps here, as well as views of the craggy granite peaks circling the meadowy basin. The lake also offers good fishing and swimming.

TIP: Some of the best vistas are from the lake's trailless north shore.

After returning to the East Eagle Trail, turn upstream and continue climbing. Keep right at the Frazier Pass junction as the trail gets narrower and rockier. Several long switchbacks moderate the climb. Cross East Eagle Creek and enter the high meadows of the headwall basin. Watch for deer and elk in this area. A long climb is required to exit this lovely basin as the trail winds up moderately steep granite slopes to Horton Pass.

WARNING: Snow often obscures this high route well into summer, so be sure to navigate carefully.

A cairn marks the top of windswept Horton Pass with its excellent views.

The outstanding side trip to the summit of Eagle Cap should not be missed. The summit trail begins beside a pond below the north side of Horton Pass.

TIP: It's easier to simply walk up the rocky ridge directly from the pass for about 0.4 mile to where you meet the official path.

The trail climbs steadily over rocks and snowfields, eventually switchbacking up the exposed slopes to the top. From here the rugged topography of the entire Wallowa Range spreads out in all directions. There are especially good views down the huge U-shaped gorges of East Eagle Creek and East Lostine River. To the east, Glacier Lake shimmers in its basin, and granite peaks rise in all directions. *Wow* pretty much sums it up.

From Horton Pass the main trail crosses meadows and semipermanent snowfields and then drops to tiny Upper Lake at the head of East Lostine Canyon. You turn right at a junction and right again just 100 yards later to reach popular Mirror Lake. On a calm morning or evening, this lake lives up to its name, with fine reflections of towering Eagle Cap. Continue down the trail to the east to reach deep and beautiful Moccasin Lake (with excellent camps), and turn right at the junction at the lake's west end. This next stretch is also part of the Wallowa River Loop (Trip 21).

The trail now makes a long, strenuous climb to Glacier Pass, traveling first through forest, then meadows, and finally alpine terrain. Once again the views from the pass are terrific, but even better scenery is just ahead at Glacier Lake. Deserving a place on any list of Oregon's most spectacular lakes, this large alpine jewel ranks second only to incomparable Crater Lake in the southern Cascades. When free of ice (only about two or three months out of the year), this clear pool, surrounded by white granite peaks and permanent snowfields, is unbelievably beautiful. Camping here is not recommended due to the fragile terrain and cold nights.

From Glacier Lake the easiest route to continue your trip drops 2.5 miles to Frazier Lake, where the trail turns right and climbs to Little Frazier Lake and on to Hawkins Pass. For hikers who don't mind some steep cross-country travel, a more scenic alternative crosses the outlet creek of Glacier Lake and follows a boot-beaten path along the lake's east shore. Look carefully for an unmarked route that goes by a smaller upper lake, continues south over a saddle, and then drops to Prospect Lake. The stark granite basin holding this deep lake is only slightly less spectacular than the setting for Glacier Lake, and it is much more private. Unfortunately, the camps here are rocky and exposed. Reaching Little Frazier Lake requires a steep downhill scramble following the outlet creek of Prospect Lake.

TIP: In general, the right (south) side of the creek provides more manageable trail conditions, but you'll still have to crawl around some boulders and small cliffs.

The creek itself is a joyful series of cascades and waterfalls with lots of flowers. At the bottom, go left along the north shore of Little Frazier Lake to pick up the trail.

Turn right and follow the path as it makes a moderately steep climb in several small switchbacks to Hawkins Pass.

WARNING: Snow remains on the north side of Hawkins Pass practically all summer.

The trail then drops into the basin at the head of the South Fork Imnaha River, which features outstanding views and acres of wildflowers. The prominent pinnacle to the southwest is Jackson Peak. There are several inviting camps both here and a bit below a lovely waterfall about 0.4 mile past where the trail crosses the stream. Farther down the canyon, the views become more restricted as the forests grow thicker, but it's still a pleasant walk. Near the junction with Cliff Creek Trail, about 4.5 miles from the headwall basin, are some clearings with more nice camps.

Turn south on Cliff Creek Trail and immediately face a chilly ford of the Imnaha River. The path then climbs steadily through forests and brushy meadows on its way up Cliff Creek. Wildflowers add color in summer, and larch trees make October equally attractive in this area. Look for deer in the meadows—and often in your camp at night. Aptly named Red Mountain towers to the east, adding to the excellent scenery. You top out at a forested pass and then turn right at a junction to reach Crater Lake, which has good camps in the trees above the north shore. Unlike most lakes in the Wallowas, this one does not fill a glacial cirque but sits in a low saddle near the pass. The lake's water level fluctuates considerably during the year. The high water of early summer is more attractive. Distant Krag Peak, Red Mountain, and Granite Mountain provide lovely backdrops.

TIP: If you have an extra day, spend it on an easy flower walk to Tuck Pass and the Pine Lakes to the southeast.

To complete the loop trip, you hike west through a low saddle past a couple of shallow ponds and then make a long, fairly steep descent along the brushy avalanche slopes beside Little Kettle Creek. A seemingly endless series of switchbacks eases the grade. The trail ends at the junction with the East Eagle Trail, where your car awaits at the trailhead.

POSSIBLE ITINERARY

	CAMP	MILES	ELEVATION GAIN
Day 1	Hidden Lake	8.8	2,800'
Day 2	Mirror Lake (with side trip up Eagle Cap)	12.0	3,500'
Day 3	Upper Imnaha Basin	10.0	2,500'
Day 4	Crater Lake	8.4	1,500'
Day 5	Out	6.7	100'

24

HELLS CANYON WESTERN RIM SUMMIT TRAIL

RATINGS: Scenery 8 **Solitude** 8 **Difficulty** 5
MILES: 53 (66)
ELEVATION GAIN: 7,400' (9,300')
DAYS: 5–7 (6–9)
SHUTTLE MILEAGE: 63
MAP: USFS *Hells Canyon National Recreation Area and Wilderness*
USUALLY OPEN: Late May–November
BEST: Early to mid-June
PERMITS: Northwest Forest Pass required at trailheads
RULES: Private land along Cow Creek—no public traffic on road; close any gates you open
CONTACT: Wallowa Mountains Office, Wallowa-Whitman National Forest, 541-426-4978, fs.usda.gov/wallowa-whitman

SPECIAL ATTRACTIONS

Views, wildlife, solitude, wildflowers

CHALLENGES

Limited water sources, some road walking, large burned areas, ticks

Above: The scene from Buckhorn Lookout

HOW TO GET THERE

Reach the south starting point by taking I-84 to Exit 302 in Baker City. Head east on OR 86, and go 60.2 miles. Turn left (north) onto North Pine Road, and go 14.3 miles. Turn right onto the paved Wallowa Loop Road/Forest Service Road 39 (closed late October–early May or early June due to snow) and go 5.1 miles. Turn right (east) onto FS 490, and drive 5.5 miles, passing Hells Canyon Overlook. Continue straight on FS 3965, a rough gravel road. Drive 7.3 miles, past the turnoff to McGraw Lookout and a gate, to the developed PO Saddle Trailhead.

There are two options for exiting this hike. The first is Dug Bar (see below for directions). A slightly shorter option is to exit via Cow Creek. This route crosses private land and follows a road closed to public traffic, but hikers are allowed to walk through. This exit avoids the final steep 10 miles of Dug Bar Road, so it is easier for those with a typical passenger car. From I-84 take Exit 261 in La Grande and turn east onto OR 82. In 1.4 miles turn left (north) to remain on OR 82. Go 17.7 miles and turn right (east) to again remain on OR 82. Drive 44.2 miles to the town of Enterprise. Turn right (south) to continue another 6.3 miles on OR 82 to Joseph. Turn left (east) onto OR 350 and go 29.4 miles. After crossing the Imnaha River, turn left (north) onto Lower Imnaha Road. In 6.3 miles make a slight right (northeast) onto Dug Bar Road/FS 4260. In 6.8 miles turn left (north) to remain on Dug Bar Road. Go 6.5 miles, and the Cow Creek Trailhead is on the left just before you cross a bridge over the Imnaha River again. (For the Dug Bar Trailhead, cross the bridge over the Imnaha River, and turn left to stay on FS 4260. Go 10.7 miles to the end of the road and the trailhead.)

TIP: To avoid the time-consuming and tedious car shuttles in Hells Canyon, consider employing a shuttle service. Originally designed for rafters, these services also assist hikers by moving your vehicle between trailheads while you spend more time hiking. Fees vary, and you'll have to make arrangements in advance. One such service is Hells Canyon Shuttle (800-785-3358; hellscanyonshuttle.com).

GPS TRAILHEAD COORDINATES:

(PO Saddle) N45° 13.818' W116° 46.514'
(Dug Bar) N45° 48.277' W116° 41.207'
(Cow Creek) N45° 45.822' W116° 44.900'

INTRODUCTION

Of the three long trails in Hells Canyon described in this guide, the Western Rim National Recreation Trail is the most comfortable for backpackers. This trip has comparatively few steep ups and downs because the path follows the surprisingly gentle Summit Ridge. The unbearable heat of the lower canyon is replaced by higher-elevation temperatures that are 20 or more degrees cooler. Nights are also more comfortably cool for sleeping. There is also plenty of shade among the rim's evergreen forests. On the other hand, the rim route has fewer water sources, so camping choices are limited.

TIP 1: For more solitude, hike this route before Hat Point Road opens to traffic (usually around the second week of June, but call ahead to confirm). You will have to walk over

Hells Canyon Western Rim Summit Trail
0 2 4
Miles
To Lewiston, Idaho
Dug Bar Road
4260
Imnaha River
Dug Bar 1,030'
Thorn Spring Creek
Christmas Creek Ranch
1,300'
To Imnaha
Square Mountain 4,800'
Deep Creek
Snake River Trail
Snake River
Roland Creek
Cat Creek
Copper Creek Lodge
Bench "High" Trail
Bob Creek
Highrange Rapids
Rowley Gulch
Litch Ranch
Tryon Saddle
Lookout Creek
Cow Creek
Tryon Creek Ranch
Camp Creek
Englishman Hill
Lord Flat 5,600'
landing strip
3,100'
Pleasant Valley Creek
Pittsburg Guard Station
Long Prong
Somers Creek
Somers Point 5,676'
Pittsburg Landing
Mormon Flat
Durham Creek
Robertson Ridge
Muir Creek
Cougar Creek
Two Corral Creek
OREGON
Windy Ridge
Parliament
Salt Creek
Salt Creek Trail
Kirby Bar
Hominy Creek
Kirkwood Ranch
Ninemile Saddle
Suicide Point
Dry Gulch
Temperance Creek Ranch
Grassy Knoll 6,515'
Lightning Creek
Temperance Creek
Wisenor Place
Alum Bed Rapids
Sand Creek
Horse Creek
Warnock Corral 6,700'
game warden's cabin
Eagle's Nest
Rush Creek
To Imnaha
Bench "High" Trail
Johnson Bar 1,300'
Sluice Creek
Rush Creek Rapids
Memaloose Guard Station
Hat Point Lookout
landing strip
4240
Log Creek
Snake River Trail
Imnaha River
Freezeout Saddle 5,300'
4230
Saddle Creek
IDAHO
To Pine Creek
Freezeout Creek
Bear Mountain
Black Mountain 6,862'
Snake River
Lookout Mountain
13.1
PO Saddle Trailhead
3965

a few snowfields, but the joy of having the terrific view from Hat Point all to yourself is well worth it.

TIP 2: Don't forget to bring binoculars; wildlife is abundant.

DESCRIPTION

From the south trailhead, the Western Rim Trail follows a gravel road that drops to PO Saddle.

NOTE: From about mid-June to mid-September, this road is open to cars for the first 1.5 miles, to Saulsberry Saddle. At this point, it temporarily enters the wilderness, so the U.S. Forest Service has blocked the road with a berm.

The road continues to Saulsberry Saddle, where it crosses under a set of power lines and reverts to a dirt jeep track. The jeep road climbs a wide gully to a large flat area with a mix of forests and meadows.

TIP: Two springs can be found to the west of the trail for those in need of water.

The route continues northeast along the ridge and then breaks out of the trees at the expansive meadows near Himmelwright Spring. In June this meadow is a flower bonanza, choked with the large white blossoms of Wyethia, as well as yellow balsamroot and a smattering of other species. Views extend to the snowy peaks of the distant Wallowa Mountains. Unfortunately, cows often trample the whole area, so the trail can be smelly and muddy, and camping is problematic.

Keeping right at a junction with Morgan Ridge Trail and descending from Himmelwright Meadow, the old jeep road climbs a bit and then comes to a junction with Battle Creek Trail. This route veers off to the right on its way down to the Snake River. Continuing north, your trail makes a gradual ascent, sometimes in a tunnel of trees, to Lookout Mountain. Trees partly obscure the views, but the open area on top supports a wealth of wildflowers.

The old road pretty much ends at Lookout Mountain, though a jeep track continues as far as Squirrel Prairie. You drop a bit to Benjamin Spring, which may run dry by mid- to late summer, and continue the moderate descent to a junction. To the left is the trail to Marks Cabin and a spring. The Western Rim Trail goes right and drops to the sloping meadow and the (usually) year-round creek in Squirrel Prairie. This is an excellent place to camp, though the presence of a healthy bear population makes it prudent to hang your food. (So far, the bears in Hells Canyon have not presented a problem for campers. Proper food storage will help keep it that way.)

TIP: A superb side trip from here follows the Bear Mountain Trail east through meadows and a once-burned forest. The trail climbs a bit and then follows a wide ridge all the way to the outstanding overlook atop Bear Mountain. The perspective of the snowy Seven Devils Mountains, appearing deceptively close across the gaping chasm, is particularly noteworthy.

Back on the Western Rim Trail, the route soon becomes a footpath, but travel remains easy, with only modest ups and downs. More burned and regrowing trees provide further evidence of old fires. Views alternate between the Freezeout and Imnaha Canyons to the west and Hells Canyon and the peaks in Idaho to the east. You may even spot the lookout tower on Hat Point in the distance to the north. About 3.7 miles from Squirrel Prairie is Freezeout Saddle, where the Bench and Saddle Creek Trails cross our route.

The Western Rim Trail goes straight and makes a well-graded climb along a rocky ridge covered with wildflowers, bunchgrass, and a few evergreens. Excellent views provide interest and variety as the trail shifts from one side of the ridge to the other. A little before the final switchbacks are two (usually flowing) creeklets.

TIP: Stock up on water here because this is the last opportunity for several miles.

At the top of the climb is the gravel Hat Point Road/Forest Service Road 4240, which serves as the trail for the next several miles. If your trip is in early June, the road walk should be pleasantly quiet; otherwise, you must share the route with cars.

Turn right on the road and soon reach walk-in Saddle Creek Campground, which supplies picnic tables, campsites, and breathtaking sights but no water. The road makes a series of ups and downs through subalpine fir forests and burned areas as it tours the top of the ridge overlooking Hells Canyon. Several viewpoints along the way will keep your camera busy. The road eventually works away from the ridge, passes some buildings beside the Memaloose helitack base (for helicopter-transported wildfire crews) and airstrip, and reaches the junction with FS 315 to Hat Point. This entire area (and for many miles to come) was burned by the Summit Fire in 1989 (and again in 2022), which left behind a seemingly endless silver ghost forest that is interesting but provides little shade and is rather monotonous. Lodgepole pines and a mixture of undergrowth have sprouted a new forest, but they are still fairly sparse and short.

The quickest way to continue the Western Rim Trail is to go straight on the road toward Warnock Corral, but to come this far and skip Hat Point would be absurd. So turn right and make the moderate 1.7-mile climb along the road to the Hat Point Lookout. This 90-foot tower is staffed in summer, and the person assigned here enjoys views that defy description. The view down to the Snake River, flowing more than a vertical mile below, is amazing. Even more thrilling, however, are the seemingly endless vistas of canyon slopes, the Seven Devils mountains in Idaho, and the distant Wallowa Mountains in Oregon. In early July the meadows provide gorgeous foregrounds with a colorful array of wildflowers. A picnic area and a short interpretive trail surround the lookout, providing information as well as scenic lunch spots.

TIP: To spend the night at Hat Point, continue north another 0.3 mile to Sacajawea Campground with its year-round spring.

To continue on the Western Rim Trail, return to FS 4240 and turn right. The road immediately passes the Memaloose Guard Station, then slowly descends beside the headwaters of Lightning Creek. At a gate, the road changes from gravel to dirt and then continues down to a nice view from Sluice Creek Saddle before climbing a bit to the Warnock Corral Trailhead in a small meadow. Camping here is pleasant (especially before the road is open), with a spring and small creek for water and a few green trees providing shade amid the fallen snags of the burned area. The Temperance Creek Trail drops to the northeast from here on its way to the Snake River.

From Warnock Corral the Western Rim Trail follows a four-wheel drive road that winds north through more of the slowly recovering burn area from the 1989 fire. The road is used primarily by hunters in the fall, so early-summer hikers should have it all to themselves. There is neither water nor much shade on this rather dull segment, so it can get surprisingly hot for this elevation. The road/trail passes a marked side route to Sleepy Ridge and, 0.5 mile later, finally leaves the ghost forest and enters more attractive terrain. You keep straight at the junction with a jeep road to Windy Ridge and then climb briefly to the overlook atop aptly named Grassy Knoll.

From this high point the route cuts through a nearly pure stand of even-age lodgepole pines (the legacy of a fire several decades ago) for 2 miles to a fence line. Beyond this the terrain becomes more diverse and interesting, with better views but also several steep ups and downs—a rarity for this hike. After about 1 mile you reach a low point called Indian Grave Saddle, where you will find an excellent camp and a spring with a pipe and horse trough. Refill your water bottles here. The road now enters another recovering burn area and makes a quick climb to a ridge.

TIP: A worthwhile side trip goes south from here to an unnamed open knoll with terrific views.

The Western Rim Trail goes north along the rim before dropping to Ninemile Saddle (more views). Shortly beyond the next hill, an unmarked jeep trail to the west goes 0.2 mile to a spring and an old cabin (possible camps here).

Atop the next hill is a junction and a large meadow area identified on maps as Parliament. No other legislature on the planet could possibly have enjoyed a better view! To the east drops the enormous gorge of Hells Canyon, while to the west is a gentler slope of forests that drop off into the canyons and ridges of Imnaha River country. Elk are generally the only legislators likely to be present. Leaving "Capitol Hill," so to speak, the road remains easy walking as it gradually descends past viewpoints for 1.8 miles to a junction.

Veering off to the right is the highly recommended up-and-down route to Somers Point. Views along this path—especially the jaw-dropper from Somers Point itself—are among the most memorable on this trip. The first 200 yards follow a jeep road, but the route soon becomes a pleasant footpath. The trail passes some nice camps in a saddle after 1.1 miles. You keep right at a junction just west of an unobtrusive radio tower and then descend through attractive forests. The last mile to Somers Point goes over a wide and spectacular meadowy ridge with lots of vistas and wildflowers; there's no longer really a trail here, but you should be able to follow the ridgeline to the top.

You'll enjoy an outstanding view from the end of Somers Point. The river can be seen in two different directions, contorted canyon walls stretch for miles, and the snowy peaks of Idaho provide a fine backdrop. Pittsburg Landing, with its boat ramp and campground, lies directly below on the Idaho side of the river. Fires over the years have left some snags, but these can't diminish the scene.

TIP: Binoculars will come in handy for spotting wildlife and rafters.

A view like this is hard to leave; fortunately, an inviting camp is nearby. A spring with a pipe and horse trough sits 200 yards north of and below the trail, 0.2 mile west of Somers Point. Excellent camps are found another 200 yards west of the spring in a strip of trees.

WARNING: If you leave camp, and at night, be sure to hang your food. Curious bears have been known to come sniffing around campsites in the area.

Back at the Somers Point junction, the Western Rim Trail continues to follow the road on its gentle course to the north. After curving left, the route heads back toward the ridge but generally remains in the trees. After making a long, fairly gradual descent, the road starts to break out into more open country. A short side trail goes left near here to Dorrance Cow Camp, where a cabin and some good camps are located. The main trail continues north over a grassy hill and drops through view-packed bunchgrass meadows to the south end of the Lord Flat landing strip. Despite its remote location, this airstrip's grassy 2,000-foot "tarmac" gets a surprising amount of use by U.S. Forest Service personnel, hunters, and others. Water is also available here.

From the landing strip the Western Rim Trail veers left on a jeep track and gradually drops down open slopes. Look for wildlife such as elk and black bears here. The jeep road finally ends near a tiny pond, after which the trail descends 19 switchbacks as it closely follows the Summit Ridge. To your immediate right lies Deep Creek Canyon, while to the left is Cow Creek's rugged defile. Your route switchbacks down to a saddle and a junction, with sketchy use paths heading both left and right. Continue straight and trace an up-and-down route along the ridge for about 2 miles to Fingerboard Saddle.

A good trail crosses our route here, providing a possible exit to Cow Creek Road and back to the trailhead. This is the shortest way out for hikers in a hurry. To exit from here, turn left, drop to Cow Creek, and follow the road downstream through Litch Ranch and eventually out to your car.

If you decide to stick with the Western Rim Trail, keep straight from Fingerboard Saddle and follow a roller-coaster route along the ridge. The north end of Summit Ridge is much narrower and more rugged than the south end, but it also has more continuous views and fewer trees. The trail is often indistinct, but because it closely follows the ridgeline, you shouldn't get lost.

WARNING: Water along the ridge is scarce to nonexistent, so carry extra.

Loop around the headwaters of Little Deep Creek to the east and make a sometimes-steep descent from a high point on the ridge to a saddle. The trail goes over another hill before facing the final short climb to Square Mountain. The Rowley Gulch Trail goes left and makes a steep switchbacking descent from the saddle just south of Square Mountain. Having come this far, however, you really should make the climb to Square Mountain to enjoy its views all the way to the Snake River near Dug Bar.

If Dug Bar is your chosen exit, follow the Western Rim Trail north from Square Mountain as it follows Dug Creek through a mix of forests and meadows to a junction first with the Bench Trail and then with the Snake River Trail (beware of poison ivy near here). The trail goes over a small rise with excellent views down to Dug Bar Ranch and drops down to the river-level trailhead.

To exit via Rowley Gulch after descending back down from Square Mountain, go west at the junction with a steep route (often easy to lose) that switchbacks down a ridge. The route goes over to a side canyon before paralleling the seasonal creek in Rowley Gulch to

Cow Creek Road. Turn right (north) and follow this road through attractive, mostly open country, usually well above the stream, back to your car.

NOTE: Please be respectful of the private land here by keeping gates open or closed as you found them and by not camping.

NOTE: The three trips described in Hells Canyon are all one-way, point-to-point hikes. For those unable to arrange a car shuttle, it is also possible to devise several long and spectacular loop trips in the canyon. One of the best begins at Dug Bar, goes up the Snake River Trail to Somers Creek, and then returns to Dug Bar via the Bench Trail over Tryon Saddle. This 42-mile trip is at its best in early to mid-May. A second trip, which peaks in early June, though with some snow at the highest elevations, begins at the Freezeout Trailhead and follows the Bench Trail to Kneeland Place. The route then climbs steeply to Somers Point and returns to the Freezeout Trailhead via the Western Rim Trail. The total distance for this loop is 58 miles. With some creativity and a good map, many other loop trips of various lengths can be planned.

WARNING: Less-used connecting trails are often faint and difficult to find on the ground. Also, the canyon's great changes in elevation create radically different environments. Therefore, while one part of your planned loop is cool, green, and beautiful, the lower part of the same trip may be hot, dry, and brown. Prepare accordingly.

POSSIBLE ITINERARY

	CAMP	MILES	ELEVATION GAIN
Day 1	Squirrel Prairie (with side trip to Bear Mountain)	13.1	2,200'
Day 2	Sacajawea Campground (Hat Point)	11.4	2,300'
Day 3	Indian Grave Saddle	12.2	1,100'
Day 4	Somers Point	6.6	1,200'
Day 5	Lord Flat	8.9	1,000'
Day 6	Out	13.7	1,500'

25 SNAKE RIVER TRAIL

RATINGS: Scenery 10 **Solitude** 7 **Difficulty** 8
MILES: 41
ELEVATION GAIN: 6,000'
DAYS: 4–5
SHUTTLE MILEAGE: See transport notes below
MAP: USFS *Hells Canyon National Recreation Area and Wilderness*
USUALLY OPEN: Year-round
BEST: Mid-April–early May and September–October
PERMITS: Northwest Forest Pass required at trailheads
RULES: No fires within 0.25 mile of the Snake River; firepans required year-round
CONTACT: Wallowa Mountains Office, Wallowa-Whitman National Forest, 541-426-4978, fs.usda.gov/wallowa-whitman

SPECIAL ATTRACTIONS

Whitewater rafters to observe, historical sites, wildlife, great canyon scenery

CHALLENGES

Complicated and expensive boat transportation; rattlesnakes, ticks, and black widow spiders (especially in the spring and early summer); no shade—it can be extremely hot; lots of poison ivy

Above: View below Suicide Point
photographed by Douglas Lorain

HOW TO GET THERE

The logistics of starting this hike are unusually complicated. A very long and tedious car shuttle from Hells Canyon Dam to Dug Bar is one option. This would allow you to enjoy the trail's entire length, but it also would require making arrangements for a short boat ride downstream to Battle Creek, where Oregon's river trail starts.

For Hells Canyon Dam, take I-84 to Exit 302 in Baker City. Head east on OR 86 for 67 miles. At Copperfield, go straight for 0.5 mile onto Hells Canyon Road (also known as Forest Service Road 454), crossing into Idaho, then turn left. Follow Hells Canyon Road 22 miles to the dam.

To reach the Dug Bar trailhead, from I-84 take Exit 261 in La Grande and turn right (east) onto OR 82. In 1.4 miles turn left (north) to remain on OR 82. Go 17.7 miles and turn right (east) to again remain on OR 82. Drive 44.2 miles to the town of Enterprise. Turn right (south) to continue another 6.3 miles on OR 82 to Joseph. Turn left (east) onto OR 350 and go 29.4 miles. After crossing the Imnaha River, turn left (north) onto Lower Imnaha Road. In 6.3 miles make a slight right (northeast) onto Dug Bar Road/FS 4260. In 6.8 miles turn left (north) to remain on Dug Bar Road. Go 6.6 miles, cross the Imnaha River again, and turn left to stay on FS 4260. Go 10.7 miles to the end of the road and the trailhead. The drive is long and sometimes rough but incredibly scenic.

WARNING: The last 8 miles are especially steep and difficult. When the road is wet, a four-wheel drive vehicle is highly recommended.

A second option (with a much shorter car shuttle) is to start the trip from the Freezeout Trailhead (see Trip 26). This requires a climb over Freezeout Saddle, where there is likely to be some snow through April. The route then descends the Saddle Creek Trail to reach the Snake River Trail about 8 miles downstream from Battle Creek. To reach Freezeout Trailhead, from I-84 take Exit 302 in Baker City, and head east on OR 86. Go 60.1 miles, and in Halfway turn left onto North Pine Road. Drive 14.3 miles and turn right onto Forest Service Road 39/Wallowa Mountain Loop. In 8.8 miles turn right onto FS 39/Upper Imnaha Road. Go 2 miles and turn right onto Wallowa Mountain Loop/FS 3955/Upper Imnaha Road. Drive 18 miles, cross the Imnaha River, and turn right onto FS 4230 (marked SADDLE CREEK TRAIL). Keep left at the first fork and continue 2.7 miles to the Freezeout Trailhead at the road's end.

WARNING: The Saddle Creek Trail includes several stream crossings that in the spring can be cold and rather treacherous.

Still another plan (and the one recommended here) necessitates only one car, but you must make arrangements at least two weeks in advance with a jet boat operator to pick you up at Dug Bar and drop you off upstream. The larger companies are happy to help, but you'll have to work around their regular tour schedules. Expect to pay between $80 and $160 for boat transport from Dug Bar to about Johnson Bar. Reliable operators include Hells Canyon Adventures (800-422-3568; hellscanyonadventures.com) and Snake River Adventures (800-262-8874; snakeriveradventures.com).

A final option, which avoids bad roads altogether, is to leave your car in Lewiston, Idaho; take the jet boat upstream to your chosen drop-off; and then arrange for the boat to pick you up for the ride back down to Lewiston at the end of the hike. This option requires

Snake River Trail
To Lewiston, Idaho
Dug Bar Road
4260
Dug Bar 1,030'
Immaha River
Thorn Spring Creek
Christmas Creek Ranch
Snake River
Snake River Trail
1,300'
To Imnaha
Square Mountain 4,800'
Deep Creek
Roland Creek
Cat Creek
Bob Creek
Copper Creek Lodge
Highrange Rapids
Deep Creek Ranch
Bench "High" Trail
Rowley Gulch
Litch Ranch
Tryon Saddle
Lookout Creek
Tryon Creek Ranch
Camp Creek
Englishman Hill
Cow Creek
Lord Flat 5,600'
landing strip
Pleasant Valley Creek
3,100'
Pittsburg Guard Station
Long Prong
Somers Creek
Somers Point 5,676'
Pittsburg Landing
Mormon Flat
Robertson Ridge
Durham Creek
Muir Creek
OREGON
Windy Ridge
Parliament
Hominy Creek
Salt Creek
Salt Creek Trail
Two Corral Creek
Cougar Creek
Kirby Bar
Kirkwood Ranch
Suicide Point
Ninemile Saddle
Grassy Knoll 6,515'
Dry Gulch
Temperance Creek Ranch
Lightning Creek
Temperance Creek
Wisenor Place
Alum Bed Rapids
IDAHO
Sand Creek
game warden's cabin
Eagle's Nest
Horse Creek
Warnock Corral 6,700'
Rush Creek
To Imnaha
Rattlesnake Creek
Johnson Bar 1,300'
Sluice Creek
Rush Creek Rapids
Memaloose Guard Station
Hat Point Lookout
landing strip
Imnaha River
4240
Log Creek
Freezeout Saddle 5,300'
4230
Saddle Creek
Black Mountain 6,862'
To Pine Creek
Freezeout Creek
To Hells Canyon Dam
0 1 2 3
Miles

that you stick with a set schedule on the trail to make the prearranged pickup time, and you'll probably have to pay for two boat trips.

TIP: See the note in Trip 24 concerning car-shuttle services for hikes in Hells Canyon.

NOTE: While jet boats are recommended here as the most convenient transportation for backpackers, they are not necessary for this hike. If you are morally opposed to the use of jet boats, do not avoid this outstanding trip as a result. Use one of the other options noted above.

GPS TRAILHEAD COORDINATES:

(Dug Bar) N45° 48.277' W116° 41.207'
(Freezeout) N45° 22.548' W116° 45.715'
(Hells Canyon Dam) N45° 14.493' W116° 42.190'

INTRODUCTION

Two words sum up the experience of hiking Oregon's Snake River Trail: *spectacular* and *exhausting*. With all due respect to the marvelous canyon scenery found along the Rogue River, the Owyhee River, and many other Oregon streams, they all pale in comparison to the vastness of Hells Canyon. The Snake River Trail provides perhaps the ultimate backpacking experience in the canyon. Although the trail on the Idaho side is easier to access, Oregon's Snake River Trail sees much less traffic, reaches higher viewpoints, has more loop options, and is a bit longer and more rugged. In short, it's worth the complicated access. Only the most jaded traveler will fail to return with a sore neck from so much time spent looking up to the canyon's rim thousands of feet above. More serious threats than a sore neck, however, are rattlesnakes and poison ivy, so you must spend at least as much time looking down as up.

TIP 1: Summer days are blisteringly hot, and nights are uncomfortably warm. Dress accordingly and be prepared to sleep on top of your bag.

TIP 2: In many places poison ivy is so abundant that you simply cannot avoid the stuff. Try using a shielding product, applied before contact, and/or a special soap to wash off the toxins afterward. People who are particularly allergic should probably avoid this hike altogether.

DESCRIPTION

Pick up your prearranged boat ride at Dug Bar and plan on a long, exciting, and informative trip upriver to the recommended drop-off opposite Johnson Bar. The larger companies typically stop along the way at Kirkwood Ranch, an interesting museum that is well worth a visit. It will be early afternoon by the time you disembark. You must scramble up the bank a bit to reach the trail.

TIP: Before starting the downstream trek, consider a short exploration upstream. Rush Creek Rapids is a good nearby goal and logical turnaround point.

Downstream from Johnson Bar, the wildly scenic route stays close to the river and soon comes to a fine camp at (probably dry) Yreka Creek—obtain water from the Snake River. The path then crosses a huge rock shelf called Eagle's Nest, where the trail has been blasted into the side of the rock. Take a moment to marvel at the work involved, not to mention the quantity of dynamite it must have taken. Civilian Conservation Corps workers did an admirable job building this path in the 1930s. About 2.2 miles from the takeout point is the Sand Creek game warden's cabin. Farther downstream, at Alum Bed Rapids, the Idaho side boasts a colorful area of exposed yellow cliffs.

The trail works around a bend in the river and then tours a grassy bench above the stream. You pass a marked junction with a very sketchy "trail" up Dry Gulch and then go around a large, fenced meadowy flat. In a confusing section near the north end of this pasture, the trail crosses the fence and goes down to Temperance Creek Ranch. You make a bridged crossing of Temperance Creek and come immediately to a junction in the trees. You can camp upstream amid this creek's lush riparian vegetation.

Now the Snake River Trail goes north, passes the massive cliffs of Suicide Point (across the river in Idaho), and reaches good camps and a cabin at the flats of Salt Creek.

TIP: A possible side trip climbs the steep Salt Creek Trail to a series of excellent overlooks above the river.

Continuing on the Snake River Trail, cross Two Corral Creek, briefly follow close to the river, and then go across a large, sloping bench. Near the north end of this bench is Slaughter Gulch (often dry). The trail now drops to the riverside and hugs the shore beside steep cliffs. The route is chiseled into the canyon walls and, despite staying close to river level, is constantly making tiny ups and downs. The crossing of Cougar Creek offers good views across the river to the meadowy flat holding Kirkwood Ranch.

The rugged trail continues to hug the cliffs on the Oregon side for the next mile or two before breaking out onto a meadowy bench across from Idaho's Kirby Bar. Muir Creek supplies water and some possible spots to eat lunch or camp. The alternating pattern of steep slopes and river benches continues as you cross a set of cliffs and reach the bench at Durham Creek (more potential camps). For the next 2 miles the trail goes through a narrow section of the canyon, where both the Oregon and Idaho trails have been carved out of the hillsides and cliffs. You are likely to see far more people on the Idaho side's trail because that popular route has easy access for day hikers from Pittsburg Landing.

NOTE: Geography buffs may be interested to note that, as the trail rounds the slopes of Robertson Ridge, it crosses the easternmost point in Oregon.

Landmarks, mainly on the opposite shore, include the trailhead at Upper Pittsburg Landing and, later, the car campground at Lower Pittsburg. On the Oregon side, the trail crosses an arid bench to a junction with a steep path going up Robertson Gulch and then continues to the Pittsburg Guard Station.

In the miles ahead the Snake River cuts through a particularly narrow and steep-walled part of Hells Canyon. To avoid this difficult section, you are forced to make a long, sometimes rugged, but highly scenic detour. First your path climbs inland to the Bench Trail, some 1,500 feet above. The climb is steep in places and, as is true on the entire trail, exposed to the sun. Start with full water bottles and carry your own shade—a hat. The route contours away from Pittsburg and climbs a draw to a point about 500 feet above the river. Near the head of this draw is a spring with possible water. The trail then traces an up-and-down course about 1 mile to the crossing of Pleasant Valley Creek, with water and some shade. Now the climb really gets underway as the rocky path leads up a small ridge, gaining a little more than 1,000 feet in 1 mile. Just short of the high point is a junction with the Bench Trail in a large meadow with terrific views up to Somers Point.

The two trails follow the same route north for the next 2.8 miles. After 1.5 beautiful ridge-and-meadow miles, the fun abruptly ends as the trail steeply climbs a shadeless gully to a pass. Take a well-deserved rest at the top to enjoy the panoramas. As the trail descends toward Somers Creek, you will have some fine views down to the Snake River.

At a junction near the rounded summit called Englishman Hill, the Bench Trail goes left a short distance to Somers Creek (good camps), while the Snake River Trail (our route) turns right and continues its descent back to the river. After you make a couple of quick switchbacks, the often-steep route follows a tributary canyon of Somers Creek down to the main stream. A pleasant riparian zone of dense deciduous vegetation and a few ponderosa pines accommodates the trail as it parallels the rushing stream. The route requires three creek crossings that may get your feet wet but aren't difficult.

WARNING: Be particularly alert for poison ivy and rattlesnakes through this section.

Farm equipment relics at Kirkwood Ranch
photographed by Douglas Lorain

The area where you return to the Snake River has good campsites near an old cabin. At Camp Creek, a short distance farther north, are more camps and a junction with a trail that climbs back to the Bench Trail near Tryon Creek Ranch.

To continue your tour, closely follow the banks of the Snake River as it cuts a surprisingly straight path north for the next few miles. Steep cliffs on both sides of the canyon provide exciting scenery. The Idaho side no longer has a trail, as that path's northern terminus was Pittsburg Landing. About 0.4 mile north of Camp Creek, Tryon Creek furnishes a good camp and a chance to refill your water bottles. If this spot doesn't suit you, more camps are located at Lookout Creek just over 1 mile farther north. After Lookout Creek the trail passes along the base of some impressive cliffs, and in places it has been blasted right into the side of them.

After a junction with a sketchy trail just before Lonepine Creek (usually dry), your trail leads well above the raging Snake River as it cuts through a particularly narrow segment of the canyon. Just above the trail near Highrange Rapids, an old mine shaft is protected as a nursery for bats. The trail then works back down to river level and returns to its pattern of miniature ups and downs blasted into the cliffs.

Just past a second mine tunnel, the trail splits. The official trail climbs to the left, while to the right are a boat landing and the lush oasis of Copper Creek Lodge, a modern facility run by a commercial boat operator. In fact, you may have stopped here on the boat ride up. It includes several modern cabins, manicured lawns and shade trees, running water, gift items and souvenirs, and dining facilities. Hikers need reservations to spend the night or eat here; call 509-758-4800 or visit hellscanyontours.com. Day hikers from Copper Creek Lodge use the trails near here, so this is one of the few areas where you can expect company on this trip.

Shortly beyond the lodge you cross a wide bench where there is a junction near Bob Creek.

TIP: Shortly after crossing this creek, look for a short spur trail that goes upstream to a small waterfall.

Several trees on the flat meadow area near Bob Creek make this a particularly good campsite. As you leave the day hikers behind, the Snake River Trail remains close to the river until Cat Creek, where it detours around an abandoned ranch. A sketchy trail ascends the slopes south of here on its way to Tryon Saddle.

To continue your tour, traverse a large meadowy bench above Roland Bar Rapids and then arrive at Roland Creek. This small creek usually flows all year, so stock up on water here. For the next several miles, the Snake River Trail travels a rugged up-and-down course well away from the river over terrain that will keep your heart pounding, from both the exertion and the views.

TIP: Elk are common. Keep an eye out for wildlife.

The detour away from the river starts with a sometimes steep and rocky 600-foot climb from Roland Creek to a saddle. The trail then follows a less strenuous up-and-down course to the buildings of abandoned Dorrance Ranch. Just past the ranch the trail splits. To the right, a path drops back down to the Snake River and then continues to Christmas Creek Ranch. The official Snake River Trail keeps left, crosses Bean Creek (usually flowing), and then drops a bit around a ridge to Christmas Creek. Shortly beyond this small stream is the junction with the return loop of the trail to Christmas Creek Ranch. Next is yet another climb, though this time at a fairly moderate grade, along a view-packed slope to a junction with the spectacular path to Deep Creek Ranch.

TIP: If you have an extra day, this trail is well worth taking as a long side trip.

After crossing Thorn Spring Creek near an old cabin, the trail climbs a bit more and then begins the steep 1,100-foot descent back to the Snake River.

The trail returns to the river just above Deep Creek Bar. There is plenty of water here, as well as a collection of interesting shacks and old machinery from Chinese miners. Several luxurious camps in the vicinity cater to whitewater rafters and feature such amenities as picnic tables and an outhouse.

WARNING: You must ford Deep Creek here, which can be a bit tricky in the spring, so use caution.

To complete your adventure, continue along the Snake River another 1.1 miles to Dug Creek. You turn up this side stream and travel through the dense grasses and vegetation along the creek.

WARNING: The stinging nettles and poison ivy in this section are so thick that they are impossible to avoid.

The trail crosses and recrosses the creek, sometimes making it easy to lose. Often the easiest alternative is to simply walk up the streambed itself. After about 0.8 mile the trail finally works away from the creek (though the poison ivy remains in force) and reaches a junction. Turn right and climb a bit to reach a great view overlooking Dug Bar, and then drop steeply to the ranch. The well-marked public trail goes to the right around the ranch area.

TIP: Don't miss the short side trail to a sign referencing the Nez Perce Indians' crossing of the Snake River near this location in 1877. The courageous band of Indigenous people, led by Chief Joseph, traveled through here on a heroic (and ultimately futile) journey in search of freedom.

From here it is only a few hundred yards to the parking area near the boat ramp at the trailhead.

POSSIBLE ITINERARY

	CAMP	MILES	ELEVATION GAIN
Day 1	Temperance Creek	6.8	500'
Day 2	Pittsburg	8.5	500'
Day 3	Bob Creek	13.2	2,600'
Day 4	Out	12.5	2,400'

26

HELLS CANYON BENCH HIGH TRAIL

RATINGS: Scenery 10 **Solitude** 8 **Difficulty** 8
MILES: 63
ELEVATION GAIN: 14,900'
DAYS: 5–8
SHUTTLE MILEAGE: 46
MAP: USFS *Hells Canyon National Recreation Area and Wilderness*
USUALLY OPEN: April–November
BEST: Early to mid-May
PERMITS: Northwest Forest Pass required at trailheads
RULES: No fires within 0.25 mile of Snake River
CONTACT: Wallowa Mountains Office, Wallowa-Whitman National Forest, 541-426-4978, fs.usda.gov/wallowa-whitman

SPECIAL ATTRACTIONS

Views, abundant wildlife, wildflowers, solitude

CHALLENGES

Rattlesnakes, poor road access, poison ivy, often very hot, rough trail, several burn areas, ticks (especially in the spring)

Above: Wisenor Place
photographed by Douglas Lorain

HOW TO GET THERE

To reach the north trailhead of this hike, drive to the end of Dug Bar Road. The Freezeout Trailhead is the south trailhead for this hike. See page 163 of Trip 25 for directions to both trailheads and information about car shuttles.

GPS TRAILHEAD COORDINATES:

(Dug Bar) N45° 48.277' W116° 41.207'
(Freezeout) N45° 22.548' W116° 45.715'

INTRODUCTION

For lovers of canyon scenery and wildflowers, the Bench Trail through Hells Canyon is the experience of a lifetime. Following a mid-canyon route about halfway between the Snake River and the Summit Ridge, this spectacular tour provides a greater variety of scenery than any other long trail in the canyon. In addition to offering vistas across the canyon to the peaks in Idaho, the area delivers views down into the depths below, up to the contorted canyon walls above, and, often most impressive of all, of the scenic meadows right at the hiker's feet. Photographers must become very choosy to avoid running out of storage space and battery (bring extra!). This trail also travels through the finest examples of native bunchgrass in Oregon—a plant community lost elsewhere to the hooves of cattle and introduced plant species. In season, wildflowers and wildlife are perhaps more abundant here than on any other long trail in the state.

Despite the awesome scenery, the great distances and rugged terrain keep out all but the best-conditioned backpackers. Horse packers are much more common, though even they are rather few and far between. You'll probably have most of this wonderful hike all to yourself.

NOTE: Trail signs usually identify this as the High Trail. Users, however, more often refer to it as the Bench Trail, as this is a better description of the terrain.

WARNING: Those who choose to come here must be prepared for the rigors of this place. The second half of this hike is particularly rugged, with numerous steep climbs and descents over sunbaked slopes. (Fortunately, unlike on the Snake River Trail, there are usually enough trees to provide shade at rest stops, although a large section in the middle of this hike was affected by the 2022 Double Creek Fire.) At lower elevations you may encounter poison ivy. Rattlesnakes inhabit the entire length of the trail. Temperatures, while more comfortable than at the bottom of the canyon, can be very hot on sunny afternoons. In a few places, where game and livestock trails veer off in all directions and grasses obscure the path, the route is easy to lose–good route-finding instincts will come in handy.

TIP: Fans of watching wildlife should carry binoculars. Use them in the early morning and evening to scan the grassy slopes and rock ledges. You have a good chance of spotting elk, deer, bighorn sheep, black bears, coyotes, and maybe even a mountain lion. As you sit quietly and continue to search, more animals inevitably seem to come into view. It's great fun!

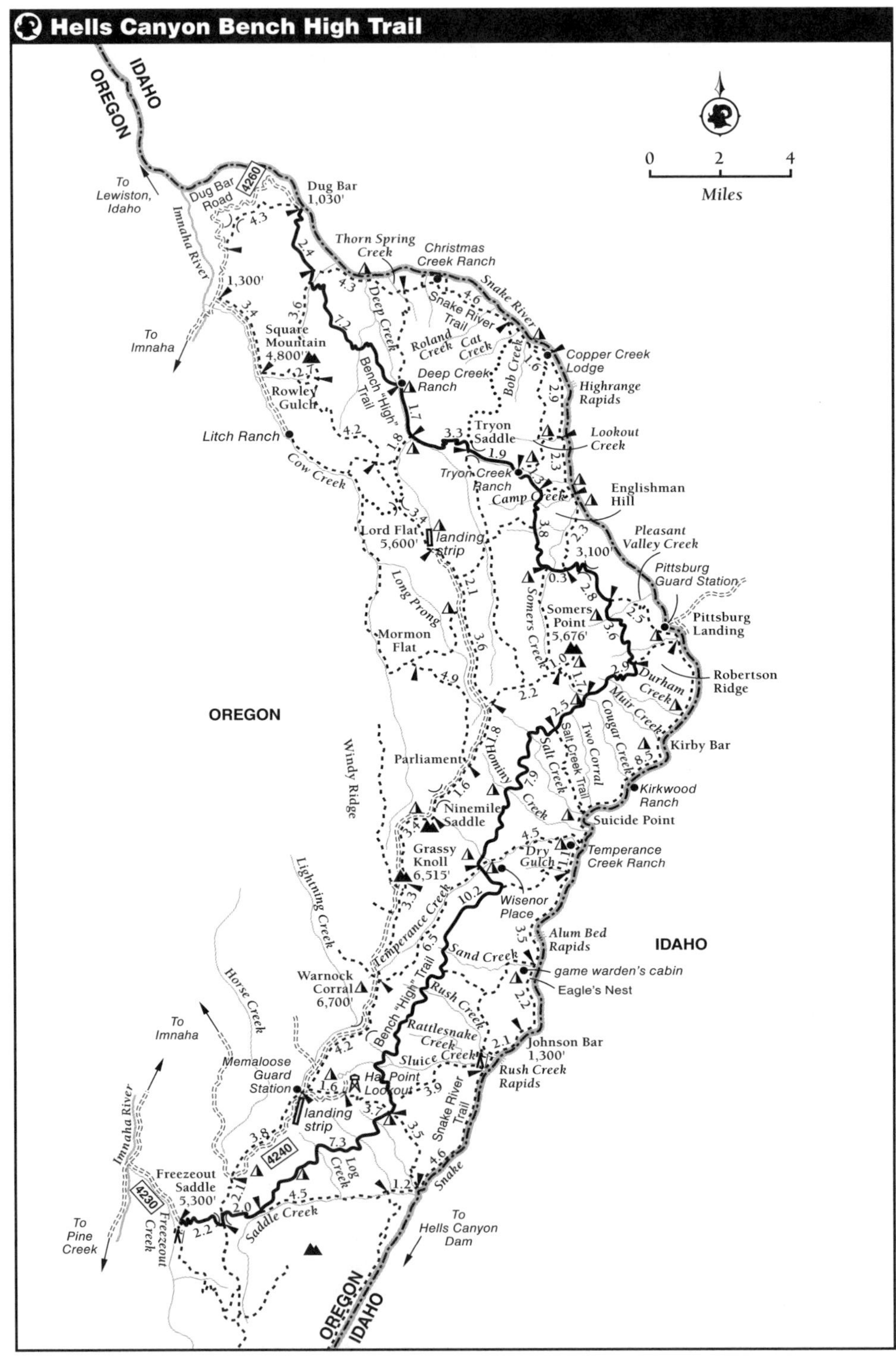
Hells Canyon Bench High Trail
IDAHO
OREGON
To Lewiston, Idaho
Dug Bar Road
4260
Dug Bar 1,030'
Imnaha River
1,300'
To Imnaha
Thorn Spring Creek
Christmas Creek Ranch
Snake River
Snake River Trail
Square Mountain 4,800'
Deep Creek
Roland Creek
Cat Creek
Bob Creek
Copper Creek Lodge
Highrange Rapids
Deep Creek Ranch
Bench "High" Trail
Rowley Gulch
Litch Ranch
Tryon Saddle
Lookout Creek
Tryon Creek Ranch
Camp Creek
Englishman Hill
Cow Creek
Lord Flat 5,600'
landing strip
Pleasant Valley Creek
3,100'
Pittsburg Guard Station
Pittsburg Landing
Long Prong
Somers Creek
Somers Point 5,676'
Mormon Flat
Robertson Ridge
Durham Creek
Muir Creek
Cougar Creek
Two Corral
Salt Creek Trail
Salt Creek
Kirby Bar
OREGON
Windy Ridge
Parliament
Hominy Creek
Kirkwood Ranch
Ninemile Saddle
Suicide Point
Grassy Knoll 6,515'
Dry Gulch
Temperance Creek Ranch
Wisenor Place
Lightning Creek
Temperance Creek
Alum Bed Rapids
IDAHO
Sand Creek
game warden's cabin
Eagle's Nest
Warnock Corral 6,700'
Rush Creek
Horse Creek
To Imnaha
Rattlesnake Creek
Johnson Bar 1,300'
Sluice Creek
Rush Creek Rapids
Memaloose Guard Station
Hat Point Lookout
Snake River Trail
landing strip
4240
Log Creek
Imnaha River
Freezeout Saddle 5,300'
4230
Saddle Creek
Snake
To Pine Creek
Freezeout Creek
To Hells Canyon Dam
OREGON
IDAHO
0 2 4
Miles
2.4
4.3
3.6
7.2
3.4
2.7
1.7
1.8
4.2
3.3
1.9
4.6
1.6
2.9
2.3
1.3
3.8
2.3
0.3
2.8
2.5
3.6
2.9
2.1
3.6
4.9
2.2
1.0
1.7
2.5
8.5
1.8
7.9
1.6
3.4
4.5
1.1
3.3
10.2
3.5
6.5
2.2
4.2
2.1
1.6
3.9
3.7
3.5
3.8
7.3
4.6
2.1
2.0
4.5
1.2
2.2

DESCRIPTION

Your route begins with a long series of moderately steep switchbacks up a grassy slope to Freezeout Saddle. (Odds are very good that you will be hot and sweaty after the 1,700-foot climb, and "freezing" will be the last thing on your mind.) In many ways Freezeout Saddle is the focal point of hiking in Hells Canyon. In addition to the Bench Trail, the Western Rim Trail (see Trip 24) cuts through here on its way south to McGraw Lookout and north to Hat Point, and the Saddle Creek Trail grants access to the Snake River. Finally, this is one of the few locations in the canyon with reasonable access for day hikers to such landmarks as Bear Mountain.

To hike the Bench Trail, go straight from the saddle and descend a mostly open slope with several exceptional views of smooth-sided Bear Mountain and craggy Black Mountain to the south. The trail passes through a repeatedly burned area—the first of many on this trip—whose snags provide habitat for a large population of Lewis's and other woodpeckers. After 2 miles you turn left at a junction with the Saddle Creek Trail.

As the Bench Trail goes north, several patterns that will hold true for most of this trip soon become apparent. For the most part, the trail is gently graded, following the canyon slopes at elevations between 3,500 and 4,500 feet. To allow this, it contours out across the ridges and into the creek canyons in a seemingly endless series of zigzags. Large meadowy benches sometimes provide a platform for the trail, but the in-out pattern predominates. The river, flowing some 3,000 feet below, is rarely visible. The vegetation provides another interesting pattern. Surprisingly lush forests of Douglas fir and ponderosa pine, along with numerous shrubs and ground cover plants, grow on the north-facing slopes. On drier, south-facing slopes, only the occasional ponderosa pine survives amid rocky meadows sprinkled with wildflowers. The meadowy benches and ridges are perhaps most scenic of all, with breathtaking views and thousands of flowers. Look for balsamroot, lupine, phlox, wallflower, yarrow, Indian paintbrush, Lomatium, gilia, brodiaea, and countless others.

With these patterns in place, your route begins with a long, undulating approach to a prominent ridge about 5 miles northeast. The trail has only moderate ups and downs, and numerous small creeks provide water, so the hiking is easy and enjoyable. Log Creek has the first good campsites. Upon finally reaching the ridge, you are rewarded with a large grassy area and excellent views of the cliffs above. Shortly beyond the ridge, the route crosses Rough Creek above a small falls and then continues through forest to crossings of the several branches of Hat Creek.

About 100 feet after the last branch of Hat Creek, a sheepherder's cabin appears on the right, and just beyond is a junction with the trail from Hat Point. The cabin, usually open, is a good shelter if it rains.

WARNING: Lots of mice inhabit this cabin. Hang your food and be prepared for a long night of listening to the sounds of scurrying rodents.

Keep straight at the junction with the Hat Point Trail and drop another 100 yards to a second junction; the trail to the right goes past a corral on a grassy bench before descending to the Snake River.

TIP: This bench area is a wonderful place to camp, with nearby creek water, shade, and truly outstanding cross-canyon vistas.

Now the Bench Trail goes north 0.2 mile to yet another junction. You turn left and immediately enjoy terrific views of the impressive cliffs below Hat Point—it still sports plenty of snow in early May.

Continuing on the Bench Trail, the route traces a surprisingly gentle course as it circles the headwaters of Sluice Creek. The awesome cliffs and rock pinnacles of Hat Point tower above. At the final branch of Sluice Creek, the route passes below an impressive waterfall—the best on the entire trip. The trail then crosses Rattlesnake Creek (a reminder to keep an eye out for these creatures) and Rush Creek. A little beyond Rush Creek is the simple grave site of Charlie Gordon (1901–1918) for whom there is no epitaph, but the years indicate that he died far too young. A little farther along is a junction with a faint trail to Sand Creek and the Snake River.

Continuing north, the rambling route passes through scattered decades-old burn areas as it gradually gains elevation and works toward the top of the rugged divide separating Temperance Creek from the main canyon. The trail reaches the top of this wide and very beautiful meadowy ridge and then follows it about 1 mile. You pass a fenced corral and then go around the right side of a grassy knoll to a saddle with a junction. Turn left and descend very steeply on a rocky trail (watch your step), losing 1,200 feet to a ford of Temperance Creek. The old Wisenor Place homestead is on the opposite bank. There are excellent camps in the surrounding area.

The Temperance Creek Trail meets the Bench Trail here. To continue your tour, keep right and contour 0.2 mile to a crossing of Bull Creek (more camps). The trail then makes a series of ups and downs as it traverses open, grassy ridges and canyons. After crossing Cove Creek (beware of poison ivy), the trail makes a determined assault up a side canyon on its way to Hominy Saddle, almost 1,000 feet above. From the saddle the trail turns left and follows a fence line up the ridge before dropping to Hominy Creek (good camps).

Returning to its familiar "into canyon–out ridge" course, the 8-mile tour between Hominy Creek and Kneeland Place is easy, mostly level hiking over open, view-packed slopes. The only problem may be losing the sometimes overgrown path as your attention turns to the view rather than the trail. The Salt Creek Trail intersects your route at one of the many meadowy ridges. Watch for elk in this area. Cross Two Corral Creek and continue to Cougar Creek at the site of the old Kneeland Place (long gone). Lots of ponderosa pines and riparian shrubs make this a choice campsite—though horse packers seem to think so, too, so you may be crowded out.

TIP 1: The best camps are about 200 yards upstream near a spring.

TIP 2: An excellent but steep side trip from here climbs to the outstanding overlook at Somers Point, though this high ridge may still have some snow in May.

Not far beyond the Kneeland Place, the previously gentle character of the Bench Trail begins to change as the canyon's topography requires the trail to go more radically up and down. After contouring around a ridge and crossing South Durham Creek, the path drops in a series of short, steep switchbacks to North Durham Creek (water, but no camps). The path then contours out to a ridge, where a confusing ditch trail goes straight, while the Bench Trail switchbacks to the left and drops to a junction. The road and developed area visible on the Idaho side of the canyon are at Pittsburg Landing. The trail drops into Buckpasture Gulch before crossing yet another view-packed ridge and descending steeply to Pleasant Valley. Look for bears and some excellent campsites in this aptly named location.

Now the Bench Trail climbs gradually through a large meadow to a junction with the Snake River Trail. In a rugged detour around river-level cliffs, this lower trail has been forced to climb to meet the Bench Trail at this point. The two trails follow the same route north for the next 2.8 miles.

WARNING: Beware of poison ivy in this section.

After about 1.5 joyful ridge-and-meadow miles, the fun is over because the trail climbs a shadeless gully *steeply* to a pass. Take a well-deserved rest at the top to enjoy the great panoramas. As the trail descends toward Somers Creek, you will have some fine views down to the Snake River.

At a junction near the rounded summit called Englishman Hill, the Snake River Trail departs to the right while the Bench Trail makes a short jog left to Somers Creek at the site of burned-down Somers Ranch. This is a fine spot for lunch or to camp for the night. After passing a junction with a trail to Somers Point, the Bench Trail climbs gradually along grassy slopes and through lush riparian areas to Hog Creek. Keep right at a junction and then cross some beautiful grassy terraces before dropping very steeply over loose, boot-skidding rocks to splashing Camp Creek. Climb to a grassy saddle and then traverse an open terrace dotted with bushes on the way to inviting Tryon Creek Ranch. This ranch house and its outbuildings are still used by U.S. Forest Service crews, so the area is well maintained. A hose provides a steady flow of water from an unseen spring.

TIP: If you have some extra energy in the evening, invest it in the fine side trip out to Tryon Viewpoint–0.6 mile northeast along the trail to Lookout Creek.

From Tryon Creek Ranch the Bench Trail makes a long, wickedly steep 2,000-foot climb to Tryon Saddle.

TIP: Try to tackle this section in the shade of the evening or the cool of the morning.

Views from the windswept saddle are outstanding, especially of Deep Creek Canyon to the west. Elk populate the nearby slopes. Low-growing phlox and other flowers help to give this treeless pass an alpine feeling.

To continue your tour, keep right at the saddle, contour around a basin, and then begin the long descent to Deep Creek. The route drops through a mix of rocky areas and trees before following a small creek for the final 0.5 mile. An excellent camp is located in the trees next to Deep Creek at the bottom of the descent.

The trail turns north and takes a joyful course as it follows the clear, rushing waters of Deep Creek. You pass through a surprisingly lush and shady forest of ponderosa pine, Douglas fir, grand fir, and mixed deciduous trees. The hiking is easy and beautiful through this environment, which is unusual for Hells Canyon—it more closely resembles the higher-elevation forests of the Blue Mountains. Familiar forest residents like red-breasted nuthatches, porcupines, Douglas squirrels, and chipmunks find good habitat here. In early May look for huge serviceberry bushes, some as big as trees, putting on a showy display of white blossoms.

You pass the junction with a trail headed for Cow Creek before reaching a nice campsite. Continue straight to Deep Creek Ranch, which marks the end of the easy creekside forest walk.

TIP: A little downstream from the ranch is a nice flat area where backpackers can make a comfortable camp.

You ford Deep Creek next to the ranch house and then begin to climb a mostly open slope above the cliffs lining lower Deep Creek's canyon. The climb tops out several hundred feet above Deep Creek Ranch, where you can savor terrific views of the lower canyon. Sadly, the trail now loses virtually all of that hard-won elevation as it drops to Little Deep Creek. This area would make a good campsite if it weren't so badly churned to dust and used as a toilet by cattle.

The trail climbs gradually away from Little Deep Creek along an open grassy slope. Eventually you'll come to a fence line at a high pass, which delivers outstanding views. From this vantage point you can see all the way to Dug Bar Ranch, the end point of your hike. The path makes a long descent to Dug Creek and to a junction with the trail to Lord Flat.

WARNING: Beware of poison ivy near Dug Creek. The thickets here are the worst on the entire trip.

A short distance farther is a second junction, this one with the Snake River Trail coming up from the right. Keep straight, climb a bit to reach a great view overlooking Dug Bar, and then drop steeply to the ranch. The well-marked public trail goes to the right around the ranch area.

TIP 1: Don't miss the short side trail to a sign referencing the Nez Perce Indians' crossing of the Snake River near here in 1877. While crossing the flooding river as they did is not advisable, it does feel great to jump in briefly, both to cool down and to wash off a few layers of dirt before hiking the last few hundred yards to your car.

TIP 2: Don't forget to allow plenty of time for the long, slow drive back along Dug Bar Road to Imnaha.

POSSIBLE ITINERARY

	CAMP	MILES	ELEVATION GAIN
Day 1	Hat Creek	11.5	3,700'
Day 2	Temperance Creek	10.2	2,100'
Day 3	Kneeland Place	10.4	2,300'
Day 4	Tryon Creek Ranch	14.7	2,800'
Day 5	Little Deep Creek	9.3	2,800'
Day 6	Out	7.2	1,200'

27

STEENS MOUNTAIN GORGES LOOP

RATINGS: Scenery 10 **Solitude** 8 **Difficulty** 9
MILES: 24 (31)
ELEVATION GAIN: 4,700' (5,700')
DAYS: 2–4
SHUTTLE MILEAGE: NA
MAPS: USGS *Fish Lake* and *Wildhorse Lake*
USUALLY OPEN: Mid-June–October
BEST: Late June and late September
PERMITS: Free and self-issued at trailhead
RULES: Fires strongly discouraged
CONTACT: Burns District, Bureau of Land Management, 541-573-4400, blm.gov/office/burns-district-office

SPECIAL ATTRACTIONS

Solitude, incredible scenery, fall colors, wildflowers

CHALLENGES

Steep and very difficult scrambles up and down canyon headwalls; difficult stream crossings; thunderstorms; early season snowfields; limited shade; ticks (especially in spring and early summer); rattlesnakes

Above: Big Indian Headwall

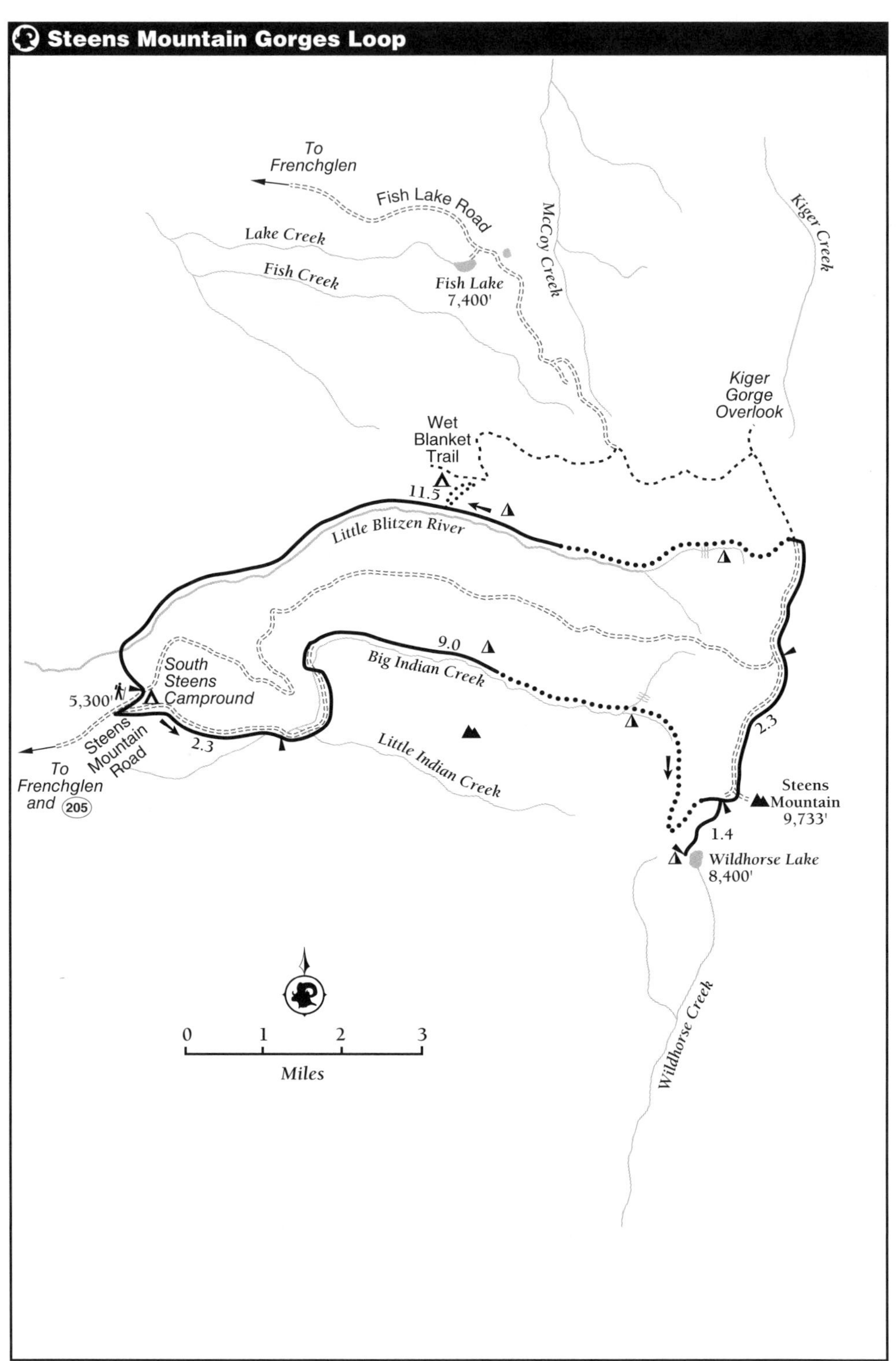

Steens Mountain Gorges Loop
To Frenchglen
Fish Lake Road
Lake Creek
Fish Creek
Fish Lake 7,400'
McCoy Creek
Kiger Creek
Kiger Gorge Overlook
Wet Blanket Trail
11.5
Little Blitzen River
9.0
Big Indian Creek
South Steens Campround
5,300'
Steens Mountain Road
2.3
To Frenchglen and 205
Little Indian Creek
2.3
Steens Mountain 9,733'
1.4
Wildhorse Lake 8,400'
Wildhorse Creek
0
1
2
3
Miles

HOW TO GET THERE

From the intersection of US 20 and US 395 in Burns, head south on Fly Road/OR 205, and go 60 miles to Frenchglen. Continue another 9 miles to a junction with a well-marked gravel road and turn left (east). This is the southern end of Steens Mountain Loop Road. Ominous signs here warn of possible blizzards. (When completely open, this is the highest road in Oregon, so they're not kidding.) Drive east on this decent gravel road about 17 miles to a bridge at Blitzen Crossing. About 2.2 miles beyond the bridge is the South Steens Campground. Turn into this campground and park near the marked trailhead at the far (eastern) end.

GPS TRAILHEAD COORDINATES:
N42° 39.379' W118° 43.449'

INTRODUCTION

Steens Mountain dominates the landscape of southeastern Oregon. At 9,733 feet it towers over the hills and marshes of the surrounding desert, and it can be seen for hundreds of miles in all directions. People are drawn to this landmark for many reasons, not least of which is the scenery.

The majestic beauty of this desert mountain has no equal in Oregon or, arguably, anywhere else in North America. The cliffs on the mountain's eastern escarpment drop more than 5,500 feet to the flat expanse of Alvord Desert. On the gently sloping west side of the mountain, ice age glaciers carved immense U-shaped gorges that are among the most impressive in the world. In most of North America, forests now obscure the evidence of past glaciation. Here, however, the only trees are scattered mountain mahogany and a few aspen and cottonwood groves near the bottom of canyons. Thus, the geologic history is spectacularly displayed for all to see. Waterfalls stream down steep walls that rise thousands of feet above the canyon floor. Clear, rushing streams flow through meadows sprinkled with wildflowers. Wildlife, including bighorn sheep, badgers, coyotes, bobcats, and the occasional rattlesnake (especially in the lower parts of the canyons), is plentiful. Best of all, the isolation and the lack of official trails mean that there's plenty of solitude—except, perhaps, during the fall hunting season. If you do this hike just before the higher parts of the loop road open to cars, you may have the entire trip to yourself. The road's lower elevations usually open in May (but call ahead to be sure).

NOTE 1: The snowpack on Steens Mountain is extremely variable. The highest parts of the loop road typically open around July 1; therefore, the last week of June is ideal for this trip. Call ahead to the Bureau of Land Management office in Burns for the latest conditions.

NOTE 2: Steens Mountain is a fragile island in a desert. Leave No Trace techniques are especially critical here. Fires, in particular, should be avoided. The country is dry, and wood is scarce, so bring a backpacking stove.

DESCRIPTION

From the parking area for the trailhead at the east end of the campground, the trail (an old jeep track) almost immediately enters the wilderness. Follow this jeep track east as it gains elevation across juniper-scented meadows, with views of Rooster Comb in the distance. The trail then drops steeply to a berm and a sign indicating the point beyond which all vehicles were prohibited in the days before the wilderness designation. The route now crosses Indian Creek.

WARNING: In spring or early summer, this can be a cold and potentially difficult ford. By fall, and sometimes even early summer, it looks fast but is shallow and easy.

TIP: A sturdy walking stick and wading shoes will come in handy.

On the opposite side, continue on the abandoned jeep track and quickly reach another crossing, this time of Little Indian Creek (possibly wet but not a problem). This side creek flows down from its own scenic gorge—a worthwhile day hike if you have the time. Your route now goes north, following the main canyon of Big Indian Creek. Look for the ruins of an old cabin tucked into the trees beside the trail. Less than 1 mile beyond the first crossing is the second ford of this creek. The streambed is a bit wider here, so the crossing is easier.

The old road provides easy walking as it slowly gains elevation. Springs and small tributaries provide ample water early in summer. The mostly flat canyon bottom and the nearby stream mean that you can camp almost anywhere. The canyon turns east and grows ever more dramatic, with continuous and awe-inspiring views of the high peaks and cliffs. Sagebrush and juniper give way to more frequent meadows and occasional groves of aspen, and wildflowers become more numerous. Patches of snow from the previous winter add to the scenery.

TIP: Photographers will need an extra-wide-angle lens to capture the vastness of this gorge.

About halfway up the canyon, the route fades out in a meadow. A large grove of aspen trees makes this a particularly inviting campsite. Though the road disappears, a sketchy trail continues up the canyon. It is sometimes lost amid sagebrush, aspens, or lush meadows, but the trail isn't really necessary. Be sure to look downstream from time to time to enjoy ever-improving views of this huge gorge. The relatively easy hiking ends at the sloping basin beneath the canyon headwall, one of Oregon's most spectacular locations. Flowers bloom in abundance, waterfalls cascade down the lava walls, and the surrounding cliffs rise almost 2,000 feet. There are plenty of possible campsites but not much shade.

Up to this point the going has been fairly easy, but sturdy boots and strong lungs are needed for the next section. Exiting the basin requires a steep uphill scramble over sometimes loose rocks. There is no single "best" route, but the recommended way turns north, following the right side of one of the creek's larger branches. Scramble up the grassy and rocky slopes, gaining 2,000 feet of elevation in about 1.6 miles, until you eventually reach the top of the headwall and the gravel Steens Mountain Loop Road.

Depending on your capacity for road-walking and/or your appetite for cross-country navigation, you have a good opportunity here for a side trip to very scenic Wildhorse Lake. From the road, it's easy; turn left (east) and walk to a signed turnoff for East Rim

Overlook and Steens Summit Road. Take a hard right and follow the summit road 2 miles to the Wildhorse Lake trailhead. This basin often remains snow-covered into July, but later in the season the lake sits in a lovely meadow filled with wildflowers. It's a 1-mile descent along the trail to established campsites at the lake, but first take a moment to follow the half-mile spur trail up to the highest point on Steens Mountain. A radio tower and buildings intrude on the wilderness setting, but the panorama is amazing! Even the peaks of the Cascade Range are visible on clear days. Best of all, though, is the view east to the large playa called Alvord Desert, more than a vertical mile below.

TIP: Bring binoculars to look for bighorn sheep here and at other spots overlooking the eastern cliffs.

If the Steens Mountain Loop Road is not yet open to traffic, you should have this overlook all to yourself. The trade-off for solitude is the need to walk over some large snowfields.

Back on the Steens Mountain Loop Road, continue walking north. The high alpine grasslands in this area are alive with wildflowers in summer, through early August. Continue north along the road to a sign indicating the overlook of massive Little Blitzen Gorge.

Here you have a choice to make: The safest route is to continue along the Steens Mountain Loop Road north to the Kiger Gorge Overlook and west to the beginning of the Wet Blanket Trail. It's a lot of road walking, and you'll want to avoid doing this in the heat of the day. The other option is to scout an off-trail descent from here, where you overlook the Little Blitzen Gorge.

If you choose the second option, brace your knees because it's a very steep descent down the headwall cliffs. Directly below the overlook, the cliffs are ridiculously steep, so try the slopes either 0.5 mile farther north or about 0.3 mile south for a marginally easier route.

The view from Little Blitzen Overlook

(You can usually see faint tread where others have gone.) It's about 1,600 feet down to the floor of the canyon, and there is no trail, so carefully pick your way down the rocky terrain. This effort is amply rewarded because the large, boggy basin below the headwall is only slightly less impressive than the one in Big Indian Gorge. Here you will enjoy more of the cliffs, wildflowers, clear streams, and generally outstanding scenery characteristic of Steens Mountain. There are numerous possible campsites to spend a night amid this grandeur.

From the top of a small waterfall that drops from the headwall basin, you'll enjoy a marvelous view down the canyon. Soon you'll catch a faint, rough trail that follows the north bank of the stream. This path gradually improves and becomes a reasonably good trail as it continues downstream.

If you have opted to continue along the loop road, make sure to stop for a look at the Kiger Gorge Viewpoint, then continue to a signed junction with the start of Wet Blanket Trail, veering off through the grass and over the edge of the cliff. This trail is steep but well used and easy to follow down into the gorge, where it meets the Little Blitzen Trail 2 miles west of the headwall.

Your route travels west past more little waterfalls and through lovely meadows filled with grasses, wildflowers, and pungent sage. Near the creek, aspen and cottonwood trees provide frames for photographs, as well as welcome shade. Dark canyon walls rise on either side. About 4 miles down the canyon, a sketchy pack trail (called Nye Trail on some maps) meets our route from the north. This little-used path switchbacks steeply up the north wall to a jeep track south of Fish Lake. The canyon floor is wide and almost level near this junction, with several nice meadows and good campsites.

The Little Blitzen River Canyon slowly angles southwest as the stream's descent gets a bit steeper. The sage, mountain mahogany trees, and brush get thicker at lower elevations, so views are somewhat limited the rest of the way. After passing a massive buttress on the south wall, the river and the trail angle a little more to the south before breaking out into the rolling sagebrush country at the mouth of the canyon. At a fence line, the trail turns left and fords the river.

WARNING: This crossing can be waist-deep in early summer.

The trail continues south, away from the river, as it climbs over a low ridge and gradually descends to the loop road at a signed trailhead. An easy 0.5-mile walk through the campground across the road leads back to your car and the close of an incredibly scenic trip.

POSSIBLE ITINERARY

	CAMP	MILES	ELEVATION GAIN
Day 1	Big Indian Gorge	8.0	1,500'
Day 2	Wildhorse Lake	6.0	2,500'
Day 3	Little Blitzen Gorge via Wet Blanket	9.0	1,200'
Day 4	Out	8.4	500'

28

DESERT TRAIL: PUEBLO MOUNTAINS SECTION

RATINGS: **Scenery** 8 **Solitude** 9 **Difficulty** 7
MILES: 22 (28)
ELEVATION GAIN: 3,700' (5,700')
DAYS: 2–3 (3–4)
SHUTTLE MILEAGE: 20
MAP: Oregon Natural Desert Association *Oregon Desert Trail Region 3 (Section 16: Fields to Denio Creek)* (available as a free download at onda.org/discover-oregons-desert/trail-resources)
USUALLY OPEN: Mid-May–November
BEST: Mid-June and September–October
PERMITS: None
RULES: Fires strongly discouraged (check locally for seasonal fire bans)
CONTACT: Burns District, Bureau of Land Management, 541-573-4400, blm.gov/office/burns-district-office; Oregon Natural Desert Association, 541-330-2638, onda.org

SPECIAL ATTRACTIONS

Expansive views, solitude, wildflowers

Above: The trail's south exit, near Denio Cemetery

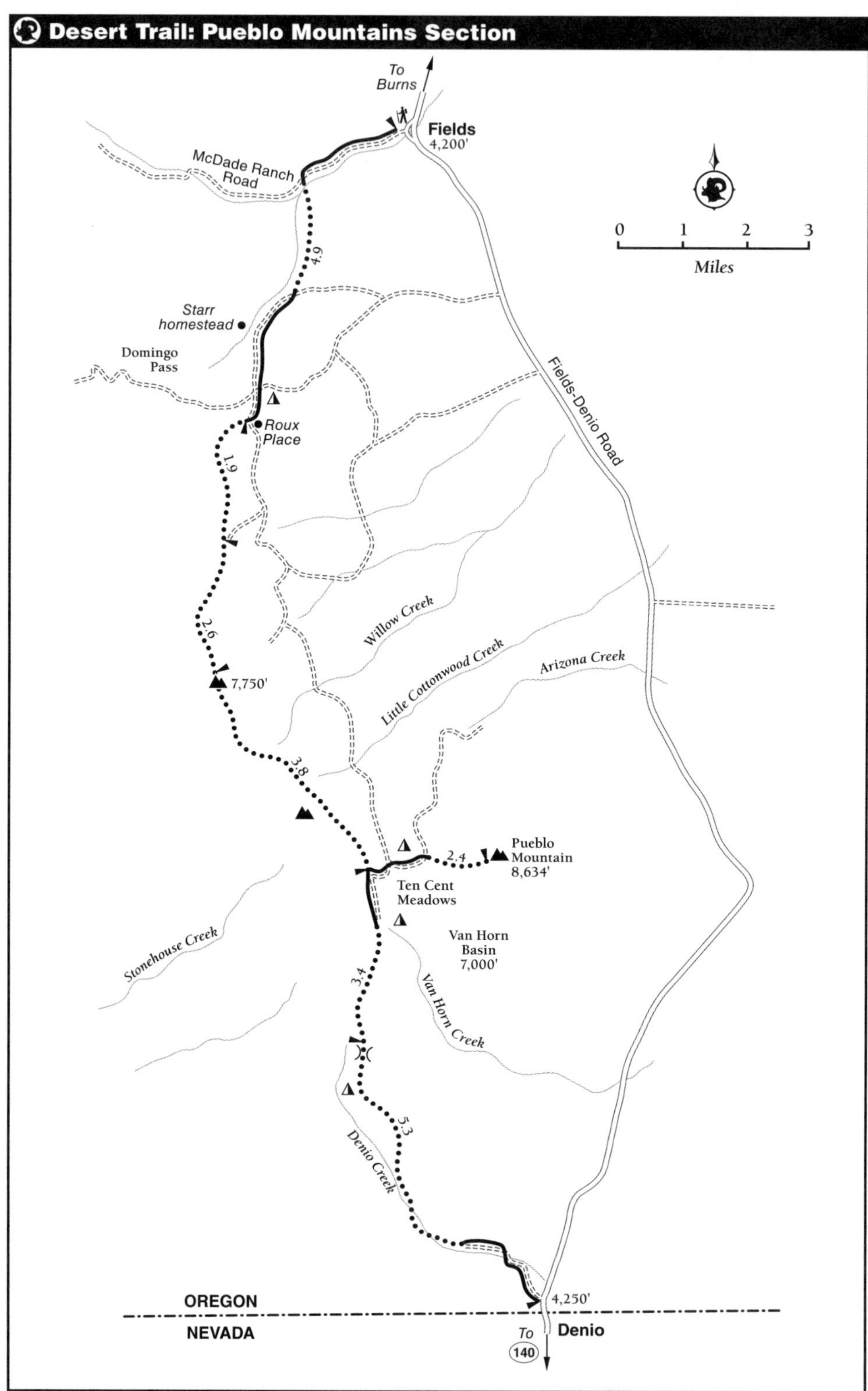
Desert Trail: Pueblo Mountains Section
To Burns
Fields
4,200'
McDade Ranch Road
0 1 2 3
Miles
4.9
Starr homestead
Domingo Pass
Roux Place
1.9
Fields-Denio Road
Willow Creek
2.6
7,750'
Little Cottonwood Creek
Arizona Creek
3.8
Pueblo Mountain
8,634'
2.4
Ten Cent Meadows
Van Horn Basin
7,000'
Stonehouse Creek
3.4
Van Horn Creek
5.3
Denio Creek
OREGON
NEVADA
4,250'
To
140
Denio

CHALLENGES

Route-finding difficulties, no shade, limited water, rattlesnakes

HOW TO GET THERE

Both ends of this trip are on a good paved highway with an easy car shuttle between them—a real blessing in an area where road access is typically over poor dirt tracks. This hike begins in the tiny town of Fields. To reach it, from the intersection of US 395 and US 20 in Burns, head south on OR 205 (which becomes Fields–Denio Road) and go 112 miles to the Fields General Store, where you can also get a famously excellent milkshake and good advice on camping and travel in the area.

The trail's south exit is beside a cemetery on OR 205 just north of the small town of Denio on the Oregon–Nevada border; there's space to park a couple of cars outside the front gate.

GPS TRAILHEAD COORDINATES:

(Fields) N42° 15.854' W118° 40.520'

(Denio Cemetery) N42° 0.144' W118° 38.087'

INTRODUCTION

This trek is likely to take many casual backpackers outside their comfort zones. For one thing, it's a long way from nowhere, about as far southeast as you can get and still be in Oregon (you exit the hike about a mile from the Nevada border). For another, there isn't actually a trail. The recommended route follows a section of the Oregon Desert Trail, which itself is largely conceptual—often unmarked and stitched together from an evolving network of existing trails, dirt roads, and cross-country routes. For this segment, you'll want to download a copy of the Oregon Natural Desert Association's (ONDA's) guidebook, carry a GPS device, and have good way-finding skills using a map and compass. Even with all that, the trip is a bit like a scavenger hunt. Your route is marked by numbered rock cairns that set a general course through the terrain, but they may be hard to see, or kicked over, and there's no defined footpath between them except for occasional zigzagging cattle trails. So you'll need a pretty good sense of direction as well as a sense of adventure.

WARNING: Bring a good map, a compass, and binoculars to help locate each cairn. The ONDA's downloadable maps and guidebook include detailed directions and waypoints for each cairn.

Partly for these reasons, and despite good road access, the Pueblo Mountains remain isolated and receive few visitors. But this desert range has a great deal to offer. The terrain is radically different from elsewhere in the state. Views seem to stretch to eternity. There are permanent streams and springs (rare for southeastern Oregon). Enough snow falls that the high cliffs and peaks are picturesquely streaked with white into June, and spring wildflowers put on a beautiful show. Don't expect much shade, however, as trees are limited to a few mountain mahogany and aspen. This hike is best early or late in the season.

Road walk at the start of the trail from Fields

DESCRIPTION

From the north end of "downtown" Fields (that is, the cluster of buildings that serve as store, motel, post office, and gas station), hike 2 miles west alongside Fields Creek on McDade Ranch Road (called Williams Creek Lane Access Road on some maps) and then turn south at a cattle guard. Cross a (usually dry) creek and follow a fence line 0.5 mile. Head briefly west about 100 yards along another fence to reach a jeep road and once again turn south. Stick with this jeep road about 2 miles (with a short detour around the Starr homestead) to Domingo Pass Road. Shortly thereafter, head southwest along a fence line. Follow this fence to its end, then continue southwest about another 100 yards to a grove of aspens at Roux Place Springs, the first reliable water.

NOTE: The springs are on private land. If you wish to camp, do so on public land, 200 yards or more to the south.

From the springs, go west and then south to contour at a roughly constant elevation around two hills; in about 2 miles, a jeep track comes up from the east. Here you should find the first in the series of cairns that you'll be following for the remainder of this trip. Ahead is a long and difficult climb along a steep gully and hillside. Views to the north of distant Alvord Desert and Steens Mountain steadily improve as you climb. Closer at hand are the crags of the Pueblos, as well as small flowers and colorful lichen on the rocks underfoot.

WARNING: The route often crosses areas of loose rocks, so exercise caution.

TIP: Be sure to check out an interesting rock with a large hole in it near cairn #7.

Reach the ridgecrest near cairn #8 and enjoy grand sights in all directions, particularly to the west over the Rincon Valley and beyond. Stick with the up-and-down ridgecrest, often on game trails, to the top of a mountain. The bulk of your climbing is now complete, so congratulate yourself and enjoy the hard-won view. As you drop down the east side of the ridge, you pass a welcome spring and then contour around the cliffs above the head of Willow Creek.

Now you round a ridge at a saddle near cairn #22 and turn south. Towering cliffs rise to the west for the next 2 miles, and twisted mountain mahogany adds to the scenery. Cross a small tributary of Cottonwood Creek and then pass a grove of stunted aspen trees on the way to Ten Cent Meadows, set in a mile-wide saddle between the main ridge of the Pueblos on the west and hulking Pueblo Mountain on the east. There are possible campsites here, with nearby spring water.

TIP: Don't miss the side trip from here to the summit of Pueblo Mountain. It's about 2.5 miles to the top, and the route often travels over steep and loose rocks, but the view is well worth the effort. There is, of course, no trail, but you don't really need one.

You meet a jeep road coming up from Arizona Creek and follow it south 1.2 miles as it drops into beautiful Van Horn Basin. There are many possible places to camp near Van Horn Creek, with aspen groves providing shade.

TIP: The morning view over the creek and the aspen groves of Van Horn Basin to the snow-streaked ridge of the Pueblos is a photographer's dream.

To continue your tour, leave the jeep road at cairn #32 and climb, often steeply, along a sidehill. You walk on top of a long rock ledge as the route works toward the pass between Van Horn and Denio Basins. The sights, as expected, are outstanding, especially to the east of massive Pueblo Mountain and of Van Horn Basin with its many aspen groves. After a well-deserved stop at the pass, proceed south into the Denio Creek drainage as you rapidly lose elevation. Wildflowers are particularly abundant here. At a large aspen grove, there is room to make a pleasant camp beneath the trees, with nearby water.

Now the route makes a long, poorly marked detour to the east around a parcel of private land in Denio Basin. You cross a fence line marking the end of private property and meet a jeep road going east toward Propeller Meadows, where the remains of an old plane crash can be found. Turn right (south) onto a dirt track here for 1.2 miles to a small pond and building at the end of the track. Continue southeast along a ridge parallel to the Denio Creek drainage until you meet the creek at the bottom of the hillside. Follow the creek toward Denio Cemetery and the end of the hike.

POSSIBLE ITINERARY

	CAMP	MILES	ELEVATION GAIN
Day 1	Roux Place Springs	5.2	1,100'
Day 2	Van Horn Basin (with side trip up Pueblo Mountain)	15.0	3,600'
Day 3	Out	8.0	1,000'

29

FREMONT NATIONAL RECREATION TRAIL: SOUTHERN SEGMENT

RATINGS: Scenery 7 **Solitude** 9 **Difficulty** 5
MILES: 17
ELEVATION GAIN: 3,100'
DAYS: 2
SHUTTLE MILEAGE: 24
MAPS: USFS *Fremont National Forest: Paisley Ranger District, Silver Lake Ranger District, Lakeview Ranger District*
USUALLY OPEN: Year-round (roads may be inaccessible in winter)
BEST: June and September
PERMITS: None
RULES: Follow posted rules (on camping, fire bans, etc.) at trailheads; leave all gates as you find them
CONTACT: Fremont-Winema National Forest Headquarters, 541-947-2151; Lakeview Ranger District, 541-947-6300, fs.usda.gov/detail/fremont-winema/about-forest/offices

SPECIAL ATTRACTIONS

Epic views from three peaks, gentle terrain, wildflowers, butterflies, solitude

Above: Rock formations above the Fremont National Recreation Trail

CHALLENGES

Cattle, heat, potentially confusing forest road crossings

HOW TO GET THERE

To reach the Mill Trailhead from Lakeview, take US 395 north for 11 miles, then turn right onto Forest Service Road 3721/Deter Ranch Road. After 0.3 mile bear right onto a narrow, bumpy road and continue 0.5 mile, staying right again at an intersection; at 0.7 mile keep right again at a junction with a private road. In 0.3 mile cross a cattle guard and continue to the trailhead and parking loop at the road's end.

To reach Vee Lake from Lakeview, take US 395 north for 13 miles, then turn right (east) onto OR 140 (signs to Adel/Plush) and drive 7.9 miles. Turn left (north) at the Camas Sno-Park onto FS 3615 and go 17 miles. Bear right onto FS 3616 and continue 4 miles to the lake and small trailhead at the road's end.

GPS TRAILHEAD COORDINATES:

(Mill) N42° 20.229' W120° 16.238'
(Vee) N42° 25.335' W120° 09.569'

INTRODUCTION

The Fremont National Recreation Trail (NRT) overlaps parts of the Oregon Desert Trail and the Southern Oregon Intertie Trail, but it's an ambitious project all its own. In three main segments, the long-distance trail extends through much of the Fremont National Forest, starting at Yamsay Mountain in the north, crossing Winter Rim, and then traversing the crest of the Warner Mountains. Parts of the trail are faint or primitive, and there are small gaps between the segments, but the Fremont NRT gets more cohesive every year. Forest roads provide access to the trail at various points along the way, so hikers can choose how much they want to attempt (and, equally important, can work around frequent weather- and fire-related closures).

The northernmost section offers sweeping views from Yamsay Mountain and Hager Mountain. The middle section runs south from Government Harvey Pass along the spectacular crest of Winter Rim, a fault block rising more than 2,000 feet above Summer Lake. This southern segment, the shortest and currently most accessible, wanders from the Mill Trailhead in the Crooked Creek Drainage north to tiny Vee Lake. The scenery is surprisingly lush and varied, the grade is mellow, and views from the often-bare ridgeline are dramatic. Within just a few miles, the trail goes from a quiet, woodsy creekbed to a trio of high peaks that are easy to summit, then back down into a colorful little canyon. Think of it as a quick and easy sampler of a region that deserves more attention and further exploration.

DESCRIPTION

From the Mill Trailhead, cross Crooked Creek (there may be a log bridge, but if not it's an easy ford) and follow the old roadbed east. The gently graded trail follows the creek through a shady forest of ponderosa pine, aspen, willow, and cottonwood, with interesting rock formations on the ridges above. In about half a mile, near a spring in a grassy

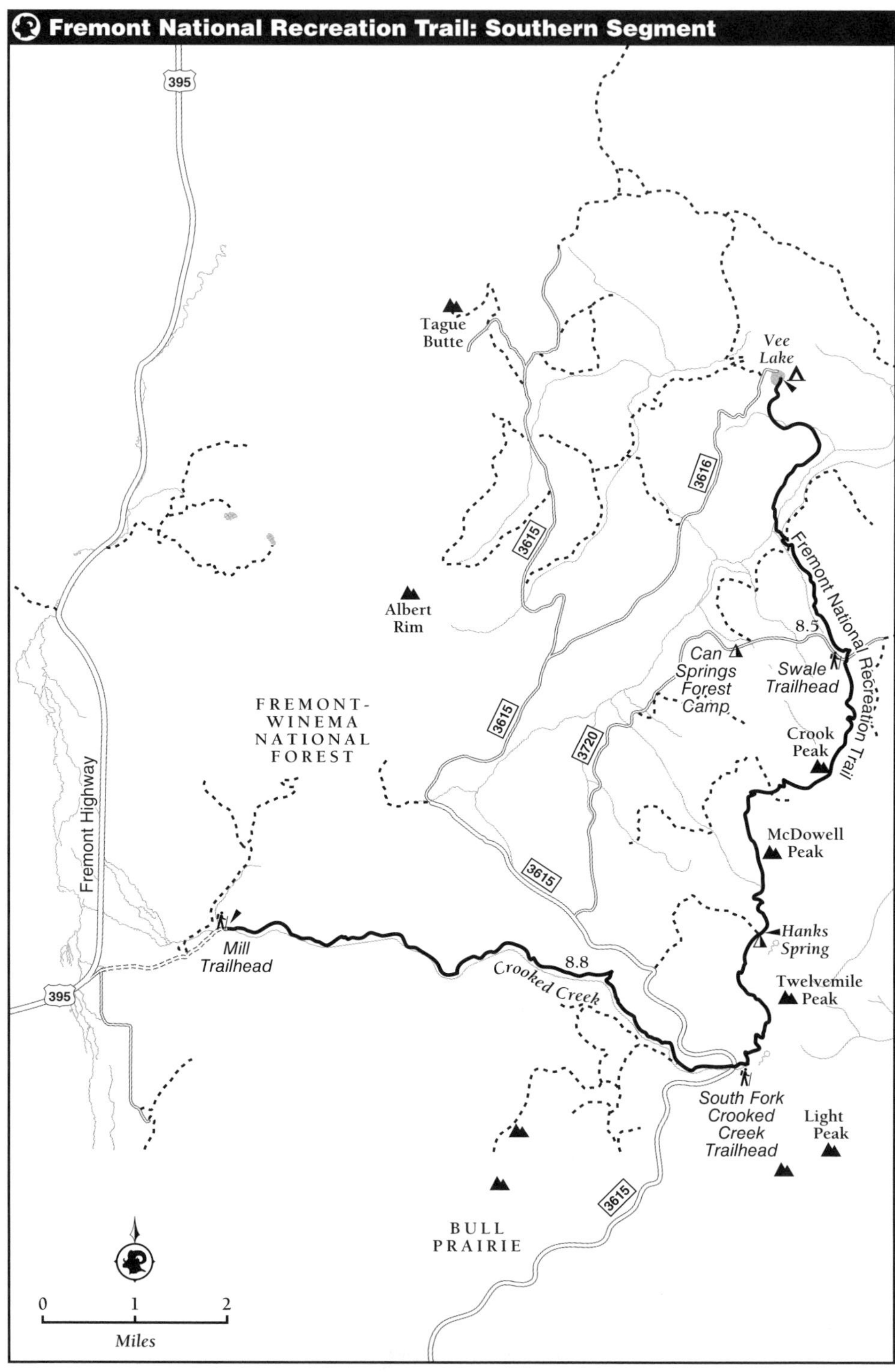
Fremont National Recreation Trail: Southern Segment
395
Tague Butte
Vee Lake
3616
3615
Albert Rim
Fremont National Recreation Trail
8.5
Can Springs Forest Camp
Swale Trailhead
FREMONT-WINEMA NATIONAL FOREST
3720
Crook Peak
Fremont Highway
McDowell Peak
3615
Hanks Spring
Mill Trailhead
8.8
Crooked Creek
Twelvemile Peak
395
South Fork Crooked Creek Trailhead
Light Peak
3615
BULL PRAIRIE
0 1 2
Miles

meadow, there's an interpretive sign beside the trail that describes the history of logging in the area.

The path begins to narrow into a small canyon as you continue up the creek. Then the terrain opens up again to spring-laced meadows full of butterflies and wildflowers. The sloping canyon walls hold pine trees, juniper, and mountain mahogany, and you pass through more lush wildflower meadows. At a dirt track leading off to the right, you bear left, cross Big Cove Creek, then cross Crooked Creek again (there may be several strands of the creek to cross here). After this crossing, ignore use trails to the left and right and instead go straight on a trail marked with white diamond blazes as it winds uphill slightly away from the creek.

Continue heading east with the creek below to your right. North Warner Viewpoint is at the top of the ridge to your left. At about 5.5 miles the trail makes a sharp right turn to cross the North Fork of the creek before continuing southeast. In just over a mile, your trail meets paved FS 3615. Carefully cross this road to reach the South Fork Crooked Creek Trailhead, where there's a pit toilet and a large parking area.

TIP: Top up your water bottles here; there are occasional springs on the next stretch of trail, but they're often muddied, cow-trampled, a ways off-trail, and hard to locate.

An obvious dirt track exits the trailhead parking lot and starts to climb. You're following the overlapping Oregon Desert Trail/Fremont NRT as it zigzags uphill and north toward Twelvemile Peak. Several dirt tracks cross your path, but you stay on the single-track trail as it winds up the hill; the wider tracks lead to another crossing at the top of the hill, but the proper trail ascends at a more reasonable grade.

Views start to open up as you climb the west side of Twelvemile Peak. You can see across invitingly bare ridges to the Drake Peak Lookout (rentable and reachable by car), as well as Drake Peak and Light Peak (aka "other Drake Peak"), to the south.

TIP: Informal trails that go along this ridgeline and up around Twelvemile Peak are well worth exploring.

Your route continues to switchback up and then skirt the west side of Twelvemile Peak just at treeline. Rounding the north side of the peak, the path drops briefly into thick forest, then continues to alternate between wide-open sage-covered slopes and patches of mixed forest, with intermittently awesome views to the north and west. A mile and a half past the South Fork Crooked Creek Trailhead, you go through a not-very-effective-looking gate and continue to traverse the hillside. Half a mile later, you reach a small cluster of woods and a sign for Hanks Spring, which could be more of a cattle-stomped bog depending on the time of year, but it has spots to set up camp or at least take a break among the trees before setting off on the next stretch.

From Hanks Spring, guideposts point the way up a hilly meadow (or meadowy hill), with excellent views to the north and east but no shade. You continue heading north, traversing the bare western slopes of McDowell Peak. Once you round the northern edge of McDowell, you cross a forest road in a wooded saddle, then traverse the south side of Crook Peak.

TIP: On a clear day, views from the top of each of these peaks extend in pretty much all directions, and they're both easy to summit.

Then the trail drops again toward First Swale Creek, where it comes to a gravel road that leads to Swale Trailhead. A mile west on FS 3720 is the small, primitive Can Springs Forest Camp beside a spring-fed creek.

From Swale Trailhead, the route follows First Swale Creek for 0.7 mile, crosses a gravel road, then crosses the creek before dropping into the tree-lined canyon of Honey Creek. Your route follows this very scenic canyon for about a mile, giving you ample time to admire the colorful rock walls opposite. Then the trail leaves Honey Creek behind, curving northwest around a plateau through mixed forest, before turning north once again and dropping to Vee Lake, where a small campground sits among pine and aspen trees.

POSSIBLE ITINERARY

	CAMP	MILES	ELEVATION GAIN
Day 1	Hanks Springs	8.8	2,500'
Day 2	Out (Vee Lake)	8.5	600'

A spring-fed creek beside the Fremont National Recreation Trail

30

HONEYCOMBS LOOP

RATINGS: Scenery 9 **Solitude** 10 **Difficulty** 8
MILES: 17 (29)
ELEVATION GAIN: 3,500' (6,400')
DAYS: 2–3 (3–4)
SHUTTLE MILEAGE: NA
MAPS: USGS *Three Fingers Rock* and *Pelican Point*
USUALLY OPEN: April–November
BEST: Early May and September
PERMITS: None
RULES: Fires strongly discouraged (and periodically banned; check regulations in advance); camping in Leslie Gulch is allowed only at Slocum Creek Campground
CONTACT: Vale District, Bureau of Land Management, 541-473-3144, blm.gov/office/vale-district-office

SPECIAL ATTRACTIONS

Colorful rock formations, solitude

CHALLENGES

Limited water, poor road access (or complicated boat transport), no trails, rugged hiking, rattlesnakes

Above: Owyhee Reservoir

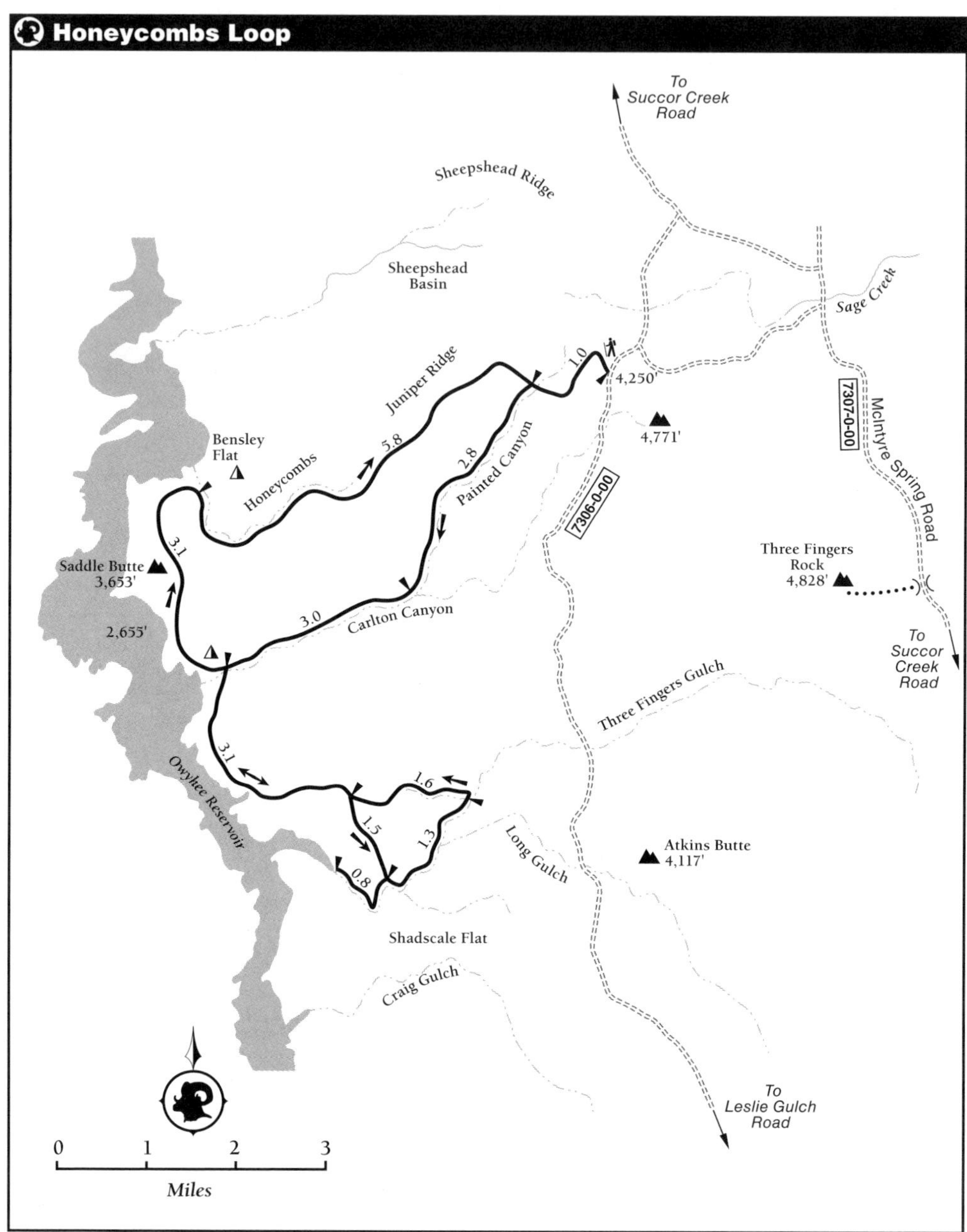

HOW TO GET THERE

For those without boat transportation, access to the closest roads is easier from the south. Drive north from Jordan Valley on US 95 for 18.2 miles, then turn left onto gravel Succor Creek Road. Follow this route 8.5 miles and turn right to remain on Succor Creek Road. Go another 6.6 miles (5 miles north of the well-marked Leslie Gulch Road turnoff) and turn left onto McIntyre Spring Road. The driving difficulties start here. With mud, rocks, and little or no maintenance, this road will never be mistaken for a superhighway. On the positive side, the drive provides wonderful views of cliff-edged McIntyre Ridge and the chance to see wild horses.

In 3.8 miles, pass a trailhead sign for prominent Three Fingers Rock (well worth the relatively short walk to explore) and continue north another 3.5 miles. Turn left in a grassy little valley holding Sage Creek, which is dry by early summer. This road, even worse than the one you've been on, climbs about 2.8 miles to a gate (close it behind you) and then a junction. Bear left. In a low pass 0.2 mile south of this junction, park beside a livestock watering tank.

GPS TRAILHEAD COORDINATES:
N43° 28.653' W117° 14.143'

INTRODUCTION

A land of striking beauty lies on the east side of the Owyhee Reservoir. In the dry canyons of this desert country, you will discover a collection of oddly shaped rock pinnacles, towers, and cliffs painted in a colorful array of browns, reds, and oranges. In spring, especially after a wet winter, the sagebrush and grasses turn green, and wildflowers like balsamroot and Indian paintbrush add yellows, reds, and other colors to the scene. Hikers familiar with the canyon lands of southern Utah will feel right at home.

Getting there, however, is not easy. A good gravel road goes down Leslie Gulch, so this canyon has become popular with hikers, photographers, and other admirers. Stretched out to the north are several equally spectacular canyons whose remoteness provides much more solitude. For the backpacker, the best access is either by boat from Owyhee Reservoir or over rough and poorly marked dirt roads that are torture on cars. Boat access requires finding someone willing to shuttle you down the reservoir about 25 miles to Bensley Flat and then return to pick you up after your trip. There is no commercial service, and relatively few private boaters go this far down the lake. As for the roads, after it rains, only high-clearance four-wheel-drive vehicles should try them. One option is to park on one of the area's good roads (through Leslie Gulch or Succor Creek Canyon) and then take a mountain bike to the starting point for your hike.

WARNING: Water ranges from scarce to nonexistent. The only reliable year-round source is Owyhee Reservoir, and this should be treated with both chemicals and filtering before drinking. On the other hand, beware of occasional thunderstorms that may cause flash floods.

DESCRIPTION

Having survived the drive, strap on a pair of sturdy boots (good ankle support is essential in this steep, rocky, trailless terrain) and head northwest on a jeep track. You top a low hill and then turn south and drop to a gully at the head of Painted Canyon. Hike down this ravine as it grows narrower and more spectacular. In places you may be forced to make rugged detours around cliffs and dry waterfalls.

TIP: Bring a rope to lower your pack over especially steep and dangerous sections before climbing down yourself.

The long, steep descent ends as the canyon bottom widens and levels out. Multicolored cliffs and spires rise on both sides, and as you continue down the canyon, the geologic scenery does nothing but improve. Near the mouth of Painted Canyon, the walls narrow considerably before breaking out into Carlton Canyon.

TIP: To see more towers and cliffs, drop your pack and explore east into upper Carlton Canyon for 0.5 mile.

Turning west, you'll find that the scenery remains good, though not as continuously dramatic as Painted Canyon.

TIP: After about 1 mile look for a side canyon to the north that is well worth exploring.

About 2 miles from Painted Canyon and 1 mile from the mouth of Carlton Canyon, you'll reach some high buttresses on either side that are especially dramatic. You can make camp in the flats where the canyon widens near Owyhee Reservoir—just don't count on any shade.

You can make an excellent but rugged day trip to Three Fingers Gulch from a base camp at the mouth of Carlton Canyon. Pack some water and hike south along the up-and-down slopes beside Owyhee Reservoir. After about 2 miles cross the mouth of a good-size canyon and then climb along this canyon's south ridge for 1.5 miles to where it levels out. From here you turn south up a second ridge, bordered on the west by cliffs and pinnacles.

NOTE: These cliffs go steeply down to the reservoir, which explains why you have to make this detour. Access beside the water is not feasible.

Descend east to a saddle, then *carefully* scramble down a *very* steep and narrow gully between two cliffs. You should reach the base of Three Fingers Gulch near a fork in the canyon at Shadscale Flat, where a very faint jeep road approaches from the south. Be sure to explore downstream through this scenic, narrow gulch to the Owyhee Reservoir.

WARNING: The last 0.2 mile to the reservoir requires some tough scrambling.

TIP: If you're really ambitious, scramble up the canyon's steep south slope to enjoy clifftop views of Three Fingers Gulch. Once on top, turn west and go about 0.5 mile to reach the terrific overlook atop the impressive cliffs rising directly from the waters of Owyhee Reservoir.

Turning east (upcanyon), keep left at the forks where you entered Three Fingers Gulch, and travel between two impressive cliffs. After about 0.8 mile you'll reach the mouth of Long Gulch at a point distinguished by a tall pinnacle. Keep left, following Three Fingers Gulch, and 0.3 mile later turn left again into a small canyon. You can climb this canyon all the way to the top of the ridge that you came in on earlier in the day, then retrace your route back to Carlton Canyon.

To complete the recommended backpack loop, go north from the mouth of Carlton Canyon along the sagebrush-covered hills beside Owyhee Reservoir. After about 1 mile you'll reach the base of Saddle Butte. Scramble over the pass on the east side of this landmark, then drop down a ravine to the large expanse of Bensley Flat. You can comfortably camp almost anywhere on this bench. There are even a few boaters' cabins and willow trees near the reservoir's shore.

Tall reddish-brown cliffs rise to the east of Bensley Flat.

TIP: These cliffs are best photographed in the low light of late evening.

From the south end of the cliffs, you walk up a scenic draw that heads initially south and then loops around to the northeast. This gulch goes through the heart of the Honeycombs—a spectacular region with a dizzying display of colorful rock formations, many pockmarked with holes and small caves. The north side of the canyon is particularly impressive.

About 2 miles from the canyon's mouth, you pass to the left of a large rock monolith and then continue to follow the canyon bottom as it climbs and turns east. At the head of the canyon, scramble very steeply to the right to reach the top of long, rolling Juniper Ridge, where the walking is much easier as you follow game and cattle trails.

WARNING: The crisscrossing trails along this ridge can be confusing. The correct route follows a generally northeast course along the top of this wide ridge.

After about 2 miles turn east, drop down a gully, and look for the jeep track coming down to the head of Painted Canyon.

TIP: If Juniper Ridge reaches a little saddle and starts to climb moderately steeply toward a 4,500-foot-high point, then you've gone about 0.5 mile past the proper turnoff.

Pick up the jeep route and follow it back to your vehicle (either car or mountain bike).

POSSIBLE ITINERARY

	CAMP	MILES	ELEVATION GAIN
Day 1	Mouth of Carlton Canyon	6.8	200'
Day 2	Day trip to Three Fingers Gulch (return to mouth of Carlton Canyon)	12.0	2,900'
Day 3	Out (via Honeycombs)	9.9	3,300'

Just north of Hanks Springs on the Fremont National Recreation Trail
(See Hike 29, page 188)

OTHER BACKPACKING OPTIONS

Though this book includes what the authors consider the *best* long backpacking trips in Oregon, there are many other options for the adventurous backpacker. With some creativity and a good set of contour maps, a backpacker could easily spend a lifetime in this diverse state. What follows is an overview of some additional recommended trips, with just enough description to whet the appetite. Because many of these hikes are in lesser-known areas, they are excellent options for solitude lovers. (Unless specifically noted, none of these trips requires a permit.)

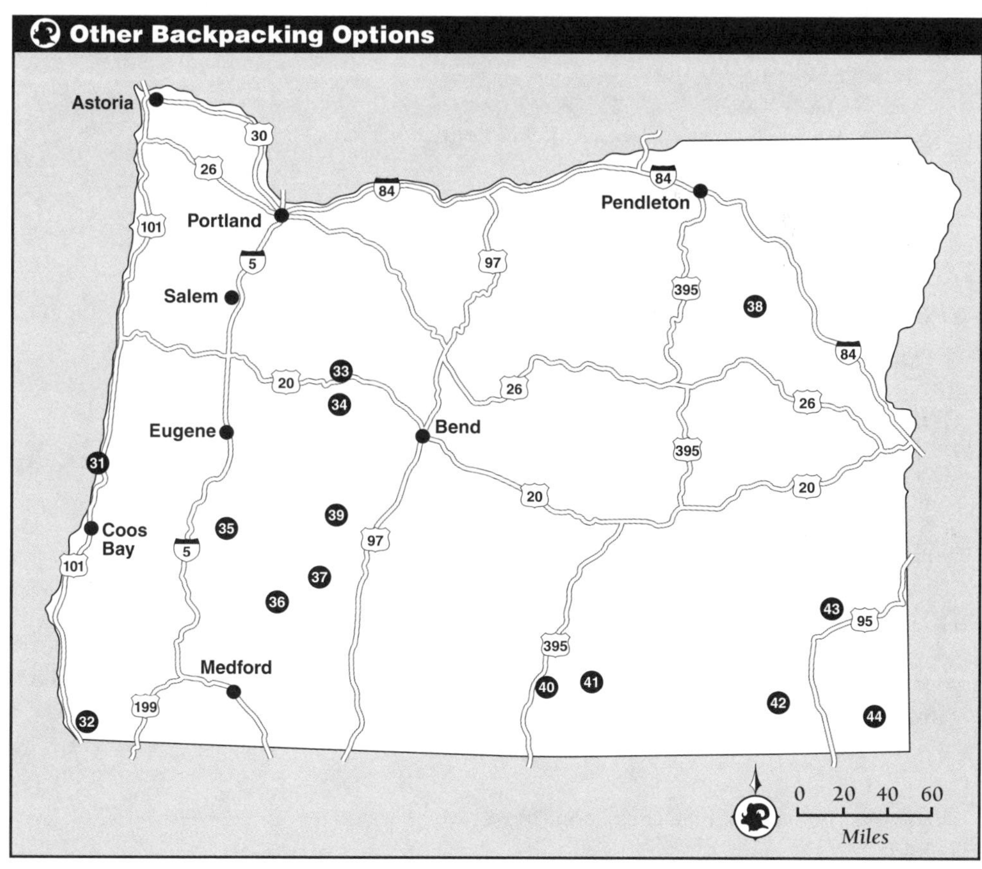

31

OREGON DUNES LOOP

RATINGS: Scenery 7 **Solitude** 3–8 **Difficulty** 5
MILES: Varies
DAYS: Varies
MAP: USFS *Oregon Dunes National Recreation Area*
USUALLY OPEN: Year-round
BEST: Winter and mid-May

SPECIAL ATTRACTIONS

Extensive sand dunes

CHALLENGES

Summer crowds, quicksand in winter

GPS TRAILHEAD COORDINATES:
(Tahkenitch Creek Trailhead) N43° 48.783' W124° 09.261'

Though this area is crowded in summer, it is blessedly quiet in winter. Mid-May features blooming rhododendrons in the forests. Backpackers have several options, but your best choice is some combination of beach and inland dune hiking south from the Tahkenitch Creek Trailhead, to Threemile Lake, and back north along the beach.

Above: Part of the Oregon Dunes Loop (Trip 31)

32

SOUTH COAST

RATINGS: Scenery 10 **Solitude** 4 **Difficulty** 5
MILES: Varies
DAYS: Varies
MAP: USGS *Brookings, Gold Beach,* and *Cape Sebastian*
USUALLY OPEN: Year-round
BEST: Mid-April–May

SPECIAL ATTRACTIONS

Spectacular coastal scenery

CHALLENGES

Very limited camping options, some road walking

GPS TRAILHEAD COORDINATES:
(Brookings) N42° 03.934' W124° 18.366'

Between Gold Beach and Brookings, the Oregon coast is at its most spectacular. By connecting beach walks with trail segments, a *stunningly* scenic hike is possible. Lack of campsites, proximity to the highway, and sometimes-crowded trails make this area more popular with day hikers than backpackers. Hike north from Brookings through Samuel H. Boardman State Scenic Corridor as far as time and ambition allow. Two possible stopping points are Arch Rock and Cape Sebastian.

33

OLD CASCADES LOOP

RATINGS: Scenery 4 **Solitude** 9 **Difficulty** 5
MILES: 42
DAYS: 4–5
MAP: USFS *Willamette National Forest: Sweet Home Ranger District*
USUALLY OPEN: June–November
BEST: Late June–July

SPECIAL ATTRACTIONS

Solitude, old-growth forests

CHALLENGES

High elevation gain, mountain bikes

GPS TRAILHEAD COORDINATES:
N44° 25.758' W122° 01.815'

The star attraction of this route is the old-growth forest. Several sloping wildflower meadows and ridgetop viewpoints add variety and scenic interest. You start from the Maude Creek (also known as Crescent Mountain South) Trailhead; from Bend, take US 20 northwest about 52 miles, then turn right (north) onto Forest Service Road 2067 (signs for Lava Lake Sno-Park). Follow the road 1.7 miles to the Maude Creek Trailhead. Hike over Crescent Mountain and the Three Pyramids and then loop counterclockwise via Scar Mountain, Knob Rock, Donaca Lake, and Pyramid Creek back to Crescent Mountain and your car.

34

MCKENZIE RIVER NATIONAL RECREATION TRAIL

RATINGS: Scenery 8 **Solitude** 5 **Difficulty** 3
MILES: 26
DAYS: 2–3
MAP: USFS *Willamette National Forest: McKenzie River National Recreation Trail*
USUALLY OPEN: Year-round
BEST: August–September

SPECIAL ATTRACTIONS

Beautiful riverside scenery, waterfalls, easy access, gentle terrain

CHALLENGES

Traffic noise, crowds, mountain bikes

GPS TRAILHEAD COORDINATES:
N44° 17.423' W122° 02.131'

Ramble alongside the mighty McKenzie River, a designated Wild and Scenic River, through old-growth forest and lava beds, past waterfalls and deep pools. The trail starts just outside the town of McKenzie Bridge, but it can be accessed via any of 11 trailheads along OR 126. Developed campgrounds along the river make for easy, family-friendly overnights.

TIP: Don't miss the scenic viewpoints at Sahalie Falls, Koosah Falls, and Tamolitch Blue Pool—they're touristy, but for good reason.

A gentle section of the McKenzie River National Recreation Trail (Trip 34)

35

NORTH UMPQUA TRAIL

RATINGS: Scenery 7 **Solitude** 5 **Difficulty** 3
MILES: 47
DAYS: 3–5
MAP: USFS *North Umpqua Ranger District*
USUALLY OPEN: March–November
BEST: April–May

A rock spire next to the North Umpqua River (Trip 35)

SPECIAL ATTRACTIONS

Whitewater rafters, beautiful river and canyon scenery, wildlife, waterfalls, fishing

CHALLENGES

Wildfire closures, poison oak, near highway, ticks

GPS TRAILHEAD COORDINATES:
(Swiftwater) N43° 19.902' W123° 00.304' **(Toketee Lake)** N43° 16.347' W122° 24.348'

The North Umpqua Trail, completed in 1997, follows the beautiful North Umpqua River from Idleyld Park all the way to the river's source. Even though the trail parallels busy OR 138, it has a surprisingly wild character. A series of bridges and road crossings allows for one-way trips of 5–70 miles; access points are easy to find all along OR 138. Some sections are still closed for repair after recent wildfires, but many have reopened.

36

ROGUE–UMPQUA DIVIDE

RATINGS: Scenery 7 **Solitude** 7 **Difficulty** 5
MILES: 27
DAYS: 3
MAP: USFS *Boulder Creek Wilderness, Rogue–Umpqua Divide Wilderness, Mount Thielsen Wilderness, Oregon Cascades Recreation Area*
USUALLY OPEN: Late May–November
BEST: Mid- to late June

SPECIAL ATTRACTIONS

Wildflowers, rock formations, views, solitude

CHALLENGES

Long car shuttle, burned areas

GPS TRAILHEAD COORDINATES:
(Abbott Butte) N42° 55.160' W122° 35.087'

This little-known wilderness is a pleasant surprise to most Oregon hikers. The hike features meadows filled with a stunning array of wildflowers, subalpine lakes, fascinating rock formations, and expansive views. The best tour of the area starts in the south at a pass on gravel Forest Service Road 68 northwest of Prospect. Hike north past Abbott Butte, Elephant Head, Anderson Butte, and Hershberger Mountain.

TIP: Don't miss the short side trip to the Hershberger Lookout.

Continue along spectacular Rocky Ridge, descend to Fish Lake, and exit at the Fish Lake Creek Trailhead off FS 2840 in Umpqua National Forest. Side trips abound.

37

UPPER ROGUE RIVER

RATINGS: Scenery 6 **Solitude** 4 **Difficulty** 3
MILES: Varies
DAYS: Varies
MAP: USFS *Rogue River National Forest*
USUALLY OPEN: Late May–November
BEST: Late October

SPECIAL ATTRACTIONS

Beautiful river and canyon scenery, fall colors, waterfalls

CHALLENGES

Some crowded areas, near major highway

GPS TRAILHEAD COORDINATES:
N43° 05.449' W122° 13.290'

Although it's never far from a busy highway, this long river path is a real treat. While a few of the more geologically interesting attractions, such as Natural Bridge, are crowded with tourists, other areas are quiet. Late October brings few people and exceptional fall colors. Start from the Crater Rim viewpoint along OR 230 west of Diamond Lake, and hike downstream past waterfalls, past campgrounds, and through attractive old-growth forests all the way to Prospect (48 miles). Numerous access points allow for shorter options.

38

NORTH FORK JOHN DAY RIVER

RATINGS: Scenery 6 **Solitude** 8 **Difficulty** 4
MILES: 25
DAYS: 3–6
MAP: USFS *North Fork John Day Ranger District*
USUALLY OPEN: June–November
BEST: June–October

SPECIAL ATTRACTIONS

Excellent fishing, canyon scenery

CHALLENGES

Some burned areas

GPS TRAILHEAD COORDINATES:
N44° 54.935' W118° 24.272'

This forested canyon hike is especially appealing to anglers. Opportunities to try your luck in the rushing waters of the North Fork John Day River are found around every bend. Several historical old cabins are also interesting. For a one-way downhill hike, start from the North Fork Trailhead along paved Forest Service Road 73 northwest of Sumpter. The trail stays close to the stream's north bank for its entire length. The lower trailhead is on dirt FS 5506, most easily reached from Ukiah to the west.

39

DIAMOND PEAK LOOP

RATINGS: Scenery 8 **Solitude** 6 **Difficulty** 5
MILES: Varies
DAYS: Varies
MAP: USFS *Middle Fork Ranger District*
USUALLY OPEN: July–October
BEST: Mid- to late July

SPECIAL ATTRACTIONS

Relative solitude, scenic lakes

CHALLENGES

Mosquitoes, burned areas

GPS TRAILHEAD COORDINATES:
(Trapper Creek Campground Trailhead) N43° 34.970' W122° 02.729'

The high, snowy ridge of Diamond Peak rises impressively over the lush forests and quiet lakes south of Willamette Pass. A couple of large fires in 2024 closed the entire wilderness for months, but there is still plenty of beautiful scenery to explore. Some trails on the southwest side of the mountain may be closed for a few years, but you can make a good loop using the Yoran Lake Trail and the PCT toward Yoran Lake, Mt Yoran, and Diamond Peak, then returning via Whitefish Creek. As always, check conditions with local officials first, especially in a recently burned area.

40

ABERT RIM

RATINGS: Scenery 9 **Solitude** 10 **Difficulty** 7
MILES: 24
DAYS: 3
MAP: USGS *Little Honey Creek and Lake Abert South*
USUALLY OPEN: June–November
BEST: June

SPECIAL ATTRACTIONS

Bighorn sheep, views!

CHALLENGES

No trail, almost no water

GPS TRAILHEAD COORDINATES:
N42° 23.292' W120° 14.051'

Abert Rim is the tallest and perhaps the most impressive fault scarp in the world. An extended backpacking trip is the ideal way to appreciate the vastness of this scenic rim. Off OR 140 northeast of Lakeview, go north on Forest Service Road 3615 and then dirt FS 377 to the Abert Rim overlook. Walk cross-country north along the view-packed rim's edge. Exit either at Mule Lake (poor road access) or via the steep use path down to US 395 at Poison Creek.

Bunchberry dogwood on Mount Hood

41

HART MOUNTAIN–POKER JIM RIDGE

RATINGS: Scenery 8 **Solitude** 10 **Difficulty** 8
MILES: 30
DAYS: 3
MAPS: USGS *Hart Lake, Warner Peak, Campbell Lake,* and *Bluejoint Lake East*
USUALLY OPEN: Mid-May–November
BEST: June

SPECIAL ATTRACTIONS

Wildlife, views, solitude

CHALLENGES

Poor road access, no trails, rugged route, ticks, very limited water

GPS TRAILHEAD COORDINATES:

N42° 23.589' W119° 49.772'

This is a long but very scenic hike along Hart Mountain's desert escarpment. The area was temporarily closed due to the Warner Peak Fire but is due to reopen in 2025. From Plush (northeast of Lakeview) drive south along the rough, narrow, dirt track beside Hart Lake's east shore for about 4 miles and park. You start with a difficult scramble up to the high plateau of Hart Mountain. Turn north to Warner Peak and Rock Creek and then cross the refuge access road and continue along Poker Jim Ridge to the recommended exit at Bluejoint Lake. Wildlife and views are abundant throughout. Except for Rock Creek, water is nonexistent. Permits are required.

42

TROUT CREEK MOUNTAINS LOOP

RATINGS: Scenery 8 **Solitude** 9 **Difficulty** 8
MILES: 44
DAYS: 4–6
MAPS: USGS *Doolittle Creek* and *Little Whitehorse Creek*
USUALLY OPEN: Mid-May–October
BEST: June and early October

Near the confluence of Whitehorse and Cottonwood Creeks (Trip 42)
photographed by Douglas Lorain

SPECIAL ATTRACTIONS

Solitude, fishing, wildlife, fall colors (especially aspens), wildflowers

CHALLENGES

Poor roads, no trails, private land to circumvent

GPS TRAILHEAD COORDINATES:

(Sweeney Ranch) N42° 15.043' W118° 10.709'

These little-known desert mountains near the Nevada border are a treat for hikers. One of several possible trips is a long loop hike that starts near privately owned Sweeney Ranch and goes up scenic Whitehorse Creek Canyon. Turn west along a jeep road on the high ridge of the Trout Creeks and then return via Little Whitehorse Creek Canyon.

43

LOWER OWYHEE CANYON RIM

RATINGS: Scenery 9 **Solitude** 10 **Difficulty** 6
MILES: 44
DAYS: 4–6
MAPS: USGS *Lambert Rocks* and *Rinehart Canyon*
USUALLY OPEN: April–November
BEST: May

SPECIAL ATTRACTIONS

Wildlife, magnificent canyon scenery

CHALLENGES

Awful road access, very limited water, poison ivy near the river, rattlesnakes

GPS TRAILHEAD COORDINATES:

N42° 52.039' W117° 43.328'

The *best* way to experience the wild and scenic canyon of the Owyhee River is to float the stream. The *next* best way is to backpack the rim—a highly rewarding adventure, despite the lack of trails.

WARNING: The "roads" here are passable only for high-clearance four-wheel-drive vehicles.

From the tiny community of Rome, go northwest on gravel and then dirt county roads through a private ranch (leave all gates the way you found them) to the start of public land near Crooked Creek. Park and walk east and then north along the canyon rim.

TIP: Don't miss exploring Chalk Basin and the side trip to the vista from Iron Point.

Exit at Rinehart Canyon "Road" (more of a jeep track) northwest of the Jackson Hole Basin.

44
LOUSE CANYON

RATINGS: Scenery 8 **Solitude** 10 **Difficulty** 10
MILES: 50
DAYS: 4–7
MAPS: USGS *Rawhide Springs, Drummond Basin,* and *Three Forks*
USUALLY OPEN: May–October
BEST: September

SPECIAL ATTRACTIONS

Solitude, desert canyon scenery

CHALLENGES

Poor road access, very rough scrambling required, rattlesnakes, lots of wading (or even swimming)

GPS TRAILHEAD COORDINATES:
N42° 07.839' W117° 18.958'

This is an *extremely* remote and rugged hike down the canyon of the West Little Owyhee River. The canyon features towering cliffs, colonnades and pinnacles, pools of water reflecting canyon walls, and wildlife. The hike is *extraordinarily* rough and should be contemplated only by very experienced and well-equipped hikers willing to expend an enormous amount of both physical and mental energy to enjoy this adventure. Start from Anderson Crossing at the mouth of Massey Canyon and end near Three Forks—both reached by very poor dirt roads. Good maps are essential.

LONG-DISTANCE TRAILS

Oregon has a handful of long-distance trails, both well known and less so, ideal for backpackers who really want to immerse themselves in a challenging thru-hike. Consider tackling all or part of these iconic trails:

- **Oregon Desert Trail** (onda.org): 750 miles of hiking trails, jeep tracks, old roads, and cross-country routes stitched together across eastern Oregon.
- **Oregon Coast Trail** (oregoncoasttrail.org): Around 362 miles of breathtaking coastline, and, like many long-distance trails, still a work in progress.
- **Pacific Crest Trail** (pcta.org): Oregon's section of the famous trail stretches 455 miles.
- **Corvallis-to-the-Sea** (c2ctrail.org): 60 miles from the Willamette Valley to the coast on little-used roads and trails.
- **Blue Mountains Trail** (hellscanyon.org/blue-mountains-trail): 530 miles through northeastern Oregon, between Wallowa Lake and John Day.

INDEX

OPPOSITE: Reaching the beach on the Oregon Dunes Loop (Trip 31, page 200)

D

E

F

G

K

L

M

R

S

ABOUT THE AUTHORS

Douglas Lorain moved with his family to the Pacific Northwest in 1969, and he has been obsessively hitting the trails of his home region ever since. Spurred by an unquenchable thirst for new trails to explore and a great enthusiasm for backpacking, he has now hiked more than 30,000 miles through every corner of the American Northwest and many thousands more in other western states and Canadian provinces. Despite a history that includes being bitten by a rattlesnake, being shot at by a hunter, being charged by grizzly bears (twice!), and donating gallons of blood to mosquitoes, Douglas claims that he wouldn't trade one moment of it because he has also been blessed to see some of the most beautiful scenery on Earth.

His other books for Wilderness Press include *Afoot & Afield Portland/Vancouver, Backpacking Idaho, Backpacking Washington, Backpacking Wyoming, One Best Hike: Mount Rainier's Wonderland Trail, One Night Wilderness: Portland,* and *Top Trails: Olympic National Park & Vicinity.*

Douglas is a photographer and recipient of the National Outdoor Book Award. His photographs have appeared in numerous magazines, calendars, and books.

photographed by Becky Lovejoy

Becky Ohlsen is an outdoor adventurer, travel writer, and part-time nomad who moved to Portland in 1995 from a small town in southern Colorado. Becky updated and revised this fourth edition of *Backpacking Oregon,* as well as the previous edition; she's also the author of *Walking Portland* and coauthor of *Best Tent Camping Oregon* and *One Night Wilderness: Portland.* In the summer, Becky spends most of her time out in the wild, only braving civilization when she needs supplies (or a shower). She travels with a pack raft and climbing shoes, just in case. She has written dozens of travel guidebooks for Lonely Planet, covering Sweden, Oregon, and Washington, among other destinations, and was recently named one of "50 Portland Writers We Admire" by *Willamette Week* newspaper. In the off-season, Becky can usually be found at her desk typing or reading with a cat on her lap, taking frequent breaks to ski or snowshoe in the Colorado mountains.

The Story of AdventureKEEN

We are an independent nature and outdoor activity publisher. Our founding dates back more than 40 years, guided then and now by our love of being in the woods and on the water, by our passion for reading and books, and by the sense of wonder and discovery made possible by spending time recreating outdoors in beautiful places.

It is our mission to share that wonder and fun with our readers, especially with those who haven't yet experienced all the physical and mental health benefits that nature and outdoor activity can bring.

In addition, we strive to teach about responsible recreation so that the natural resources and habitats we cherish and rely upon will be available for future generations.

We are a small team deeply rooted in the places where we live and work. We have been shaped by our communities of origin—primarily Birmingham, Alabama; Cincinnati, Ohio; and the northern suburbs of Minneapolis, Minnesota. Drawing on the decades of experience of our staff and our awareness of the industry, the marketplace, and the world at large, we have shaped a unique vision and mission for a company that serves our readers and authors.

We hope to meet you out on the trail someday.

#bewellbeoutdoors